KU-423-305

An Introduction
to Political Sociology

Nelson's Political Science Library
Editor: K. W. Watkins PhD, University of Sheffield

MAURICE DUVERGER
Party Politics and Pressure Groups

MAURICE DUVERGER
The Study of Politics

L. J. MACFARLANE
Modern Political Theory

MICHAEL RUSH
The Selection of Parliamentary Candidates

MICHAEL RUSH and PHILLIP ALTHOFF
An Introduction to Political Sociology

JOHN W. SPANIER
American Foreign Policy Since World War II

JOHN W. SPANIER
Games Nations Play: Analyzing International Politics

W. THORNHILL
The Nationalized Industries

An Introduction
to Political Sociology

MICHAEL RUSH and PHILLIP ALTHOFF

NELSON

THOMAS NELSON AND SONS LTD
36 Park Street London W1Y 4DE
PO Box 18123 Nairobi Kenya

Thomas Nelson (Australia) Ltd
597 Little Collins Street Melbourne 3000

Thomas Nelson and Sons (Canada) Ltd
81 Curlew Drive Don Mills Ontario

Thomas Nelson (Nigeria) Ltd
PO Box 336 Apapa Lagos

Thomas Nelson and Sons (South Africa) (Proprietary) Ltd
51 Commissioner Street Johannesburg

First published in Great Britain 1971
Reprinted 1972
Copyright © Michael Rush and Phillip Althoff 1971
Diagrams © Thomas Nelson and Sons Ltd 1971
All Rights Reserved. No part of this publication may be
reproduced, stored in a retrieval system, or transmitted, in
any form or by any means, electronic, mechanical,
photocopying, recording or otherwise, without the prior
permission of the publishers.

ISBN 0 17 712034 7

Printed in Great Britain by
Fletcher & Son Ltd, Norwich

To Jean and Barbara

Acknowledgments

The authors gratefully acknowledge the permission of the undermentioned to reprint material as indicated in the text:

The American Academy of Political and Social Science, Philadelphia, Pennsylvania for material from *The Annals*; the American Institute of Public Opinion, Princeton, New Jersey, the American Political Science Association and Professor V. Subramaniam for material from the *American Political Science Review*; Attwood Statistics (Nederland) N.V., Rotterdam; the Editors of the *British Journal of Sociology* and Dr Mark Abrams; Doubleday & Co Inc, New York, Heinemann Educational Books Ltd, London and Professor Seymour M. Lipset for material from *Political Man*, New York, 1959 and London, 1960; the DOXA Istituto per le Ricerche Statische e l'Analisi dell'Opinione Pubblica, Milan; the European Co-ordination Centre for Research and Documentation in Social Sciences, Vienna for material from a comparative three-nation study on 'Images of a Disarmed World', 1964–5; Eyre & Spottiswoode Ltd, London, Essential Books Inc, Fair Lawn, New Jersey and the Oxford University Press, New York for material from J. F. S. Ross, *Elections and Electors*, London, 1955; Gallup, London and Gallup International; Granada Publishing Ltd (MacGibbon & Kee Ltd), London and Basic Books Inc., New York for material from J. F. S. Ross, *Elections and Electors*, London, 1955; Gallup, London and Gallup International; Granada Publishing Ltd (MacGibbon & Kee Ltd), London for material from W. L. Guttsman, *The British Political Elite*, London, 1963; the Controller of Her Majesty's Stationery Office and Dr A. H. Halsey and Mr I. M. Crewe for material from *The Civil Service* (*Fulton Report*), Vol. 3 (I), Cmnd. 3683, 1968; the Indian Institute of Public Opinion Private Ltd, New Delhi; Institut Français d'Opinion Publique, Paris; Institut für angewandte Sozialwissenschaft, Bonn–Bad Godesberg; Institut für Demoskopie Allensbach GmbH, Allensbach am Bodensee; Instituto de la Opinión Pública, Madrid; the Journal Press, Provincetown, Mass. and Dr Holger Iisager for material from the *Journal of Social Psychology*; Little, Brown & Company Inc, Boston, Mass., Faber & Faber Ltd, London and Professor Richard Rose for material from *Politics in England*, Boston, 1964 and London, 1965; Little, Brown & Company Inc, Boston, Mass. for material from Richard R. Fagen, *Politics and Communication*, Boston, 1966; McGraw-Hill Book Co, New York and Professor David Easton and Professor Jack Dennis for material from *Children in the Political System*, New York, 1969; Professor Dwaine Marvick of the University of California, Los Angeles; METRA DIVO Beratungen GmbH, Frankfurt am Main; the *Minneapolis Tribune* for material from the Minnesota Poll; National Opinion Polls Ltd, London; Professor Marvin E. Olsen of the University of Chicago; Mr Roger Pethybridge of the University College of Swansea; Princeton University Press, Princeton, New Jersey, Professor Gabriel A. Almond and Professor Sidney Verba for material from *The Civic Culture*, Princeton, New Jersey, 1963 (Little, Brown edition, Boston, 1965); Princeton University Press and Professor Gabriel A. Almond and Professor James S. Coleman for material from *The Politics of the Developing Areas*, Princeton, New Jersey, 1960; the Editor of the *Public Opinion Quarterly*; the Public Opinion Survey Unit, University of Missouri, Columbia, Missouri; Random House Inc and Professor Donald R. Matthews for material from *The Social Background of Political Decision-Makers*, New York, 1954; the Society for the Psychological Study of Social Issues and Professor Alex Inkeles for material from the *Journal of Social Issues*; UNESCO and Professor Robert D. Hess for material from the *International Social Science Journal*; and Yale University Press and Professor Bruce M. Russett, Professor Hayward R. Alker Jr, Professor Karl W. Deutsch and Professor Harold D. Lasswell for material from the *World Handbook of Political and Social Indicators*, New Haven, Conn., 1964.

Contents

List of Abbreviations

AIOP American Institute of Public Opinion, Princeton, New Jersey
ALP Australian Labour Party
APOP Australian Public Opinion Polls
ATTS Attwood Statistics (Netherlands)
CAL California Poll, San Francisco
CHP Republican People's Party (Turkey)
CPSU Communist Party of the Soviet Union
DIVO METRA DIVO Beratungen GmbH, Frankfurt am Main
DMS Institut für Demoskopie Allensbach GmbH, Allensbach am Bodensee
DOXA DOXA Istituto per le Ricerche Statische e l'Analisi dell'Opinione Pubblica, Milan
EGA Encuestas Gallup de la Argentina
EMNID EMNID Institut, Bielefeld
ENA École Nationale d'Administration
GMA Gallup Markedanalyse, Denmark
IFOP Institut Français d'Opinion Publique
IIPO Indian Institute of Public Opinion
INFAS Institut für angewandte Sozialwissenschaft, Bonn–Bad Godesberg
IOP Instituto de la Opinión Pública, Madrid
MINN Minnesota Poll of the *Minneapolis Tribune*
NDP New Democratic Party (Canada)
NIP National Institute of Psychology, Teheran
NOP National Opinion Polls, Great Britain
POSU Public Opinion Survey Unit, University of Missouri
PRIO International Peace Research Institute, Oslo
SOC Gallop (Social Surveys), Great Britain
VC European Co-ordination Centre for Research and Documentation in Social Sciences, Vienna

Note: the opinion poll designations are those used in the periodical *Polls*.

Preface

This book was originally conceived when we were both teaching at the University of Western Ontario in 1967–8. It was during this time that the conceptual framework which forms the basis of the book was evolved, and the preliminary work of gathering the material begun. Since then a complex – and we hope fruitful – trans-Atlantic collaboration has continued, resulting in the present volume.

We have attempted to draw together into this one volume the many strands of social and political behaviour which constitute political sociology and to offer a unified concept of its many facets. In so doing we have sought to contribute to the increasing attention being paid to political sociology and to demonstrate its crucial importance in the study of politics.

We would like to express our grateful thanks to our colleagues who helped and encouraged us at various stages in the writing of this book, and to Mrs Susan Ridler, who typed the final manuscript under considerable pressure of time. A special debt is due to Dr K. W. Watkins, the editor of the series in which this book appears, without whose continuing encouragement, unlimited patience and unfailing advice this book would not have been written. A similar but much deeper debt, however, is due to our respective wives, to whom this book is dedicated.

Finally, we gratefully acknowledge permission to make use of already-published material. Although this book draws on material from many sources, we, of course, remain responsible for its contents.

M.D.R.
Department of Politics
University of Exeter

P.A.
Department of Political Science
Kansas State University
Manhattan

1 · Introductory

The term 'sociology' was coined by Auguste Comte (1798–1857), one of the founding fathers of the discipline. Simply defined, the term means the study of society, but in practice it is the study of society from a particular point of view. Both Comte and Herbert Spencer (1820–1903), another of the founding fathers, stressed that the *society* was the basic unit of sociological analysis, the various social institutions (such as the family and political, economic and religious institutions) and the interrelationship between these institutions being the sub-units of analysis. Thus, in endeavouring to emphasize this societal context, modern sociologists have variously defined sociology as, 'the science that deals with social groups',[1] and 'the study of human interactions and interrelations'.[2] The focus of sociology is therefore upon human behaviour, but it is concentrated on neither individual nor collective behaviour as such – these may be regarded as the province of psychiatry and psychology. What sociology is concerned with is human behaviour – both individual and collective, but more often collective – and its relation to society; sociology is therefore the study of human behaviour within a societal context.

Political science is less easy to define, however. Whereas sociology is concerned with human behaviour from the point of view of society and is in this respect all-embracing, politics is clearly concerned only with certain aspects of society. Thus, as W. G. Runciman has argued, 'such separate disciplines as economics, or demography, or criminology, or politics should be regarded as

[1] Harry M. Johnson, *Sociology: A Systematic Introduction*, London, 1961, p. 2.
[2] Morris Ginsburg, *Sociology*, London, 1934, p. 7.

co-ordinate but distinctive branches of sociology (or social science)'.[1] It is not difficult to suggest those aspects of society which are of central concern to the study of politics: particular social institutions, such as legislatures and executives, political parties and interest groups, immediately spring to mind, as do particular areas of human behaviour, such as the electoral or legislative processes; but it is more difficult to delimit the boundaries of political science and hence to define it. In an effort to circumvent this problem most definitions have sought to delineate the essence of politics. Thus we are told that the central concern of politics is the resolution of human conflict, or the process by which society makes decisions or evolves policies, or authoritatively allocates resources and values, or that it is the exercise of power and influence in society. Whether any of these is the essence of politics is a matter of opinion, but few would dispute that each of these concepts is of great concern to the political scientist.

It is in many respects helpful to regard power as the focal point of political studies, but, just as we have defined sociology as the study of human behaviour within a societal context, so it is important to stress that we are looking at power within the same societal context. This still avoids the question of a definition, however, and all these attempts to suggest the essence of politics point to a particular area of study – the means by which man solves his problems with his fellow-men. Looked at this way, political science involves the study of the problems themselves, of the machinery that may be evolved to deal with them, of the factors which influence men in their solution, and, by no means least, of the ideas which influence men in dealing with them.

In this sense, 'political science is a subject matter, not an autonomous discipline. . . . The subject is defined by a problem.' For the author of these words, Bernard Crick, that problem is government, which is 'the activity of maintaining order'.[2] Here, of course order means the regulation of relations between men in the very widest sense and not simply that suggested in the phrase law and order. Political science is not synonymous with the study of

[1] W. G. Runciman, *Social Science and Political Theory*, London, 1965, p. 1. See also W. J. M. Mackenzie, *Politics and Social Science*, London, 1967.

[2] Bernard Crick, 'The Tendency of Political Studies', *New Society*, 3 November 1966, p. 683. See also his *In Defence of Politics*, London, 1962.

government, but it encompasses it in that it examines, in Crick's phrase, 'the function of government in society'.

Whatever the rationale for regarding political science as an integral part of sociology, it has, academically, developed as a separate discipline. This was probably inevitable, given its original links with historical and legal studies and the efforts of many early sociologists to link their subject with the natural sciences. This is true of each of the social sciences: each has different origins and development, often accidental in nature, so that the practitioners of each 'subject' have come to regard them as separate disciplines and tended to ignore related 'subjects':

> Whatever is a 'problem' for one discipline becomes a 'given', an external factor, for the neighbouring discipline. For instance, economists assume political structures to be given. Likewise, sociologists assume economic structures to be given. In a similar vein, political scientists assume social structures to be given. Each discipline throws light on a set of variables precisely because other factors are assumed to be external, distal and equal.[1]

At the same time, political scientists have long recognized the importance of sociology to the study of politics, and the theories of men like Marx, Weber, Mosca, Pareto and Michels have had a profound effect on political studies. It has been recognized that no political system, no political institution, no politician works in a vacuum, and sociological studies have provided valuable insights into the societal environment within which politics function. This has become increasingly apparent as more attention has been paid by political scientists to comparative studies in general and developing societies in particular. In this process there has developed a considerable body of work which may legitimately be regarded as the realm of *political sociology* – the examination of the links between politics and society, between social structures and political structures, and between social behaviour and political behaviour.

THE ORIGINS AND DEVELOPMENT OF POLITICAL SOCIOLOGY
The origins of a discipline, subject or area of study are often obscure, and to suggest particular individuals as 'the founding fathers' of a particular body of knowledge is a perilous process.

[1] G. Sartori, 'From the Sociology of Politics to Political Sociology', *Government and Opposition*, 4, 1969, p. 196.

Thus some of our readers may object either to our citing of Comte and Spencer as founding fathers of sociology or to the omission of Marx or Durkheim or Weber. Nevertheless, certain figures stand out as individuals whose contributions have been of fundamental importance. In the case of political sociology two such figures stand out: Karl Marx (1818–83) and Max Weber (1864–1920).

Marx's contribution was both massive and varied, and not, of course, limited to political sociology. His contribution falls into three areas: general theory, specific theory and methodology. Following Hegel, Marx developed a theory of historical inevitability based on the dialectic of thesis, antithesis and synthesis, but unlike Hegel he based his theory on the material conflict of opposing economic forces, resulting in the ultimate overthrowal of capitalism and the creation of a classless society. Marx's interpretation of history was based on the twin pillars of economic and sociological theory. He developed David Hume's labour-value theory into the theories of surplus value and the exploitation of labour, and these formed the basis of his major sociological theory, the class struggle. He also developed a theory of alienation which argued that the working class or proletariat became increasingly alienated from the rest of society as their work became a means of avoiding starvation rather than a means of self-expression. Closely involved with the theories of the class struggle and alienation is the concept of class consciousness – the recognition by individuals in society that they belong to economically based groups – which formed an essential prerequisite of class conflict.

Many criticisms have been levelled at Marx's theories, some based on their general validity, others on their predictive value. For example, although he did not ignore the importance of ideas as sociological factors, Marx regarded them as dependent rather than independent variables, thus subordinating them to his economic interpretation of history. The role of Marxism as an *ideology* in many parts of the world would suggest that Marx over-emphasized the economic subordination of ideas. Similarly, the failure of a number of his predictions and his failure to anticipate the adaptive capacity of capitalism, have cast doubt on his theories. These criticisms, however, do little to diminish his contribution to political sociology. Both his general theories of economic determinism and dialectical materialism and his specific theories of the class struggle, class consciousness and alienation have stimulated an enormous amount of work, some of it seeking to support Marx's ideas, some of it seeking to disprove them. The result has been a vast contribution to knowledge, which has in turn often stimulated yet further work.

Quite apart from this, however, Marx made a further vital contribution in the field of methodology. His development of 'scientific socialism' laid down standards of scholarship and methods which were an example to subsequent social scientists. Marx endeavoured to give his theories a firm basis in fact by amassing a vast amount of evidence which he sought to examine in a systematic and rigorous fashion. How successful he was in this remains a matter of dispute, but the very fact that he claimed this for his theories meant that both his followers and critics had to make similar endeavours.

Perhaps inevitably, the second founding father of political sociology, Max Weber, was one of Marx's leading critics. Weber's contribution consisted not only of a major critique of Marx, but of a considerable number of specific studies and concepts of importance to political sociology. In his work *The Protestant Ethic and the Spirit of Capitalism*,[1] and in his studies of India, China and the Jewish people, Weber sought to demonstrate that non-economic factors, especially ideas, were important sociological factors. Moreover, in examining social stratification in various societies he argued that social strata could be based not only on an individual's 'class' or economic position in society, as Marx asserted, but also upon his status or social position in society, or upon an individual's position in the societal power structure. These could, Weber acknowledged, be overlapping, but not necessarily identical.

Weber also contributed several important conceptual and methodological ideas to political sociology. 'Politics', Weber declared, '. . . means striving to share power or striving to influence the distribution of power, either among states or among groups within a state', the state being defined as, ' a human community that (successfully) claims the *monopoly of the legitimate use of physical force* within a given territory.'[2]

---

[1] Originally published in 1904–5, English translation, London, 1930.
[2] Max Weber, 'Politics as a Vocation', in *From Max Weber: Essays in Sociology*, translated and edited by H. H. Gerth and C. Wright Mills, London, 1948, p. 78. (Original italics.)

Weber was thus very much concerned with the exercise of power and with the justification or legitimacy of its exercise. Weber's concept of *legitimacy* – the grounds on which the exercise of power is accepted – was one of his most important contributions to political sociology. There were, Weber believed, three major types of legitimacy:

> First, the authority of the 'eternal yesterday', i.e. of the mores sanctified through the unimaginably ancient recognition and habitual orientation to conform. This is 'traditional' domination. . . .
>
> Second, there is the authority of the extraordinary and personal *gift of grace* (charisma), the absolutely personal devotion and personal confidence in revelation, heroism, or other qualities of individual leadership. This is 'charismatic' domination. . . .
>
> Finally, there is domination by virtue of 'legality', by virtue of the belief in the validity of legal statute and functional 'competence' based on rationally created *rules*.[1]

These three types of legitimacy are an example of another of Weber's important contributions. Traditional, charismatic and legal domination were 'pure' or *ideal types* and were not therefore mutually exclusive. Weber's concept of the ideal type is simply the construction of historically observable facts into a model or bench mark against which other, similar phenomena could be measured. In using the term 'ideal' he is not passing any judgement on the models he constructed, merely plotting points on a sociological graph. The construction of ideal types has been and remains a fruitful tool in the hands of the political sociologist.

Weber's other major methodological legacy was the concept of sympathetic (or subjective) understanding, or *Verstehen*, as applied to sociology. Weber felt that human behaviour could be better understood if account were taken of the motives and intentions of those directly involved in that behaviour. It was natural that Weber should stress such a concept, given the importance he attributed to the force of ideas as sociological factors. None the less, it has led to criticism of Weber's work on the grounds that, regardless of his claims that it was value-free, the examination of men's motives involved an interpretive element which could not be ultimately objective. Inevitably, Weber's work has been criticized on other grounds, such as historical accuracy, but his work and ideas have, like those of Marx, proved a stimulus to subsequent generations of sociologists and political scientists.

[1] ibid., pp. 78–9. (Original italics.)

Although Marx and Weber may properly be regarded as the founding fathers of political sociology, there are, of course, others whose contribution, whilst less fundamental and stimulating, remains nevertheless important. Furthermore, a brief examination of some of these contributors illustrates the development of political sociology. The work of Alexis de Tocqueville (1805–59) is a case in point. In his *L'Ancien Régime et la Révolution* (1856) he argued that the Revolution of 1789 did not mark a complete break with the past and that some measure of continuity was inevitable, thus anticipating many later ideas on the process and nature of social change. One of Marx's contemporaries, Walter Bagehot (1826–77), editor of *The Economist* from 1860 to 1877 and an influential observer of the political scene during this period, also deserves mention. Bagehot examined the links between culture and personality, and between political institutions and behaviour. He argued that it was possible to delineate a national character for various countries, expounding this theme to great effect in *The English Constitution* (1867), in which he asserted that English political institutions were derived from the deferential nature of the English people. Bagehot also distinguished between constitutional theory and practice, speaking of the 'dignified' and the 'efficient' parts of the constitution, and this book remains a classic contemporary account of and commentary upon Cabinet and parliamentary government. Bagehot's other major work in the field of political sociology was *Physics and Politics* (1872), in which he applied the concept of evolution to the origins and development of societies, placing particular emphasis on the part played in this process by imitation.

It was the process of imitation as a social phenomenon that characterized the work of a French sociologist, Gabriel Tarde (1843–1904), who may also claim to have contributed to the development of political sociology. Not only did Tarde in general claim that the political system of any society was inextricably linked with the social structures of that society, but he also stressed the importance of two other areas which have become of prime concern to political sociologists. Tarde examined and stressed the social impact of modern communications in the form of the telegraph, telephone, and mass-produced books and newspapers, and sought to formulate links between the mass media and the individual. In so doing he anticipated such theories as the role of the individual 'opinion leader' and the 'two-step flow of communication'. In addition to this, Tarde emphasized the role of élites, particularly as means of diffusing ideas through society, pointing the way not only to the major counter-attack against Marxism but to the next major development in political sociology.

The élite theorists, Vilfredo Pareto (1848–1923) in *The Mind and Society*[1] and Gaetano Mosca (1858–1941) in *The Ruling Class*,[2] sought to refute Marxism by acknowledging the existence of a ruling class or élite, but arguing that this élite did not necessarily owe its position to economic supremacy and that political and social change came about by a circulation of élites which was not necessarily attributable to economic factors. We shall be examining their ideas in Chapter 4, but it should be noted that the concept of the élite has been of major importance to political socio-logy, not only in stimulating such later élite theorists as James Burnham and C. Wright Mills, but in concentrating the attention of sociologists and political scientists upon such phenomena as political parties and interest groups.

Two of the earliest contributors to the study of political parties were M. Ostrogorski (1854–1919) and Roberto Michels (1876–1936), the former in *Democracy and the Organization of Political Parties*[3] and the latter in *Political Parties: A Sociological Study of the Oligarchical Tendencies of Modern Democracy*.[4] Both authors examined the organizational development of political parties and came to similar conclusions: that such organizations were inevitably dominated by small groups of activists and that popular control was both a sham and an impossibility – for Ostrogorski party politics was inevitably 'caucus politics', for Michels all political organizations were subject to an 'iron law of oligarchy'.

As increasing attention was paid to the organization of political parties, so other observers began to look at the sources of their electoral support. In the United States, for example, Stuart Rice

[1] Originally published in 1916 and translated into English as *The Mind and Society*, London, 1935.

[2] Originally published in 1896, revised in 1923, and translated into English as *The Ruling Class*, London, 1939.

[3] London, 1902.

[4] Originally published in 1911, English translation 1915. See also his *First Lectures in Political Sociology*, translated by Alfred de Grazia, Minneapolis, 1949.

in his *Quantitative Methods in Politics*[1] published a study of the voting behaviour of a sample of respondents over a period of time (this was the first known panel study), a trend analysis of electoral statistics and the results of ecological research he had conducted. Another example is the work of Rudolf Herbele on the sources of Nazi support prior to their accession to power in 1933.[2]

At the same time trends in social science generally led some political scientists to examine the role of personality in politics. The most prominent of these was Harold Lasswell, whose *Psychopathology and Politics* and *Politics: Who Gets What, When and How?*[3] are classics of the period. This concentration on the individual as the unit of analysis produced an inevitable reaction in the form of increasing attention being paid to the links between culture and politics, and between economic development and political systems. Important examples of work in these fields are *The Civic Culture*[4] by Gabriel Almond and Sidney Verba, *Politics in the Developing Areas*,[5] edited by Gabriel Almond and James Coleman, and Seymour Martin Lipset's *Political Man* and *The First New Nation*.[6]

The circle has almost taken a full turn: the earliest work in political sociology was concerned with explaining the totality of political behaviour within a societal context – with what we now call macro-research; this was followed by criticism of this work and concentration of the details of political behaviour within their context – a concern with micro-research; finally, there have now been attempts to link the results of these efforts together. Whether these efforts have been successful or are likely to be in the future is, as we suggest in our final chapter, a matter of opinion, but this is in no way a criticism of those who make the effort.

APPROACHES AND METHODS

It should already be apparent from our discussion of those who have contributed to our knowledge of political sociology that a number of approaches and methods are appropriate to its study.

[1] New York, 1928.
[2] Rudolf Herbele, *From Democracy to Nazism: A Regional Case-Study on Political Parties in Germany*, Baton Rouge, Louisiana, 1945.
[3] Chicago, 1930, and New York, 1936, respectively.
[4] Princeton, N.J., 1963.   [5] Princeton, N.J., 1960.
[6] Garden City, New York, 1960, and London, 1963, respectively.

But, as Sartori has pointed out, approaches and 'research methods are largely decided by the kind of evidence which is available for the units and the kind of problems with which one deals.'[1]

In using the term 'approach' we mean a particular orientation or point of view. For instance, one such orientation is the historical approach, which, as we have already seen, was of particular importance to both Marx and Weber. Quite apart from this, however, such an approach provided a necessary perspective to such studies, both in a temporal and a contextual sense.

Another approach involves the use of comparative data by which studies of political phenomena in one society are used to throw light on similar or contrasting phenomena in another. This approach was used, for example, by both Ostrogorski and Michels in their studies of political parties, and in the environmental studies of Almond and his colleagues and Lipset, cited above.

The value of these two approaches is not normally questioned, but other orientations are subject to criticism. The traditional institutional approach, for instance, has long been cited as inadequate and unrealistic because it ignores the realities of political behaviour by concentrating on legalistic and constitutional factors. This is, however, to overstate the case: political behaviour takes place within an institutional framework and neither the behaviour nor the institutions can be adequately explained without an understanding of both. This is implicit in most studies of political parties and legislative behaviour.

In contrast to the institutional approach, the behavioural approach endeavours to avoid what are regarded as the faults of other approaches. It is characterized by stressing the individual as the basic unit of analysis, and the need to separate facts from values and to make verifiable generalizations. Behaviouralism has undoubtedly led to considerably greater rigour in social and political analysis by laying down high standards, but it has also been criticized for neglecting the advantages of other approaches. In practice, like the other approaches we have mentioned, behaviouralism is best seen as one of several possible orientations, all of which may be fruitful according to the nature of the problems being studied.

This particular observation is even more applicable to the methods used in the study of political sociology. Obviously con-

[1] Sartori, 'From the Sociology of Politics to Political Sociology', p. 198.

siderable reliance is placed upon quantitative methods, including the use of statistical surveys and aggregative data, such as that used in studies of political ecology. Much of the work based on these methods involves the use of sophisticated statistical techniques, in particular correlation and significance tests. It is important to appreciate, however, that statistical evidence based on such tests, however positive, is an indication of some relationship which may or may not be casual. What such evidence does do is to provide a basis for further work as well as an indication, often a very strong indication, of what are likely to be the key variables in a particular problem.

In addition to gathering quantitative material, the political sociologist also relies upon gaining considerable insight through the use of intensive interview surveys (including the use of panel studies involving the periodic interviewing of the same respondents), of case-studies, and of direct or indirect participation in the political process. The use of interviews is of particular importance in investigating the motives of those involved in the political process and as a means of testing theory against practice. Similarly, case-studies allow resources to be used intensively, whilst participation in the political process, either directly as an 'actor' or indirectly as an observer, has often been an effective method.

Finally, considerable use is made of theories and models both to provide guidelines for research and to offer explanations of the phenomena studied. A theory may be defined as 'a heuristic device for organizing what we know, or think we know, at any particular time about some more or less explicitly posed question or issue'; and a model as, 'a rather general image of the main outline of some major phenomenon, including certain leading ideas about the nature of the units involved and the pattern of their relations.'[1]

One of the major types of theory of interest to the political sociologist is that known as systems theory, which argues that all social phenomena are part of discernible, regular and internally consistent patterns of behaviour. We may therefore speak of, say, a social system and a number of interdependent sub-systems, such as those concerning economics or politics. Each of these sub-systems may be further subdivided, so that it is common when dealing with particular sub-systems to speak of the economic system or the political system and so on. One of the leading

[1] Alex Inkeles, *What is Sociology?*, Englewood Cliffs, N.J., 1964, p. 28.

proponents of systems theory is Talcott Parsons, whose book *The Social System*[1] and other work has been the basis of much academic controversy and stimulus. Parsons and a number of other sociologists, notably Marion Levy and Robert Merton, have become identified with what is known as the functional approach to systems theory. The term function is defined as 'the objective consequence of a pattern of action for the system'.[2] Functionalism depends ultimately on the Parsonian view that a system seeks to achieve particular goals and that all behaviour and phenomena are related to this end. This has led to the development of structural-functionalism, which argues that all social behaviour and phenomena (constituted as patterns of action or structures) fulfil (or fail to fulfil) particular functions for the system. There is no doubt that the structural-functional approach has thrown light on areas which have been previously overlooked or neglected and, in particular, has offered significant explanations of phenomena as fulfilling a particular need or function. None the less, as Runciman has pointed out, there has been a tendency to confuse *purpose* with *results* through the use of the term *goal*, while the fundamental precept that a system necessarily has goals in this sense may be questioned. In addition, structural-functionalism has been criticized for being unable to account adequately for systemic change and being ideologically biased in a conservative or static direction. These last two criticisms are, of course, closely connected, and we will be dealing with the problem of societal change in Chapter 2.

In the field of political studies, David Easton's *The Political System, A Framework for Political Analysis* and *A Systems Analysis of Political Life*[3] suggest an alternative to the functional approach. This is known as input-output analysis. Easton is especially concerned with how a political system continues to exist and what causes it to change. He therefore suggests that certain contributions are made to the political system in the form of 'inputs'. These may be *demands* for action or *support* for the system. Following a conversion process, 'outputs' in the form of *authoritative decisions* are produced. There is also a process of reaction to these

[1] Glencoe, Illinois, 1951.

[2] Oran R. Young, *Systems of Political Science*, Englewood Cliffs, N.J., 1968, p. 29.

[3] New York, 1953, Englewood Cliffs, N.J., 1965, and New York, 1965, respectively.

decisions which Easton terms 'feedback'. Easton's theory has been adapted to a structural-functional framework by Gabriel Almond, who has constructed what he terms a developmental approach to politics.[1] Just as Easton and Almond sought to provide theoretical frameworks which would incorporate those areas of study which they felt had been previously neglected, so their critics have complained that they, in turn, have neglected the 'traditional' area of institutions. In fact Almond was seeking to link institutions and processes and his main problems stem from his use of a structural-functional approach.

Most of these theories use models of various sorts to illustrate and clarify the arguments on which they are based. It is our intention to use a number of models which seem appropriate to the concepts which we regard as central to political sociology. In so doing we would stress that these models are intended to help explain these concepts and not act as substitutes for them.

A CONCEPTUAL SCHEME

We have defined political sociology as being a subject area (some would say discipline) which examines the links between politics and society, between social structures and political structures, and between social behaviour and political behaviour. In so doing we regard political sociology as a theoretical and methodological bridge between sociology and political science, or what Sartori has called 'an inter-disciplinary hybrid'.[2]

Our conceptual scheme is based upon four concepts: political socialization, political participation, political recruitment and political communication. These concepts are interdependent and interlocking, and we have defined them as follows:

Political socialization is the process by which an individual becomes acquainted with the political system and which determines his perceptions of politics and his reactions to political phenomena. It involves the examination of the social, economic and cultural environment of society upon the individual and upon his political attitudes and values. Political socialization is the most important

[1] See Gabriel Almond and G. Bingham Powell, *Comparative Politics: A Developmental Approach*, Boston, Mass., 1966.

[2] Sartori, 'From the Sociology of Politics to Political Sociology', p. 197.

link between the social and political systems, but may vary considerably from one system to another. From a political point of view, political socialization is extremely important as the process by which individuals may become involved, to varying degrees, in the political system – in political participation.

Political participation is the involvement of the individual at various levels in the political system. Political activity may range from non-involvement to office-holding. Because political participation varies from one society to another, and because it varies within particular societies, it is important to examine the concepts of political apathy and alienation and their role in non-involvement and limited involvement. It is also important to stress that participation may also result in motivation for increased participation, including the highest level – that of holding various types of office – which involves the process of political recruitment.

Political recruitment is the process by which individuals secure or are enlisted in the roles of office-holders. Recruitment is a two-way process and may be formal or informal. It is a two-way process in that individuals may themselves seek the opportunity or may be approached by others to become holders of such positions. Similarly, recruitment may be formal in that individuals may be recruited openly by means of institutional machinery of selection or election, and informal in that individuals may be recruited privately with little or no recourse to such machinery. This also involves some consideration of whether those who hold these offices can be said to constitute a clearly defined political group or élite.

Political communication is the process by which politically relevant information is transmitted from one part of the political system to another, and between the social and political systems. It is a continuous process involving the exchange of information between individuals and groups of individuals at all levels of society, and includes not only the expression of the views and wishes of members of society, but also the means by which the views and proposals of those in power are transmitted to society and the latter's reaction to those views and proposals. Political communication plays a crucial role in the political system: it constitutes its dynamic element and is a vital part of political socialization, participation and recruitment.

We have deliberately concentrated on political processes in formulating our four concepts, but not to the exclusion of political and social institutions: these we regard as an integral part of the processes we describe and as an essential part of any attempt to explain the connection between social and political phenomena, which is the task of political sociology.

2 · Political Socialization

Political socialization was described in Chapter 1 as the process by which an individual becomes acquainted with the political system and which determines his perceptions of politics and his reactions to political phenomena. It is determined by the social, economic and cultural environment of the society in which the individual lives and by the interaction of the experiences and personality of the individual. Political socialization is therefore the key concept of political sociology in several respects. First, the three other concepts of participation, recruitment and communication are inextricably linked with it – participation and recruitment because they are partially dependent variables of socialization and communication because it provides the dynamic element in socialization. Second, political socialization demonstrates the interaction and interdependence of social and political behaviour. And finally, as a necessary corrollary of that interaction and interdependence, it demonstrates the interdependence of the social sciences in general and of sociology and political science in particular.

In a sense, the importance of political socialization has long been recognized, though this has, until fairly recently, been implicit rather than explicit. For example, once some sort of association between the personal characteristics of individuals and voting behaviour had been established through various types of electoral studies, many of the explanations offered implied some form of socialization. In other words the experiences of and values held by, say, a British manual worker are such that he is more likely than a non-manual worker (who will have had different experiences and hold different values) to vote for the Labour party. Until the publication in 1959, however, of Herbert Hyman's *Political Socialization*,[1] political scientists' treatment of the concept had been fragmentary rather than systematic.

This relative neglect on the part of political scientists is in many respects curious, since political philosophers have long stressed the importance of what amounted to political socialization, or at least to particular manifestations of it, while many a politician has been aware of the value of political education. Both Plato and Aristotle placed importance on the training of members of society for various types of political activity; Rousseau recognized the role of education in inculcating values; and the liberal philosophers of the nineteenth century placed great stress on what Robert Lowe described as the need 'to educate our masters'. Similarly, throughout history great use has been made of formal education for political purposes: this is as apparent in the medieval church's monopoly of education as it is in the totalitarian states of the twentieth century.

If political scientists paid little attention to socialization, however, or at least took it for granted, to the anthropologist, the social psychologist and the sociologist it has long been an important concept, and it is from these disciplines that we draw our three initial definitions of socialization:

> [1.] . . . those patterns of social action, or aspects of action, which inculcate in individuals the skills (including knowledge), motives, and attitudes necessary for the performance of present or anticipated roles . . . [and which continue] throughout normal human life, in so far as new roles must be learned;[2]
>
> [2.] . . . the whole process by which an individual, born with behavioural potentialities of immense range, is led to develop actual behaviour which is confined within a much narrower range – the range of what is customary and acceptable for him according to the standards of his group;[3]
>
> [3.] . . . communication with and learning from other human beings with whom [the individual] gradually enters some sort of generalized relationship.[4]

[1] *Political Socialization: A Study in the Psychology of Political Behaviour*, Glencoe, Ill., 1959.

[2] David F. Aberle, 'Culture and Socialization', in Francis L. K. Hsu (ed.), *Psychological Anthropology: Approaches to Culture and Personality*, Homewood, Ill., 1961, p. 387.

[3] Irvin L. Child, 'Socialization', in G. Lindzey (ed.), *Handbook of Social Psychology*, Cambridge, Mass., 1954, Vol. 2, p. 655.

[4] S. N. Eisenstadt, *From Generation to Generation*, London, 1956, p. 26.

Quite clearly these definitions have a great deal in common, and they effectively introduce several important facets of socialization. First, socialization is fundamentally a process of learning, learning from experience, or what Aberle calls 'patterns of action'. Secondly, a general indication is given of what is learned in that the broad limits of the individual's behaviour are laid down and, more specifically, in terms of knowledge (or information), motives (or values) and attitudes (or opinions). Furthermore, it is stressed that we are concerned not only with the behaviour of the individual but also with the behaviour of the groups to which the individual may belong. Thirdly, socialization is not necessarily confined to childhood and adolescence (even though these may be the most significant periods), but may continue throughout adult life. Finally, it is suggested that socialization is a necessary pre-condition of societal activity, and, both implicitly and explicitly, provides an explanation of social behaviour.

There are, however, two problems associated with these definitions. First, to what extent is socialization a process of systemic perpetuation? This is of considerable importance in examining the relationship between socialization and societal change, or, in functionalist terms, system maintenance. It is important to consider this problem from a functionalist point of view for a moment because one of the major criticisms of functionalism, as we have already seen, has been its alleged inability to account satisfactorily for systemic change, and, while the concept of socialization is not exclusively the prerogative of functionalist theorists, it is none the less an integral part of functional theory. To the functionalist, the process of socialization effectively explains how a system may persist over time: the system, if it is to persist, demands that certain functions must be fulfilled by means of the roles carried out by individuals or groups of individuals, and that the performance of these roles cannot be assumed but need to be learned. In other words, a society perpetuates itself by teaching its new members those values and modes of behaviour which that society regards as appropriate and acceptable. Thus a child may acquire from his parents a number of firmly held beliefs, such as a belief in the freedom of speech, the sanctity of marriage, particular religious beliefs, a belief in the rule of law and so on, and, assuming that these beliefs are widely held in the society concerned, it is reasonable to suggest that it is unlikely that there will be fundamental changes in the attitudes towards free speech, marriage, religion or the rule of law within the forseeable future. This is not, of course, to suggest that change will never occur, but merely to posit circumstances in which change is less rather than more likely. The fault, therefore, of functionalist theory, with its emphasis on system maintenance, is that it offers an explanation of why change does not occur or is minimized without offering an explanation of why change does occur, especially when such change is fundamental.

There is, in fact, no reason at all why a theory of political socialization should not be able to account for both the absence and the existence of systemic and societal change, provided such a theory allows for the inclusion of two important variables and does not confine itself to what is learned, who is taught, who teaches it and what the results are. These two variables are *experience* and *personality* and it will later be argued that both the experience and the personality of an individual (and more particularly of groups of individuals) are fundamental to the process of socialization and to the process of change.

The second problem arising out of these definitions of socialization concerns the extent to which it is an overt or covert process, conscious or unconscious, comprising not only learning but instruction. That instruction may be an important part of socialization cannot be doubted: parents may teach their children certain modes of social behaviour; societal education systems may include a provision for civic education; the state may carefully propagate its official ideology; but it cannot be stressed too much that a great deal of socialization, perhaps the greater part of it, is experiential and as such is largely covert, unconscious, unrecognized and unacknowledged. Thus terms like 'inculcate' and, to a lesser extent, 'led to develop' tend to obscure this important facet of socialization. 'Political education . . . begins', as Michael Oakeshott has pointed out, 'in the enjoyment of a tradition, in the observation and imitation of the behaviour of our elders, and there is little or nothing in the world which comes before our eyes which does not contribute to it. . . . We are aware of a past and a future as soon as we are aware of a present.'[1] Thus, in spite

[1] Michael Oakeshott, 'Political Education', in P. Laslett (ed.), *Philosophy, Politics and Society*, Oxford, 1956, p. 17.

of the fact that socialization may be partially open, systematic and deliberate, it is totally unrealistic to assume that the significance of every experience is recognized by the agent (and, perhaps to a lesser extent, the subject) of the action or actions involved in that experience. Similarly, the contribution of the subject's personality to the experience may go equally unrecognized.

These two problems of systemic persistence or change and the deliberate inculcation of particular beliefs are, as it has been shown, of considerable importance to socialization in general, but they are of crucial importance to *political* socialization since they inevitably involve the question of the persistence or change of particular régimes as well as the deliberate inculcation of particular political beliefs. In short, political socialization becomes involved in the realm of political controversy. It is but a short step in the eyes of some critics from the academic 'neutrality' of system maintenance, equilibrium and stability to the political partisanship of conservatism, preservation of the status quo and reaction. Political socialization ceases to be a concept seeking to explain how particular beliefs and orientations are acquired in *any* political system and becomes associated with explanations of why system A is in various ways superior to system B. Such views, however, result from a tendency to confuse the concept with particular results that may stem from its use. If a study of political socialization in one country shows that through a variety of agents individuals acquire beliefs and orientations which tend to perpetuate the political system of that country, it does not follow that this is necessarily true for all other countries. What it does suggest is that the various socializing agents are working in the same direction and that any countervailing agents are weak; but this does not preclude the existence of *conflicting* agents of socialization which, far from perpetuating a particular political system, may affect radical change.

In formulating a definition of political socialization, therefore, it is important to allow for both systemic persistence and change and for both the deliberate and unplanned learning of political behaviour, and the following two definitions should be seen in this light:

[1.] . . . [the individual's] learning of social patterns corresponding to his societal positions as mediated through various agencies of society.[1]

[1] Hyman, *Political Socialization*, p. 25.

[2.] . . . the process whereby political attitudes and values are inculcated as children become adults and as adults are recruited into roles.[1]

Both these definitions suffer, however, from the problems already mentioned, in that they do not offer a means of accounting for systemic change (concentrating as they do on socialization for existing 'societal positions' and roles to the apparent exclusion of the creation of new ones); nor do they distinguish sufficiently between deliberate and unplanned learning. Fred I. Greenstein, in an article on political socialization in the *International Encyclopedia of the Social Sciences*, has sought to clarify the difference between what he has termed the narrow and broad definitions of political socialization:

> . . . the deliberate inculcation of political information, values and practices by instructional agents who have been formally charged with this responsibility;

and,

> . . . all political learning, formal and informal, deliberate and unplanned, at every stage of the life cycle, including not only explicitly political learning but also nominally non-political learning of politically relevant personality characteristics.[2]

The last definition does allow for both persistence and change (at least by implication) inasmuch as no specific purpose is attributed to the socialization process. Moreover, it emphasizes that socialization is a continuing process involving all kinds of learning. David Easton and Jack Dennis, in pleading for a neutral definition of political socialization, have provided an effective, but short definition which, because it is deliberately broad, is able to encompass the various facets of Greenstein's second definition. They define political socialization simply as:

> . . . those developmental processes through which persons acquire political orientations and patterns of behaviour.[3]

The manner in which political orientations and behaviour are acquired and the results of their acquisition remain a matter for investigation.

It is now possible to posit a model of political socialization and

---

[1] Almond and Powell, *Comparative Politics*, p. 24.

[2] Fred I. Greenstein, 'Political Socialization', in *International Encyclopedia of the Social Sciences*, Vol. 14, New York, 1968, p. 551.

[3] David Easton and Jack Dennis, *Children in the Political System: Origins of Political Legitimacy*, New York, 1969, p. 7.

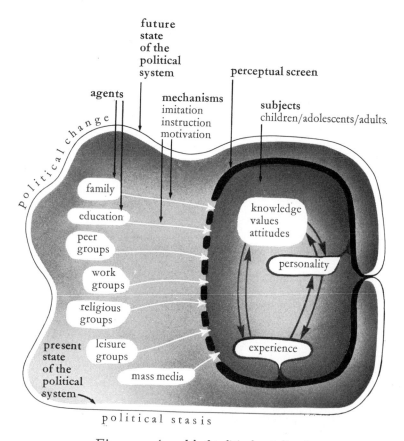

Figure 1. A model of political socialization

this is illustrated in Figure 1. The model seeks to trace the socialization process through its various stages from its beginnings in childhood to its ultimate significance in adulthood. As a model it does not suggest an absolute and arbitrary process of socialization that does not admit variation from one political system to another. Socialization is conceived as a process which continues throughout life, affecting child, adolescent and adult. At the same time, it is not suggested that each is affected equally, either within a particular system or between systems. Its temporal development, moreover, is not continuous in the sense that the individual regularly and systematically undergoes experiences which are significant and relevant to his subsequent political behaviour, even in those political systems in which regular and systematic political instruction is an important part of political socialization. Even in such systems there will be experiences which are irregular, possibly infrequent, but which are none the less of political importance in the development of an individual's political behaviour.

Similarly, although it is possible to posit the elements of political socialization, it is not suggested that these are acquired in a particular order, nor that they are of equal significance. Thus it is possible to distinguish between the acquisition of knowledge or information, values or basic beliefs, and attitudes or opinions on specific matters. While knowledge, which is basically though not exclusively factual, may precede the formation of values and attitudes, the reverse may also occur and knowledge may be used to support a particular value or attitude after its formation. At the same time, knowledge is affected by values and attitudes and cannot therefore be totally objective, if only because of the inevitable selectivity exercised by the individual. Moreover, it is also clear that attitudes are closely related to values in that an individual's basic beliefs will play a crucial part in determining his reaction to particular stimuli and to the formation of particular attitudes or opinions, but attitudes may precede values, especially on an imitative basis. It is also likely that there will be a 'feedback' process by which attitudes, or more particularly the consequences of attitudes, will affect an individual's values. Attitudes may or may not be borne out by experience, and this may serve to confirm or possibly undermine particular beliefs. Finally, values and attitudes will affect the individual's acquisition of knowledge by influencing his selection of information. Thus the three elements are analytically distinguishable but closely inter-related.

The model further suggests that the various elements of political socialization are transmitted through a variety of agents, but once again primacy is not given to any one agent or group of agents. Quite apart from the fact that some of these agents are more applicable to some of the subjects of socialization than others, they may also vary in importance from one political system to another, and sometimes within a political system. Thus children will be more likely to be affected by the influences of family and education, adults by work groups and the mass media. In communities such as the Israeli kibbutz or the Chinese commune, the role of the family may be minimized, compared with its influence in Europe or North America. Education will obviously vary in its impact, especially between those countries in which it does not go beyond the primary stage for the majority of the population and those in which there is extensive higher education. Or again, work situations differ considerably from one country to another, creating important environmental differences, quite apart from specific organizational differences, such as the degree to which the work force is unionized.

The way in which these various agents transmit the elements of political socialization also varies, and the model suggests three such ways or mechanisms: imitation, instruction and motivation. Robert Le Vine suggests that these are the mechanisms of political socialization in childhood,[1] but there is no reason why they should not be applicable to the whole socialization process. Imitation is the copying of the behaviour of other individuals and is obviously of great importance in childhood socialization, yet it need not be confined to childhood behaviour. What seems more likely is that pure imitation will be found among children, but as an adolescent and adult mechanism it becomes increasingly mixed with the other two mechanisms, so that a degree of imitation will be found in both instruction and motivation. Instruction is more or less self-explanatory, although it should be stressed that it is not confined to formal learning. An individual may be deliberately placed in a situation which is instructive in nature – this is clearly the case, for example, in various types of vocational training 'on the job', some of which may be relevant to political behaviour; while the practice of some organizations or groups of individuals to form discussion groups is an explicit but informal type of instruction. Although both imitation and instruction are specific types of experience, the third mechanism, motivation, is most closely identified with experience in general. Motivation is the learning of what Le Vine has called 'appropriate behaviour' through a process of trial and error: the individual learns directly from his experience what actions are most congruent with his attitudes and opinions. The term 'appropriate' refers not to the extent to which the individual is led to conform to some norm of group behaviour (though this may well be the result), but to the process by which

[1] Robert Le Vine, 'Political Socialization and Culture Change', in Clifford Geertz (ed.), *Old Societies and New States*, New York, 1963, pp. 280–303.

the individual relates action to attitudes and opinions to his *experience*.

Experience is one of the key variables of the model in that an individual's political behaviour is partially determined by the sum of his experience. His knowledge, values and attitudes are contributory to his experience and are in due course affected by it. In the same way the transmission of knowledge, values and attitudes through the various agents of socialization are both experiences in themselves and in time become affected by other experiences. Thus an individual's politically relevant experience arises out of and is contributory to the process of political socialization. As a result of his interviews in depth with fifteen American working men, for example, Robert Lane concludes that the individual's conception of political problems is seen through the variety of his experiences. Furthermore, his conception may be irrational in the sense that it is unplanned and unsystematic, but not necessarily within the context of his own experience. Thus the individual may ignore factors which seem to an outside observer to be important, because they fall outside his experience. It is also important to stress that where experiences are shared by a number of individuals they may acquire much greater significance in the formation of values and attitudes.[1] Group experiences are likely to reinforce commonly held values and attitudes, while the general nature of widely shared experiences often assumes considerable political significance. Widespread economic prosperity or deprivation, the rapidity of social change, frequent violence or prolonged peace, the existence or absence of social tension and so on, may provide an experiential environment which contributes to the individual's political orientations and pattern of political behaviour.

The other key variable in political socialization is the individual's personality. This too is related to his experience, but remains distinguishable from it. Political observers have long posited various types of political temperament or personality. Bluntschli, for example, linked the Hippocratic theories of temperament with various broad types of political philosophy: the reactionary was melancholic, the conservative phlegmatic, the progressive sanguine and the radical choleric. Similarly, Macaulay speaks of two classes – the conservative and the liberal.

[1] Robert E. Lane, *Political Ideology: Why the American Common Man Believes What He Does*, New York, 1962, Chapter 24.

Modern observers have sought types of political character or personality based on psychological phenomena. J. P. Guilford defines personality as an individual's 'unique pattern of traits'. Traits are defined as 'any distinguishable, relatively enduring way in which one individual differs from others', and, from the point of view of political behaviour, particular attention is paid to those traits which are 'shared' in varying degrees, by large segments of the population'.[1] Many political personality types have been posited, but there is little agreement on any range of types. Some writers have concerned themselves with a particular type, others with a general typology. Erich Fromm, for instance, describes one type as the *automaton* – a person who loses his sense of individuality by conforming to popular values.[2] Harold Lasswell suggests a range of types: the *political agitator*, who is skilled in the area of personal contact and the rousing of political emotions; the *political administrator*, who is skilled in the manipulation of organizations and situations; the *political theorist*, who is skilled in the manipulation of ideas; and the *bureaucrat*, who over-emphasizes formal rules and organization and responds habitually to given situations.[3] Similarly, David Riesman has devised a threefold grouping: the *tradition-directed* person, who lacks any conception of politics and who reacts to a limited, parochial environment; the *inner-directed* person, whose orientations stem from childhood and who is unresponsive to contemporary influences; and the *other-directed* person, who is oriented to contemporary influences.[4]

Probably the best-known attempt to posit a particular type of political personality, however, is that of T. W. Adorno *et al.*, in *The Authoritarian Personality*. By means of various attitude scales the authors posit a series of behavioural characteristics which, they suggest, comprise the authoritarian personality. These may be summarized as follows:

Attitude of dominance towards subordinates.
Attitude of deference to superiors.

[1] J. P. Guilford, *Personality*, New York, 1959, pp. 5–6, quoted in L. A. Froman, 'Personality and Political Socialization', *Journal of Politics*, **23**, 1961, p. 344.

[2] Erich Fromm, *Escape from Freedom*, New York, 1941, pp. 153–83.

[3] Harold D. Lasswell, *Power and Personality*, New York, 1948, Chapter 4.

[4] David Riesman, *The Lonely Crowd*, New Haven, Conn., 1950, Chapter 1.

A sensitivity to power relationships.

A tendency to perceive the world in a highly structured fashion.

An excessive use of stereotyped images.

An adherence to whatever values are conventional within the individual's immediate environment.

A tendency to be superstitious.

A preoccupation with virility.

A pessimistic view of human nature.

Strong moral views.

A tendency to be impatient with and generally intolerant of opposition.[1]

Earlier studies during the Second World War and in the immediate postwar period linked authoritarian (and often Fascist) attitudes with particular personality traits,[2] but the methodology used in *The Authoritarian Personality* was criticized on such grounds as its failure to take account of left-wing authoritarianism and the alleged inaccuracy and subjectivity of the most well-known of the scales used, the Fascism or F-Scale. Greenstein asserts that Adorno and his colleagues deal 'more with prejudice than with . . . psychological dispositions toward authority'.[3] In spite of the criticism of *The Authoritarian Personality*, the work is a landmark in the attempts to delineate various types of political personality and it has stimulated much of the subsequent work in the field.

There have also been attempts to delineate a 'democratic personality', but most of these have been theoretical rather than research-based. Inkeles and Lasswell, for example, offer similar, but slightly different traits:

---

[1] T. W. Adorno, Else Frenkel-Brunswik, Daniel J. Levinson and R. N. Sandford, *The Authoritarian Personality*, New York, 1950, pp. 242–62.

[2] e.g. Fromm, *Escape from Freedom*; H. V. Dicks, 'Personality Traits and National Socialist Ideology', *Human Relations*, **3**, 1950; and Ruth Benedict, *The Chrysanthemum and the Sword*, Boston, Mass., 1946.

[3] Fred I. Greenstein, 'Personality and Political Socialization: the Theories of the Authoritarian and Democratic Character', *Annals of the American Academy of Political and Social Science* (henceforth cited as *Annals*), **361**, September 1965, p. 83.

Inkeles[1]	**Lasswell**[2]
Accepting of other people	Warm attitude towards other people
Open to new experiences and ideas	Share values with other people
Responsible but watchful attitude towards authority	Wide range of values
	Confidence in environment
Tolerant of differences	Relative freedom from anxiety
Controlled emotions	

H. J. Eysenck has attempted a two-dimensional approach to the problem of political personality by the use of two attitude scales: (1) a *Radicalism-Conservatism* syndrome (the R-factor) and (2) a *Tough-minded-Tender-minded* syndrome (the T-factor). The R-factor is virtually self-explanatory, consisting merely of assessing the degree to which an individual holds radical or conservative views. The T-factor involves the following pairs of traits:

Tender minded	**Tough minded**[3]
Rationalistic (going by 'principles')	Empiricist (going by 'facts')
Intellectualistic	Sensationalistic
Idealistic	Materialistic
Optimistic	Pessimistic
Religious	Irreligious
Free-willist	Fatalistic
Monistic	Pluralistic
Dogmatical	Sceptical

According to Eysenck, both factors are psychologically based: the R-factor is based on *learning*, i.e. by a process of rewards and punishment derived from hedonistic theories of learning; and the T-factor is based on conditioning, i.e. the influence of association or continuity, and is thus a series of involuntary, emotional

[1] Alex Inkeles, 'National Character and Modern Political Systems', in Hsu (ed.), *Psychological Anthropology*, pp. 172–208.

[2] Harold D. Lasswell, 'Power and Personality', in *The Writings of Harold D. Lasswell*, Glencoe, Ill., 1951, pp. 495 ff.

[3] H. J. Eysenck, *The Psychology of Politics*, London, 1954, p. 131.

responses. Furthermore, tough-mindedness is associated with *extraversion* and tender-mindedness with *introversion*. Tough-mindedness is also closely associated with aggression, dominance and, to a lesser extent, with rigidity and narrow-mindedness.

The connection between the two factors, using British ideological positions, is as follows:

Fascism: tough-minded conservatism
Communism: tough-minded radicalism
Conservatism: intermediate tender-minded conservatism
Labourism: intermediate tender-minded radicalism
Liberalism: tender-minded intermediate radicalism-conservatism

The problem with most of these attempts to evolve a typology of political personality is that, while the various traits ascribed to particular personality types are often recognizable, they tend to remain isolated syndromes or points on a continuum. There is often the further problem of relating the particular traits to specific political behaviour. Probably the greatest problem, however, is that of linking these concepts with particular political systems. Eysenck has had some success in this, and he reports that his two-dimensional analysis has been successfully applied in a number of countries, including the United States, West Germany and Sweden, as well as Britain. How applicable it is to, say, totalitarian societies or developing societies remains an unanswered question. Even within similar political systems, there may be important differences, especially in the significance of such scales as the R-factor, and it is therefore important to take into account the particular environment concerned. For example, the extent to which violence is regarded as a legitimate means of political expression is likely to vary not only according to the personality of the individual, but also in relation to norms of the political system concerned. Any attempt, therefore, to delineate various types of 'national character' is fraught with problems. None the less, it is important to bear in mind that personality remains an important factor in the process of political socialization.

*

Political socialization is the process that results from the elaborate interplay between an individual's personality and his politically relevant experiences. These experiences are not necessarily specifically political, of course, but they are relevant because they shape his political behaviour. Experiences which are primarily social or economic may have political significance: thus movement from one neighbourhood to another may influence an individual's party identity or a period of unemployment may result in an individual becoming politically alienated. Political socialization is therefore characterized by an intricate network of knowledge, values and attitudes transmitted between individuals and groups of individuals within a political system resulting from and contributing to a set of experiences interwoven around the personality of the individual to form a syndrome of political behaviour. The knowledge, values and attitudes acquired by the individual form a *perceptual screen* through which the individual perceives political stimuli. Since the individual's knowledge, values and attitudes are subject to change, this perceptual screen is not necessarily immutable. Furthermore, some stimuli will be accepted and others rejected, so that the political behaviour, especially in respect of political participation, inevitably varies from one individual to another.[1] An individual's political behaviour, however, like his behaviour in general, develops only gradually. Clearly not all individuals develop in the same way or at the same pace, but it is possible to suggest the main lines of that development within particular political systems, and it is to this question that we now turn.

THE DEVELOPMENT OF POLITICAL SOCIALIZATION
Childhood and Adolescence Frank and Elizabeth Estvan have shown in their book, *The Child's World*, how children gradually become aware of a wider environment, how they become increasingly perceptive in response to particular situations, and how their whole outlook becomes increasingly coherent and total, where before it was fragmented and limited.[2] The children in this study were asked to identify and comment on a series of pictures depicting

[1] See Lester W. Milbrath, *Political Participation*, Chicago, 1965, Chapter 1.
[2] New York, 1959, Chapters 3–8.

various scenes in American life, including a picture of the Capitol in Washington, D.C. Just over half of the children (51 per cent) recognized the picture as a governmental (or political) scene in whole or part. Not surprisingly, older children recognized the picture as a governmental scene more frequently and made much more sophisticated comments on the scene than younger children, so that the Estvans concluded:

> Boys and girls enter school with little conception of government, only one-fourth managing to achieve a partial or structural recognition of this scene. By the time they are in sixth grade, the proportion has about trebled . . . [but] ideas and attitudes about government are slow to appear and to mature.[1]

Furthermore, the Estvans' general conclusions also have some relevance to political socialization. They found that environment was an important factor in socialization: urban children, for example, were more likely than rural children to recognize the picture of the Capitol, and this was attributed to a more local orientation on the part of children in rural areas. Children's perceptions of situations were found to be highly individual: in commenting on the picture of the Capitol, children varied considerably on the particular aspect which aroused their interest, and a number of them identified the picture as the Capitol in Madison, Wisconsin (the state in which the survey was conducted). In identifying particular points of interest, moreover, younger children were far more likely to comment on the people in the picture, whereas older children usually commented on both the people and the building, thus suggesting a progression from the merely human element to the recognition of a material element as well. The authors also found that the attitudes of the children became increasingly consistent as they got older and increasingly consistent with the various social backgrounds from which they were drawn.

As a result of survey research into political socialization, David Easton and Robert Hess suggest that in the United States political learning begins at the age of three and is well-established by the age of seven. The early stages of political learning involve the development of environmental ties, such as 'attachment to their schools' and the recognition that they live in a particular country. A simple sense of patriotism appears to be one of the earliest

[1] ibid., p. 204.

manifestations of political learning: Easton and Hess found that young children had a belief in the 'beauty of their country' and the 'goodliness and cleanliness of its people'. These early manifestations are followed by the recognition of the visible symbols of public authority, such as the policeman, the president and the national flag, but by the age of nine or ten there is increasing awareness of more abstract concepts, such as voting, democracy, civil liberty and of the role of citizens in the political system. By the age of seven or eight, moreover, the majority of American children have identified themselves with one or other of the country's two major parties.[1]

In an earlier article, Easton and Hess suggest that the child's earliest views of the President of the United States are as an authority figure and that the child's image of his father and of the President are similar during early school years. As they become older, children become increasingly aware of the President as part of a more complex governmental hierarchy:

> First, this initial socialization is to an image viewed in personal terms –
> that is, to someone whom the child sees as a person, rather than an
> impersonal group or institution; second, early in the process of political
> socialization, the President represents for the child a focus for an emer-
> ging sense of identification with a political community at the national
> level; third, to the child the President stands as a symbol of undifferenti-
> ated government that includes all levels and holds essentially all govern-
> mental authority; and fourth, the President serves as a central orientation
> point for an increasing awareness of the other elements of the political
> system . . . the Vice-President is seen as someone who helps the President;
> Congress is viewed as a group that takes orders from the President and
> performs certain tasks at his command.[2]

This progression from the simple to the complex, from the personal to the institutional, is seen clearly in the data presented by David Easton and Jack Dennis in their book *Children in the Political System*.[3] Their data was based on a national sample survey of American school-children from Grade 2 to Grade 8 (i.e. from the ages of seven or eight to thirteen or fourteen). The children were first asked which of a number of symbols they associated with government (Table 1).

[1] David Easton and Robert D. Hess, 'The Child's Political World', *Midwest Journal of Political Science*, 6, 1962.

[2] David Easton and Robert D. Hess, 'The Child's Changing Image of the President', *Public Opinion Quarterly*, 24, 1960, pp. 634–5.

[3] New York, 1969.

Table 1. *Symbols associated with government among U.S. schoolchildren*[1]

	Police-man	George Wash-ington	Uncle Sam	Voting	Supreme Court	Capitol (%)
Grade 2	8	39	16	4	5	14
Grade 8	2	2	16	47	16	7
Teachers	1	1	5	72	13	5

	Congress	Flag	Statue of Liberty	President Kennedy	Don't know (%)
Grade 2	6	16	12	46	16
Grade 8	49	12	20	23	2
Teachers	71	6	8	15	—

Grade 2 pupils were far more likely to associate government with persons, such as the President, or George Washington, or the policeman, and with visible symbols, such as the national flag or the Capitol building in Washington, whereas by Grade 8 government presented a much more complex picture to the children, which involved the recognition of institutions, such as Congress and the Supreme Court, and processes, such as voting. At the same time, the number who failed to identify government with any of the symbols suggested fell from 16 to 2 per cent between Grades 2 and 8 while the recognition of a more complex symbol like the Statue of Liberty increased from 12 to 20 per cent.

It is also clear from the data presented by Easton and Dennis that children's understanding of government is much more than a vague association with particular symbols: they also become increasingly aware of the different roles of the various governmental institutions, as Table 2 shows.

Table 2. *Understanding of the roles of governmental institutions among U.S. schoolchildren*[2]

A. Who does MOST to make the laws?

	Congress	President	Supreme Court	Don't know	Total (%)
Grade 2	5	76	11	8	100
Grade 8	85	5	8	1	99
Teachers	96	1	3	0	100

[1] Adapted from Easton and Dennis, *Children in the Political System*, Table 6–2, p. 116.
[2] Adapted from Easton and Dennis, *Children in the Political System*, Tables 6–3 and 6–4, pp. 119 and 120.

B. Who does the MOST to run the country?

	Congress	President	Supreme Court	Don't know	Total
Grade 2	4	86	3	7	100
Grade 8	35	58	4	3	100
Teachers	61	36	3	0	100

The saliency of the president in the minds of the younger children is very clear in the responses to these two questions: in both cases the president is the only figure or institution of real importance. By the time they reach Grade 8, however, children are aware that government is more complex, and although a majority still believe that the president does most to run the country, more than a third attribute this role to Congress; while the overwhelming importance of Congress as a lawmaking body is recognized by more than four-fifths of the pupils in Grade 8. It should also be noted that whereas the law-making function was largely transferred from the president to Congress between Grades 2 and 8, the question who does most to run the country is a more complicated notion and there is no comparable transfer: instead opinion is divided.

A further example of the widening political horizons of the children interviewed in the Easton and Dennis survey is shown by the extent to which they associated particular individuals with government:

Table 3. *The association of particular individuals with government among U.S. schoolchildren*[1]

Which of these people works for the government? (percentage replying 'yes')

	Milk-man	Police-man	Soldier	Judge	Post-man	Teacher
Grade 2	29	86	68	86	57	48
Grade 8	8	81	98	94	93	59
Teachers	1	77	100	91	99	45

Pupils in Grade 2 clearly associated both the policeman and the judge with government and, to a lesser extent, the soldier, but there was also evidence of some confusion and uncertainty. Thus

[1] Adapted from Easton and Dennis, *Children in the Political System*, Table 6–5, p. 122.

29 per cent said that the milkman was employed by the government and there was considerable uncertainty about the teacher and the postman. Pupils in Grade 8 had a clearer idea of which individuals did work for the government, and their political horizon had widened considerably. The overwhelming majority linked the soldier, judge and postman with government and only 8 per cent thought the milkman worked for the government. The altered positions of the policeman and the teacher are probably a reflection of an increasing awareness of the various levels of government and possibly some understandable difficulty in distinguishing between the 'government' and various other public authorities. Thus slightly fewer of the Grade 8 children said that the policeman was employed by the government, and it is as well to remember that in the United States police are employed by federal, state and city authorities. Similarly, the position of the teacher is probably a confusing one: although the survey was conducted in public (state) and not private schools, there is no immediate reason why the teacher should be associated with government employment any more than the school boards should be regarded as government agencies.

Although their data suggests a progression from the simple to the complex, from limited to broad conceptions, Easton and Dennis stress that there was no evidence to support a theory of political socialization involving a gradual and systematic linear progression or widening series of concentric circles in the development of the child's political awareness. They stress that, on the contrary, political learning appears to be fragmented and variable, so that a child may become aware simultaneously of familial authority, the role of the policeman and the existence of the President, while awareness of the three main levels of government – national, state and local – develops in a similar fashion, with the child having some knowledge of each, but far from a complete picture.[1]

As they grow older children also become aware that various individuals and groups play a role in the political process, and Easton and Dennis suggest that by Grade 4 (nine to ten years) children have some knowledge of the part played by trade unions, big business, newspapers and the churches, an awareness, in other words, of the informal areas of politics. This awareness is accom-

[1] Easton and Dennis. *Children in the Political System*, Part 2.

panied by the development of attitudes about government and politics, including party identity, and an increasing distinction between institutions and people, between political offices and the persons holding those offices.

Easton and Dennis posit four stages in childhood political socialization:

1 The recognition of authority through particular individuals, such as the child's parents, the president and the policeman;
2 The development of a distinction between internal and external authority, i.e. between private and public authority;
3 The recognition of impersonal political institutions, such as Congress, the Supreme Court, and voting;
4 The development of a distinction between political institutions and the persons engaged in the activities associated with those institutions, so that idealized images of particular persons such as the president or a Congressman are transferred to the presidency and Congress.[1]

Some differences in the rate of development were found in relation to sex, I.Q., religion and socio-economic status, but these were generally small and unsystematic, although Easton and Dennis suggest that the higher rate of development among those of higher socio-economic status might result in more deeply rooted beliefs.[2]

Easton and Dennis have also investigated the acquisition by children of political efficacy or political competence: that is, the feeling on the part of the individual that he can exert some influence in the political system. Easton and Dennis found that the feeling of political competence increased from 16 per cent in Grade 3 to 58 per cent in Grade 8, but they stress that this does not depend either on the ability to understand government or on the amount of information the respondents possessed. The feeling of competence did tend to increase, however, in relation to I.Q. and socio-economic status.[3]

[1] ibid., Part 3.
[2] ibid., Part 4.
[3] Easton and Dennis, 'The Child's Acquisition of Regime Norms: Political Efficacy', *American Political Science Review*, **61**, 1967, pp. 25–38.

The picture that Easton and Dennis draw of political socialization during childhood is clear enough, even though, as they themselves point out, it is an incomplete picture and leaves many gaps. At a fairly early age children do have some idea of what government is, even if their earliest conceptions are concentrated heavily on the figure of the president. Gradually their horizon widens and they become increasingly aware of the complexity of the political system, including some understanding of the importance of the informal facets of the political process. The child's picture becomes more complete, more coherent; his political knowledge increases, values are formed and attitudes develop; and, finally, some feeling of political competence may also arise. The whole theme of this picture, however, revolves around a single concept, for the main conclusion of *Children in the Political System* is, 'that the child is learning to orient himself to the structure of authority.'[1]

Roberta Sigel has provided more specific evidence of how important authority is to the young child: in a study of the reactions of children to the assassination of President Kennedy, she found that the greatest emotional shock at the sudden removal of the central figure of authority was suffered by the younger children in her sample.[2] If the view that attitudes towards authority are both the earliest manifestations of, and central to, political socialization is correct, then it is of immense importance to theories of legitimacy: the acceptance of a given authority – a matter which will be considered later in this chapter.

The emphasis laid on the importance of authority is closely related to theories concerning the role of the family in political socialization. We have already seen that Easton and Hess found that children had similar images of their fathers and of the president during their early school years, and that both were regarded as authority figures.[3] Such a view is in many respects crucial to the main hypothesis of Easton and Dennis. On a much wider front, however, the family has long been regarded as one of the earliest and most important agents of political socialization.

---

[1] Easton and Dennis, *Children in the Political System*, p. 399.

[2] Roberta S. Sigel, 'Some Explorations into Political Sociology: Schoolchildren's Reactions to the Death of a President', in Martha Wolfenstein and Gilbert Kliman (eds.), *Children and the Death of a President*, New York, 1965.

[3] See p. 32 above.

Robert Lane has suggested that there are three ways in which the foundations of political belief may be laid through the family:

1   By overt and covert indoctrination;
2   By placing the child in a particular social context;
3   By moulding the child's personality;

and together they constitute what Lane has called 'the Mendelian law of politics'.[1] Similarly, James C. Davies has argued that role of the family in political socialization is based on its broader task of providing for the needs of the child. Thus, by having its physical needs and its need for love and affection provided for, the child gradually acquires an identity of its own and, subsequently, is able to identify itself with others – the family serving as its earliest reference group to which the child looks for guidance as well as sustenance. This leads Davies to conclude '. . . most of the individual's political personality – his tendencies to think and act politically in particular ways – have been determined at home, several years before he can take part in politics as an ordinary adult'.[2] The evidence to support such assertions tends to be fragmentary in nature, and the exact role of the family in political socialization requires further research.

There is, however, extensive evidence linking the family with party preference. A study of the 1952 presidential election found a strong tendency for voters to support the same party as their parents, and not surprisingly, the strength of this tendency increased where both parents voted for the same party. Thus of those voters, both of whose parents were Democrats, 82 per cent were also Democrats, and of those with Republican parents, 73 per cent were Republicans.[3] Furthermore, Philip Converse and Georges Dupeux found that there was a strong correlation between an individual *knowing* his father's political identity and his

[1] Robert E. Lane, 'Fathers and Sons: The Foundations of Political Belief', *American Sociological Review*, **24**, 1959, pp. 502–11. See also *Political Ideology*, Chapter 17.

[2] James C. Davies, 'The Family's Role in Political Socialization', *Annals*, **361**, September 1965, p. 11.

[3] Angus Campbell, G. Gurin and Warren E. Miller, *The Voter Decides*, New York, 1954, p. 99.

own political identity.[1] Similarly, among a sample of college students interviewed by Philip Nogee and Murray Levin, 74 per cent had the same party preference as their parents, and this congruent identification was higher where both parents agreed and lower where there was only one parent or where the parents disagreed.[2]

What is not clear, however, is whether the influence of the family extends beyond party preference, and, even in the case of party preference, exactly how political values are transmitted from parent to child. Indeed, some doubt has been cast of the whole question of the importance of the family as an agent of political socialization by Kent Jennings and R. G. Niemi. Using a sample of Grade 12 pupils (i.e. senior high-school students), they confirmed the findings of earlier studies that the degree of party identification between parents and children is strong – only 7 per cent of their sample had a *totally different* party preference from their parents. When they investigated the transmission of attitudes on particular issues, however, and the values underlying such attitudes, they found a much lower incidence of parent–child congruence. Unfortunately, they did not take into account the fact that their sample was drawn from senior high-school students and that this in itself might account, in part at least, for differences between the attitudes of parents and children, since as seventeen- or eighteen-year-olds these students would have been subjected to other agents of socialization for a number of years, including some eleven or more years of full-time education. Even so, allowing for such considerations, this study does suggest that it is erroneous to assume that parents transmit to their children a complete set of values, let alone attitudes on particular issues.[3]

Evidence on the nature of parental transmission – *how* political values are transmitted from parent to child – is almost non-existent. One study, however, does throw some light on the matter: Karen Orren and Paul Peterson asked a sample of American

[1] Philip Converse and Georges Dupeux, 'Politicization of the Electorate in France and the United States', *Public Opinion Quarterly*, **26**, 1962, pp. 1–23.

[2] Philip Nogee and Murray B. Levin, 'Some Determinants of Political Attitudes among College Voters', *Public Opinion Quarterly*, **22**, 1958, pp. 449–63.

[3] M. Kent Jennings and R. G. Niemi, 'The Transmission of Political Values from Parent to Child', *American Political Science Review*, **62**, 1968, pp. 169–84.

parents whether they explained the assassination of President Kennedy to their children, and, if so, how. A majority (65 per cent) did *not* explain the event to their children at all. Those who did were more emotionally affected by the assassination, tended to be better informed politically, and of higher social status. This last finding was independent of the degree of political information, even though those of higher social status are normally better informed politically. The explanations offered to younger children naturally tended to be simpler in form and often involved a religious element, whereas those offered to older children tended to be broader, more historical and more political in form. In general, however, parents avoided giving negative explanations and refrained from mentioning some of the more unpleasant aspects of the event.[1]

The fact that nearly two thirds of the parents offered no explanation at all is itself significant, of course. Does this mean that they had no impact on their children's views of the assassination of the president? The study reports on the deliberate actions of those parents who *did* explain the event to their children, but this does not preclude the possibility of children being affected by the actions of their parents short of deliberate explanation – the impact of parental emotion (or even of parental silence) could be more significant than overt explanation.

If this study is any guide of the extent to which parents are overtly involved in political socialization, then we must assume that the majority of parents are covertly rather than overtly involved in transmitting knowledge, values and attitudes to their children. This is, in fact, implicit in all theories of the role of the family in political socialization: the evidence that children are likely to adopt the party preferences of their parents is overwhelming, and Jennings and Niemi probably go too far in more or less limiting the political role of the family to this. Even the evidence available on the congruence of parent–child party preference offers no specific explanation of how this preference is transmitted. Children whose parents are actively involved in politics, or strongly committed to a particular party, may be subjected to a greater degree of direct or indirect indoctrination

[1] Karen Orren and Paul Peterson, 'Presidential Assassination: A Case-Study in the Dynamics of Political Socialization', *Journal of Politics*, **29**, 1967, pp. 388–404.

than children whose parents are less interested in political activity. In the latter case, unconscious influences may be more important, and as Lane suggests, the social milieu created may be an important means of political socialization. If this is so, then it is likely to be the case for the majority of individuals, since only a fairly small minority of people are actively involved in political activity. The significance of the findings of Converse and Dupeux may be simply that the majority of American children know their fathers' political identities and that the initial reaction is to assume the same identity. As an initial reaction it may be a question of blind faith or implicit trust, but subsequent experience may well confirm, to a greater or lesser degree, the correctness of that initial reaction.

It is perhaps important to distinguish between party preference and the various values that an individual comes to adopt. Party preference is something specific in the sense that the individual identifies himself with a political party, with a party *label* – and that label is specifically contextual. An individual thinks of himself as, say, a Democrat, and this becomes a point of reference: the more closely he identifies an issue as a party matter, the more likely he is to react as a Democrat – at elections for the president, or Congress, or the state governor or legislature he will probably vote Democrat; similarly, on issues on which the party has clearly defined views, he will probably support the party line; but in an election at local level for the district attorney or sheriff he may well vote on personal rather than party grounds if he happens to know one or more of the candidates; while he may also ignore the party line in a local referendum where he feels well-informed on the issue concerned. The personnel and the issues change, but the party remains.

Compare this with the much less specific sense of identification as, say, a 'liberal'. Obviously it is possible to posit certain basic values associated with a liberal point of view, such as a belief in freedom of speech, equality before the law, and so on, but, quite apart from securing agreement as to what such beliefs mean in *practice*, their meaning may also differ over time. Can it be said with confidence that the term 'liberal' means the same from one generation to another? Even assuming a measure of agreement within a generation, the application of 'liberal' views will vary considerably in practice in response both to the situation and the individual concerned. To be a 'liberal' is a diffuse commitment; to be a Democrat is a specific commitment. The majority of Democrats may regard themselves as 'liberals', but not all 'liberals' are necessarily Democrats.

The available evidence on the role of the family in political socialization suggests that children are, on the whole, influenced environmentally rather than directly. The family provides and is part of an environment which is conducive to the acquisition of certain knowledge, values and attitudes which are commonly held by that family. At the same time, the child becomes increasingly subject to other influences which may or may not reinforce the effect of early socialization, and one of the most important of these is education.

Education has long been regarded as an important variable in the explanation of political behaviour, and there is considerable circumstantial evidence to suggest that it is important as an agent of political socialization. In their five-nation study, for example, Almond and Verba found that the more extensive an individual's education the more likely he was to be aware of the impact of government, to follow politics, to have more political information, to possess a wider range of opinions on political matters, to engage in political discussion with a wider range of people, to feel a greater ability to influence political affairs, to be a member of and to be active in a voluntary organization, and express confidence in his social environment and exhibit feelings of trust.[1] Similarly, innumerable studies have shown a correlation between electoral behaviour and education, while other studies have found significant correlations between education and subjective class identification. Moreover, many of the studies cited earlier traced the development of political knowledge, values and attitudes through the various school grades, and the figures already given in Tables 1, 2 and 3 show a convergence between the attitudes of the children and the attitudes of their teachers.

Although, in a number of instances, marked differences remain, the attitudes of Grade 8 pupils are, for the most part, closer to those of the teachers than they are to those of the Grade 2 pupils. For Grade 2 pupils the two most important symbols associated with government were President Kennedy and George Washing-

[1] Almond and Verba, *The Civic Culture* (Little, Brown, Boston, Mass., 1966), pp. 315–24.

ton; but for Grade 8 pupils they were Congress and voting, and for teachers voting and Congress (Table 1). Grade 2 pupils felt that the president did most to make the laws, but Grade 8 pupils and teachers attributed this role to Congress (Table 2). On the more difficult question of who did most to run the country, a majority of pupils in both grades nominated the president, but whereas this was the view of 86 per cent of those in Grade 2, the proportion dropped to 58 per cent in Grade 8, compared with 36 per cent of the teachers. Conversely, only 4 per cent of the pupils in Grade 2 but 35 per cent in Grade 8 nominated Congress, compared with 61 per cent of the teachers (Table 2). The association of various individuals with the government showed a less clear-cut dichotomy, but a general convergence between the views of pupils and teachers remains (Table 3).

In spite of the evidence offered above, the influence of education as an agent of political socialization remains implicit rather than explicit. The evidence is, in fact, almost entirely circumstantial – persons with differing levels of education tend to possess differing levels of political knowledge, hold differing values and attitudes, and exhibit different political behaviour. There is no reason to believe that the connection is spurious, but the problem of ascertaining the exact relationship is a difficult one. For example, what is the relationship between education and class or status? If members of a particular social class or group are more likely to receive higher education, then some relationship will exist between the two. Conversely, the same will be true if those who do receive higher education come, as a result of that education, to regard themselves as members of a particular class or group. Education may therefore be a dependent or an independent variable. The position is complicated, as the findings of the study by Raymond Murphy and Richard Morris of the relationship between occupation, subjective class identification and party affiliations show: when they controlled their statistics for education the relationship between subjective class identification and occupation persisted for those with an elementary or high-school education, but disappeared for those with a college education. They also found a strong correlation between party affiliation, income and occupation, but these income and occupational differences tended to disappear among those with higher education, so that the latter were more likely to identify themselves as middle class and Republican regardless of income and occupation.[1]

A number of studies have endeavoured to establish what effect various aspects of education have on children and adolescents. Kenneth Langton and Kent Jennings examined the impact of the civics curriculum in American schools and came to the conclusion that it was in no way 'significantly associated with students' political orientations'.[2] Another study found no direct relationship between attitudes towards politics and participation in extra-curricular high-school activities;[3] while a survey of freshmen and senior college students in California found no differences in their levels of political knowledge nor in the values they held.[4]

Once again, the evidence available suggests general rather than specific influence, environmental rather than direct socialization. As children emerge from the early influence of the family into the wider world of school and peer groups,[5] they become subject to other influences which may reinforce or conflict with early politicization. Thus Hyman has shown that political discussion not only tends to increase in the family between the ninth and twelfth grades, but among friends within the child's own grade.[6] Furthermore, Martin Levin found a tendency for individuals to adopt the majority view within peer groups, so that in a school in a predominantly Republican area the children of Democratic parents tended to become Republican and vice versa.[7]

As far as political socialization during childhood and adolescence is concerned, we can say with some confidence *what* is

[1] Raymond J. Murphy and Richard J. Morris, 'Occupational Situations, Subjective Class Identification and Political Affiliation', *American Sociological Review*, **26**, 1961, pp. 383–92.

[2] Kenneth P. Langton and M. Kent Jennings, 'Political Socialization and the High School Civics Curriculum in the United States', *American Political Science Review*, **62**, 1968, p. 866.

[3] D. Ziblatt, 'High School Extra-Curricular Activities and Political Socialization', *Annals*, **361**, September 1965, pp. 20–31.

[4] Charles G. McClintock and Henry A. Turner, 'The Impact of College upon Political Knowledge, Participation and Values', *Human Relations*, **15**, 1962, pp. 163–75.

[5] Peer groups are properly defined as groups of equals, but are commonly regarded as synonymous with age-groups.

[6] Hyman, *Political Socialization*, p. 101.

[7] Martin L. Levin, 'Social Climates and Political Socialization', *Public Opinion Quarterly*, **25**, 1961, pp. 596–606.

learned and *when* it is learned, but it is with less confidence that we can say *how* it is learned. The acquisition of political orientations and patterns of behaviour seems to owe far more to the influence of environment and experience than to specific learning or indoctrination.

Adult Socialization If the emphasis already laid upon environmental and experiential influences is correct, then it is reasonable to assume that these influences will continue to be of importance during adult life and that the process of socialization continues beyond childhood and adolescence. The main outlines of future political behaviour may well be determined in the earlier period, but this is more likely to create a situation in which there is interaction between early political socialization and the environmental and experiential influences of later life than to preclude adult socialization. A limited example will illustrate our point: there is evidence to suggest that members of legislatures undergo a process of socialization following their election, and that their subsequent legislative behaviour is determined partly by their knowledge, values and attitudes as these existed prior to election, and partly by their experiences within and reactions to their new environment in the legislature.[1] In such circumstances some degree of socialization is inevitable, but probably no more inevitable than the day-to-day experiences of ordinary men and women.

Political socialization during adult life has not been the subject of much study, although there is some evidence arising from studies of electoral behaviour, class consciousness, the influence of work situations and the development of ideology. Even so, it is at least possible to suggest those areas in which adult socialization may be important. Just as the child is gradually brought into contact with more and more of the world around him, so also is the adolescent, and the change from adolescent to adult life marks

[1] See Kenneth Prewitt, Heinz Eulau and Betty H. Zisk, 'Political Socialization and Political Roles', *Public Opinion Quarterly*, **30**, 1966, pp. 569–82; Duncan Macrae Jr and Edith K. Macrae, 'Legislators' Social Status and their Votes', *American Journal of Sociology*, **66**, 1960–1, pp. 599–603; Donald R. Matthews, *U.S. Senators and their World*, Chapel Hill, North Carolina, 1960; Allan Kornberg, *Canadian Legislative Behaviour*, New York, 1967; and Anthony Barker and Michael Rush, *The Member of Parliament and His Information*, London, 1970.

another important stage in political socialization. Some of the contacts made during childhood and adolescence may continue in a somewhat similar form through friendship and acquaintance; others may continue or be renewed through other mediums, such as work, leisure, religion or the mass media; but some, and the experiences they bring, will be new. For some, these new experiences will simply reinforce early socialization, but for others varying degrees of conflict will occur which may result in important changes in political behaviour. Movement from a rural to an urban area, change of employment or experience of unemployment, membership of voluntary organizations, the development of leisure interests, religious conversion, the absorption of fact and opinion via the mass media – these may all have some significant effect on an individual's political behaviour.

Electoral studies have again and again found correlations between party preferences and characterics of the voters which are related to environment and experience.[1] The study by Murphy and Morris already cited found that respondents who worked in commerce, finance and records were more likely to identify themselves as middle class and vote Republican, whereas those who worked in manufacturing, building and maintenance were more likely to identify themselves as working class and vote Democrat. Lewis Lipsitz, in a study of auto-workers in Detroit, found greater work dissatisfaction among unskilled workers, and these workers tended to be more pessimistic about the future, both individually and generally, more radical politically and less tolerant than skilled workers.[2] Robert Lane's study, *Political Ideology*, suggests that for the American 'common man' his experience of democracy through small voluntary groups and 'a *general* sense of satisfaction . . . leads him to accept and endorse the political system of his society'.[3] In addition, Lane's 'democrats' had a belief in at least the partial control of their own existence; they accepted the realities of politics in that they recognized that politicians are human and that delays, contradictions and confusion are, to some extent, part of the process; and this tended to be part of their

---

[1] See R. R. Alford, *Party and Society*, Chicago, 1963, and S. M. Lipset and Stein Rokkan (eds.), *Party Systems and Voter Alignments*, New York, 1967.

[2] Lewis Lipsitz, 'Work Life and Political Attitudes: A Study of Manual Workers', *American Political Science Review*, 58, 1964, pp. 951–62.

[3] Lane, *Political Ideology*, p. 91. (Original italics.)

general attitude to life rather than a specifically *political* attitude. Lane argues that the individuals he interviewed saw political problems, whether local, national or international, through the variety of their experiences. These experiences were not necessarily political, however: their total experience provided one perspective and those experiences which seemed especially relevant to the situation provided others. Moreover, their attitudes on particular situations were closely identified with the various groups to which they belonged, and these *reference* groups, acting as guides or touchstones in the individual's reaction to his experiences, provide further evidence of a continuing process of socialization during adult life.

The knowledge, values and attitudes acquired during childhood and adolescence will be measured against the experience of adult life: they may be reinforced, undermined or modified by that experience; to suggest otherwise is to suggest a static political behaviour. If the processes of adult socialization tend to reinforce those of childhood and adolescence, the degree of change may be limited to that of increasing conservatism with age, but where conflict occurs, then radical changes in political behaviour may result: such conflict may have its roots in early political socialization, but it may also be attributable to the experiences of later socialization. Bernard Berelson and his co-authors found that among their sample of voters the agreement in party preference between the voter and his three closest friends increased markedly with age between twenty-one and forty-five. Of those in the twenty-one to twenty-five age group, 53 per cent voted the same as their three closest friends; in the twenty-six to thirty-four group this had increased to 69 per cent; and in the thirty-five to forty-four group to 75 per cent; but thereafter it levelled out to 77 per cent for those of forty-five or over.[1] Similarly, the tendency for husband and wife to agree on party preference is very strong and the impact of adult socialization in general may be one of increasing social homogeneity. Conversely, the impact of social mobility introduces an element of conflict: one study suggests that upward mobility often results in the individual adopting the party of the social group he has joined, without, however, fully adopting the values and attitudes of that party; while downward mobility

[1] Bernard Berelson, Paul F. Lazarsfeld and William N. McPhee, *Voting*, Chicago, 1954, p. 97.

often results in the retention of party preference, but the partial acceptance of the values and attitudes of the lower social group.[1] In the United States the evidence on adult socialization points largely to a tendency to reinforce early socialization, but there is also evidence to link adult socialization with changes in political behaviour.

Almond and Verba have effectively summarized the results of political socialization in the United States in their study *The Civic Culture*. They found that 85 per cent of their American respondents cited their governmental and political institutions when asked what they were proud of in the United States – far behind came those who cited the economic system (23 per cent) and social legislation (13 per cent).[2] This widespread pride in the country's political system was matched by an identical proportion who felt that the national government had some effect on their daily life; while 76 per cent felt that the effect of the national government was beneficial.[3] Similarly, the overwhelming majority felt that they received equality of treatment from the government officials (83 per cent) and from the police (85 per cent), although much lower proportions (48 and 56 per cent) expected serious consideration of their point of view in encounters with officials and the police.[4] While only 27 per cent said that they regularly followed accounts of political and governmental affairs, a further 53 per cent said that they did so from 'time to time', a total of 80 per cent thus taking some interest in political matters; while 76 per cent said that they sometimes discuss politics with other people.[5] Finally, 75 per cent felt that they could do something about an unjust national regulation.[6]

A picture of considerable political homogeneity is thus presented, in which the political system of the United States is accepted by the vast majority of Americans. This does not, of

---

[1] Eleanor E. Maccoby, Richard E. Matthews and Anton S. Morton, 'Youth and Political Change', *Public Opinion Quarterly*, **18**, 1954, pp. 33–6. See also Fred I. Greenstein and Raymond E. Wolfinger, 'The Suburbs and Shifting Party Loyalties', *Public Opinion Quarterly*, **22**, 1958, pp. 473–82.

[2] Almond and Verba, *The Civic Culture*, p. 64.

[3] ibid., pp. 46 and 48. The proportion for local government was 88 per cent.

[4] ibid., pp. 70 and 72.

[5] ibid., pp. 54 and 79.

[6] ibid., p. 142; the proportion for a local regulation was 77 per cent.

course, preclude conflict *within* the political system, but what Oakeshott has called 'the arrangements of society' are broadly accepted. Even among those who accept these arrangements, conflict occurs over the policies to be pursued and who is to pursue them. While recognizing this general homogeneity it is, nevertheless, important not to overlook variations in the process of political socialization. This is important in two senses: first, there may be variations within the general homogeneity; and, second, there may be variations (or deviations) from it.

Almond and Verba's data support the view that the political system is broadly accepted in the United States, but within that acceptance there are likely to be many gradations, ranging from total acceptance to near rejection. It is also likely that the paths to that acceptance have varied – the agents of socialization, the relevant experiences and the significant environmental influences may differ from individual to individual. Thus a study of political socialization in one area of the United States led its authors to conclude:

> Children in the relatively poor, rural Appalachian region . . . are dramatically less favourably inclined toward political objects than their counterparts in other parts of the nation.[1]

Similarly, in investigating political socialization among American Negroes, Dwaine Marvick found that not only could a meaningful distinction be made between the socialization of white persons and Negroes, but between various sub-groups:

Table 4. *Proportions of various sub-groups in the U.S. who have never tried to influence a local decision*

SUB-GROUP	%
Southern Negroes	95
Young Negroes	89
All Negroes	86
Old Negroes	83
Northern Negroes	76
'Poor whites'	73
National white cross-section	70

SOURCE: Dwaine Marvick, 'The Political Socialization of the American Negro', *Annals of the American Academy of Political and Social Science*, **361**, September 1965, p. 120.

[1] D. Jaros, H. Hirsch and F. J. Fleron Jr, 'The Malevolent Leader: Political Socialization in an American Sub-Culture', *American Political Science Review*, **62**, 1968, pp. 574–5.

Apart from variations of this sort, however, there are those who may not accept the political system or who have considerable reservations about it. Just as those who accept the system come to do so through the process of political socialization, so also do those who totally or partially reject it – those who are totally or partially *alienated*; and these individuals will form an important part of our discussion of political participation in Chapter 3.

*

The data available on political socialization in other parts of the world is much less extensive and more fragmentary than that available on the United States. None the less, it is possible to make some comparisons which illustrate some of the similarities and differences, while a good deal may be inferred from our knowledge of the political systems of these other countries in general. Furthermore, some of the research conducted in other countries not only throws light on the process of political socialization in general, but deals with areas which have, as yet, received little or no attention in the United States.

Some useful comparative material is available on the subject of party identification. Converse and Dupeux, for instance, found that whereas 75 per cent of the respondents of a national survey in the United States identified themselves with one or other of the two major parties, less than 45 per cent of their French respondents identified themselves with political parties and a further 10 to 15 per cent with broad categories, such as 'left' and 'right'. As we have already noted, however, they also found a strong correlation between an individual *knowing* his father's political identity and his own political identity, and whereas 82 per cent of the Americans could recall the political identities of their fathers, this was the case with only 28 per cent of the Frenchmen.[1] There is also evidence that the age at which the individual adopts a party preference varies from one country to another. It was noted earlier that by the age of seven or eight most American children have adopted a party preference, but Hyman points out that in Sweden a survey showed that 66 per cent of the thirteen- to fifteen-year-olds were undecided, and that it was not until the

[1] Converse and Dupeux, 'Politicization of the Elecorate in France and the United States', p. 9.

age of nineteen that a majority expressed a party preference.[1] Opinion polls in other countries have also shown substantial minorities of adolescents who have shown no party preference: in a survey of the fifteen to twenty age-group in Australia, 33 per cent said they were undecided when asked which party they supported (APOP, March 1967); while 34 per cent in a poll of eighteen- to twenty-year-olds in Britain were undecided (SOC, August 1967). Similarly, a study of Danish students in the period 1946–8 found that the great majority had formed political *attitudes* by the time they had reached the age of eighteen, but nearly a quarter did not do so until they were nineteen years of age or over.[2] It is in fact instructive to compare the respective ages at which these Danish students said they first formed political and religious attitudes (Table 5).

Table 5. *Date of the formation of political and religious attitudes among Danish students*

Date of formation of attitude	ATTITUDE	Political %	Religious %
School years: 7–14		21	74
Adolescence: 15–18		55	19
Adult: 19 or over		24	7
	Total	100	100

SOURCE: Iisager, 'Factors Influencing the Formation of and Change of Political and Religious Attitudes', Table 5, p. 257.

The contrast between the ages at which the students formed political and religious attitudes is marked: approximately three-quarters had formed religious attitudes by the age of fourteen, whereas by the same age little more than a fifth had formed political attitudes. Conversely, nearly a quarter, as we have already noted, did not form political attitudes until they were nineteen or more, compared with only 7 per cent in the forming of religious attitudes.

The study undertaken by Iisager also provides some information on another aspect of political socialization which awaits fuller

[1] Hyman, *Political Socialization*, p. 62.

[2] Holger Iisager, 'Factors Influencing the Formation of and Change of 'Political and Religious Attitudes', *Journal of Social Psychology*, **29**, 1949, pp. 253–65.

investigation. A good deal has been said about the distinction between overt and covert socialization, but little work has been undertaken on what factors the *subjects* of socialization feel influenced their values and attitudes. The students in Iisager's sample were asked what factors had contributed to the formation of their political and religious attitudes. The factors which contributed to the formation of their political attitudes showed considerable variety and included reading, friends, parents, discussions, reasoning and dramatic incidents, but those influencing religious attitudes were heavily concentrated on the home and the school. Moreover, when they were asked which of these factors had been the most important for politics, the first three were reasoning, dramatic incidents and discussions, with parents coming sixth; whereas those for religion were reading and parents (first equal), and school.[1] The results of another study which illustrates the same point are shown in Table 6.

Table 6. *Agents of socialization among children in Chile: who teaches you all you know about the President?*

CLASS	Father or Mother	School	Other	Total (%)
Working class	6	56	38	100
Middle class	42	22	36	100

SOURCE: Robert D. Hess, 'The Socialization of Attitudes Toward Political Authority: Some Cross-National Comparisons', *International Social Science Journal*, 15, 1963, Table 2, p. 554.

It is possible in both the Danish and the Chilean studies that the perceptions of the respondents coincide with the actual agents of socialization, but it is also possible that they have underestimated or overestimated some of the factors involved – the influence of their parents in the formation of their political attitudes may have been greater than the Danish students and working class Chilean children realized, for example. There may, in other words, have been a degree of covert socialization of which they were unaware. If these respondents are accurate in their perceptions, however, then the data suggests that not only does the timing of particular aspects of political socialization vary from one political system to

[1] ibid., Table 3, p. 256.

another, but that the agents of socialization may also vary. The evidence available on socialization in the United States suggests that the family is an important agent of socialization, but this may not be true for all countries, as research on Japan suggests. In a survey of Japanese law students in 1960, Yasumasa Kuroda found that although the overwhelming majority of his respondents were supporters of the Socialist party, most of their parents supported other parties or no party at all. Kuroda concludes that the family is not a major agent of political socialization in post-war Japan and suggests that in a country like Japan, which has undergone considerable and rapid change in a short period of time, the major agencies of political socialization are likely to be more diffuse.[1] It may well be that party preferences of these Japanese students is, among other things, a reaction *against* the political values and attitudes of their parents, and it may therefore be possible to speak of *negative* socialization on the part of the family in this case. Whichever is the case, however, Kuroda produces strong evidence to suggest that in Japan the family plays a different role in political socialization.

A greater contrast may be seen in the Israeli kibbutz, where the traditional role of the family has been reduced and socialization is much more the concern of the whole community. Children are separated from their parents in the kibbutz: they sleep, eat and study in groups in special houses, although they do spend time with their parents during the latter's periods of leisure. The principles and framework of the education they receive is decided by the kibbutz community and embodies formal education (including ideological instruction), periods of manual work (normally agriculture), and instruction in the social and cultural life of the kibbutz. The children not only learn about the political organization of the kibbutz, but actually experience the working of that organization through their own parallel political institutions. The highest authority in the kibbutz is the general assembly, comprising all adult members of the community, and this body elects a management committee, which is subject to a fairly frequent rotation of membership. Similarly, the children have their own general assembly and elected committee, which serve both as a mark of

[1] Yasumasa Kuroda, 'Agencies of Political Socialization and Political Change: the Political Orientations of Japanese Law Students', *Human Organization*, **24**, 1965, pp. 328–31.

their separation from adult life and as a preparation for their assumption of adult roles.[1]

Some evidence has been offered on the differences in political socialization both within a particular political system and between political systems of a broadly similar nature – that is, those which may be termed modern democracies. It is, however, obvious that, compared with the United States and those other countries of which brief mention has been made, countries which have very different political systems from those of modern democracies are likely to have important differences in political socialization, and it is to these that we now turn.

POLITICAL SOCIALIZATION IN TOTALITARIAN SOCIETIES

Only by radically remoulding the teaching, organization, and training of the young shall we be able to ensure that the results of the efforts of the younger generation will be the creation of a society that will be unlike the old society, that is a Communist Society – V. I. LENIN, 'The Tasks of the Youth Leagues', speech delivered to the Third All-Russian Congress of the Russian Young Communist League, 2 October 1920 (Lenin, *Selected Works*, II, Moscow, 1947, p. 661).

. . . we have set before ourselves the task of inoculating our youth with the spirit of this community of the people at a very early age . . . And this new Reich will give its youth to no one, but itself take youth and give to youth its own education and its own upbringing – ADOLF HITLER, 1 May 1937 (*Speeches of Adolf Hitler, April 1922–August 1939*, London, 1942, p. 549).

By definition, the totalitarian state seeks to control all aspects of society, and as these speeches by Lenin and Hitler show, great stress is inevitably laid on socialization in general and political socialization in particular. The ideology of the state becomes the official basis of all action and pervades all activities. Political socialization is not and cannot be left to find its own channels; nor to purvey uncontrolled knowledge, values and attitudes which may contradict or undermine that ideology. The minds of men must be captured, guided and harnessed to the needs of the state

[1] See Eisenstadt, *From Generation to Generation*, pp. 104–7, and Rivkak Bar-Yoseph, 'The Pattern of Early Socialization in the Collective Settlements of Israel', *Human Relations*, 12, 1959, pp. 345–60.

through the vehicle of its ideology. Thus totalitarian societies differ from modern democracies in the degree of control they exercise over the political socialization of their members. All governments seek, directly or indirectly, to socialize members of society to varying degrees by the control of information, but in the totalitarian society that control is all-pervasive. None the less, the basic process of political socialization as the acquisition of political orientations and patterns of behaviour is as applicable to totalitarian societies as it is to modern democracies, but the emphasis placed on particular subjects, agents and mechanisms may vary both in kind and effectiveness.

The transition from the non-totalitarian to the totalitarian illustrates the differences that are likely to be found in political socialization. The pre-totalitarian generation of individuals will probably have been subjected to a process of political socialization markedly different from that of subsequent totalitarian generations. It is likely that their knowledge, values and attitudes will be markedly different and that these will be carried over into the new régime. It is likely, of course, that the new régime will subject them to a substantial degree of adult socialization through its control of the mass media. The first totalitarian generation may find itself in an ambiguous position since it will be subjected to extensive socialization by the régime, but it may also find that their parents and other members of the older generation represent a counter-force to that socialization. Later generations, however, will be subject almost exclusively to socialization by the state. Thus in the early stages of its rule the totalitarian régime must undermine the process of pre-totalitarian socialization, 're-educate' the pre-totalitarian generation, and prepare for the socialization of the 'new' generation. This was abundantly clear in Nazi Germany and in the U.S.S.R.

Adolf Hitler was, as his speech quoted above makes clear, fully aware of the contribution that political education or socialization could make to the entrenchment and continuance of the régime he had established. He was also aware that the control by the Nazi régime of the mass media was a necessary but insufficient condition for the inculcation of National Socialist ideology among the German people: the political experiences of Imperial Germany and the Weimar Republic were no guarantee of support for Hitler. The political socialization resulting from those experiences could be reinforced and undermined where appropriate, and Hitler made every effort to see that they were, but of much greater importance was the political education of German youth. It was necessary, however, to minimize any anti-Nazi influence that the older generation brought up under the Imperial and Republican régimes might have over the generation growing up under the Nazi régime. Hitler therefore paid not only considerable attention to formal education but also sought to control and limit the role of the family in political socialization.

Children in Nazi Germany were taught that their first loyalty was to the state, personified by the *Führer*, and that any evidence of disloyalty should be reported to the authorities. Children were encouraged to watch, indoctrinate and, if necessary, report their parents and other relatives: the privacy of the family was breached and its influence undermined. Even where the family unit resisted infiltration by its own members, it was vulnerable through the activities of 'friends' – fellow pupils of the children, fellow workers and neighbours of the parents: the establishment of a system of denunciation rendered all vulnerable.

Of greater importance, however, especially for the future, were the twin pillars of political socialization in Nazi Germany – formal education and the youth movements. Inevitably all teachers had to be trained in National Socialist ideology and to be politically reliable. Education was centralized and an order of priorities laid down:

> Hereditary tendencies; general racial picture.
> The character (degree of adherence of National Socialism).
> The physical make-up or 'body' (degree of usefulness in the event of a future war).
> (And last) Knowledge (Here the knowledge of objective reality, regarded as a last offshoot of liberalism, is often punishable where it is not merely regarded as absurd and reprehensible).[1]

All lessons revolved around the official ideology and the learning of 'useful' knowledge. All subjects were redefined in the light of National Socialist ideology and all textbooks were rewritten. History became 'the essence of political education' and 'the crown of all teaching of history consists only of following the *Führer*'.[2]

[1] Erika Mann, *School for Barbarians: Education under the Nazis*, London, 1939, p. 48.
[2] ibid., p. 51, quoted from official textbooks.

Mathematics became 'an expression of the Nordic fighting spirit', while the textbooks in mathematics were essentially 'practical'. For example, one textbook, entitled *National Political Practice in Arithmetic Lessons*, contained problems based on Germany's former colonies, such as the total loss in area and population, their proportional distribution between the mandatory powers, and comparisons with the area and population of Germany; other problems dealt with the capacity and performance of military aircraft and other military problems. Another textbook was called *Aerial Defence by Numbers* and contained problems on the effectiveness of air-raid shelters and defence against gas attacks. Nor did the Jewish 'problem' escape mathematical treatment: another textbook, *Germany's Fall and Rise – Illustrations Taken from Arithmetic Instruction in Higher Grades of Elementary School*, contained problems based on the number and proportion of Jews in Germany.[1] All subjects were subordinated to the supreme discipline of racial science, to which even the natural sciences had to conform.

Socialization through formal education was paralleled and strengthened through the Nazi youth movements. There had been strong youth movements in Germany prior to Hitler's accession to power and before the First World War. These were taken over by the new régime, and in 1936 all non-Nazi youth organizations were declared illegal:

> . . . All of the German Youth in the Reich is organized within the Hitler Youth.
> . . . The German Youth, besides being reared within the family and schools, shall be educated physically, intellectually and morally in the spirit of National Socialism . . . through the Hitler Youth.[2]

In 1939 membership of the Hitler Youth became compulsory, and any parents who resisted the indoctrination of their children were liable to have them taken out of their care. Between the ages of six and ten German children received preliminary training in history, camping, athletics and ideology. At the age of ten they were tested and, if suitable, the boys graduated to the *Jungvolk*, the girls to the *Jungmädel*, at which point they swore an oath of allegiance to the *Führer*. At the age of fourteen boys entered the Hitler

[1] ibid., pp. 61–2.
[2] Decree outlawing all non-Nazi youth organizations, quoted in William L. Shirer, *The Rise and Fall of the Third Reich*, New York, 1959, p. 253.

Youth proper and received systematic instruction in ideology and physical and military training. At the age of eighteen they joined the Labour Service, followed by military service. The pattern for girls was similar, but they had their own organizations, the *Jungmädel* (from ten to fourteen) and the *Bund Deutscher Mädel* (from the age of fourteen to twenty-one), followed by a year's service in agriculture.

The whole apparatus of the state was geared to the socialization of German youth, and this was, as Hitler declared in 1933, to be the foundation of the Third Reich:

> When an opponent declares, 'I will not come over to your side', I calmly say, 'Your child belongs to us already . . . What are you? You will pass on. Your descendants, however, now stand in the new camp. In a short time they will know nothing else but this new community.'[1]

A similar pattern of socialization is found in the Soviet Union, with emphasis on both formal education and youth movements. All teaching must conform to Communist ideology, and textbooks are similarly used as a means of political instruction. The Communist youth movement is similar in many respects to that found in Nazi Germany, but differs in that it is increasingly selective as children become older. Thus while all children are subject to early political learning through play, singing, story-telling and so forth, and membership of the Young Pioneers between the age of nine and fourteen is virtually universal, membership of the principal youth organization, the Komsomol, is much more selective. The recommendation of a Communist party member or two Komsomol members is necessary and the Komsomol is an important channel of recruitment into the Communist party itself. Komsomol members receive direct political instruction and military and para-military training.[2]

A further parallel with Nazi Germany is found in the attempts made to undermine the influence of pre-totalitarian experiences in general and family influence in particular.[3] A number of studies

[1] Speech of 6 November 1933, quoted in Shirer, *The Rise and Fall of the Third Reich*, p. 249.

[2] Merle Fainsod, *How Russia is Ruled*, Cambridge, Mass., 1963 (revised edition), Chapter 9.

[3] See also James R. Townsend, *Political Participation in Communist China*, Los Angeles, 1967, who reports that the Communist régime in China 'has tried, albeit with mixed success, to replace loyalties to the family and other particularistic units with loyalty to the political community' (p. 221).

of refugees from the U.S.S.R. carried out at Harvard University in the early 1950s found evidence of conflict between different generations in Russia. Those with parents whose political experience stretched back well into the Tsarist period found that their parents often contradicted what they had learned at school and in the various youth organizations: although some were confused as a result of this, it is some indication of the effectiveness of political socialization in Russia after the Revolution that many simply did not believe what their parents said. One study in particular examined the child-rearing values held by various generations of Russian parents. The values were as follows:

1   Tradition: mainly religion, but also including family ties and tradition generally.
2   Achievement: industriousness, attainment, material rewards, social mobility.
3   Personal: honesty, sincerity, justice, mercy.
4   Adjustment: 'getting along', 'staying out of trouble', 'security and safeness'.
5   Intellectual: learning and knowledge as ends.
6   Political: attitudes, values and beliefs dealing with the government.

Table 7.   *The child-rearing values of the two generations of Russian parents.*

VALUES	Tsarist generation	Revolutionary generation
	%	%
Tradition	75	44
Achievement	60	52
Personal	32	44
Adjustment	16	21
Intellectual	12	22
Political	12	20

SOURCE: Alex Inkeles, 'Social Change and Social Character: the Role of Parental Mediation', *Journal of Social Issues*, **11**, 1955, pp. 12–23.

The Tsarist or pre-revolutionary generation placed overwhelming stress on tradition, followed by achievement as child-rearing values, whereas the revolutionary generation placed achievement first, with tradition, although second, much reduced in importance, while increased emphasis was placed on personal values, on adjustment, and intellectual and political values. Inkeles suggests that these changes may be attributed to the impact of change upon the values of the respondents, to a process of socialization following the 1917 Revolution. He further tested this hypothesis by asking his respondents what values they held in respect of occupation, but this time he used three generations – Tsarist, revolutionary and Soviet, the latter having been brought up by parents of the revolutionary generation. The Tsarist generation stressed rewards and tradition as the most important values, but the two subsequent generations overwhelmingly stressed self-expression, although there was a significant increase in political values as well. It may be surmised that both self-expression, in the form of the individual's contribution to the welfare of society, and a greater stress on political fulfilment may be regarded as in accordance with Communist ideology, together with a reduction in the value of tradition, and that these may be attributable to a process of socialization.

The Soviet case is particularly interesting because, unlike the National Socialists in Germany, the Communists have been in power long enough to see generations born and growing up which have no direct contact with pre-Soviet Russia through personal experience and whose parents were born under the Soviet régime. Furthermore, generations are now growing up who have little or no contact with those who grew up in the earliest years of the régime, the years of the New Economic Plan, the Five-Year Plans, of collectivization, and of industrialization; similarly Stalin's Russia and the Second World War are to them history, not experience. These and future generations will have experienced the full process of political socialization under a totalitarian régime, a fact which may have important implications for the continuance of that régime.

Evidence from East European countries tends to support the data presented on the Soviet Union. Opinion polls among young people in Yugoslavia, for example, found that although 57 per cent of high school pupils said that their parents were the most important factor influencing their views, only 37 per cent said that their views were the same as their parents and 25 per cent said they were completely different. A poll of university students found that 63 per cent accepted Marxism as a 'true revolutionary theory'.[1] Another study of Polish respondents in 1964 found a relationship between knowledge of Communist doctrine and whether or not the respondents had been educated under the Communist régime (Table 8).

Table 8. *Knowledge of Communist doctrine and education under the Communist régime in Poland, 1964*

	Educated before 1946–8	Educated since 1946–8
Knew of the theory of the withering away of the state	7	22
Total respondents	34	36

SOURCE: Roger Pethybridge, 'The Assessment of Ideological Influence on East Europeans', *Public Opinion Quarterly*, 21, 1967, pp. 38–50.

The implication of the data in the table is clear as far as *knowledge* of the theory of the withering away of the state is concerned, but Pethybridge presents additional data which casts some doubt on the effectiveness of formal instruction in Marxism-Leninism in Poland. He found that whereas five of those educated before 1946–8 believed that the state would wither away, this was still the case with only eight of those educated under the Communist régime. It is important to note, however, that most of the former were either self-taught in Marxism-Leninism or else were militant Communist party members. Poland, with a substantial Catholic population, may, of course, be a special case, but the relatively recent accession to power of the Communist régime may also be an important factor in political socialization.

The evidence available on political socialization in totalitarian societies is inevitably limited and fragmentary, but the evidence and data presented does give some idea of the nature of the process in such societies. Political socialization is not left to run its course, but becomes an integral part of a totalitarian system, a means by which the régime overtly seeks to perpetuate itself and the ideology on which it is based. Thus close attention is paid to socialization throughout adult life in the Soviet Union: the general population receives carefully controlled information through a

[1] Stanislaw Skrzypek, 'The Political, Cultural and Social Views of Yugoslav Youth', *Public Opinion Quarterly*, 29, 1965, pp. 87–106.

vast network of face-to-face contacts with 'agitators'; Communist party members and candidates for party membership receive ideological instruction in political schools – more general instruction is achieved through discussion groups or seminars, through public lectures organized by the All-Union Society for the Dissemination of Political and Scientific Information; and by making standard works in Communist and Marxist-Leninist literature available at low cost; while more general socialization is sought through the strict control of the mass media.[1] Indeed, the term *political* socialization' is almost a misnomer: given the nature of totalitarian societies, in which all is legitimately 'political', the process becomes one of socialization in general. The orientations and patterns of behaviour acquired are not specifically political but societal in nature. In this sense, at least, there is a parallel between socialization in totalitarian societies and in primitive societies, in that the distinction between the social and the political is minimal. Moreover, a number of totalitarian societies place considerable emphasis on ritual in the socialization process, and this is also a feature of the process in primitive societies. The comparison must not, of course, be taken too far; none the less, the similarities are noticeable and possibly significant.

POLITICAL SOCIALIZATION IN PRIMITIVE SOCIETIES

It is in primitive societies that the role of socialization in general is seen most vividly, especially in those societies which have or had existed long enough to establish strong societal traditions which define the structure and roles of society. Although differences in socialization exist between various primitive societies, such societies lack the differentiation found in complex modern societies, and the process of socialization is characterized by an intrinsic unity emphasizing ritual, the legitimization of societal roles and, often, the achievement of status. Political socialization is an integral part of learning societal roles in general rather than political roles in particular. The Buganda people of East Africa, for example, lived in a highly-centralized monarchical system with a hierarchy based not on classes or groups but upon the status of

[1] See Alex Inkeles, *Public Opinion in Russia: A Study in Mass Persuasion*, Cambridge, Mass., 1958.

the individual. This allowed considerable social mobility within the hierarchy, but did not prevent the principle theme of socialization being respect for parents and deference to superiors, a theme which was of great importance in maintaining the hierarchical system.[1]

Primitive societies may differ considerably, however, in their socialization processes, even though they may have certain common characteristics, as Robert Le Vine has shown.[2] Le Vine examined socialization among two tribes in south-west Kenya, both of which were uncentralized and patriarchical groups, had a similar subsistence base and were characterized by blood feuds. The Nuer, however, were basically egalitarian and passive in attitude, whereas the Gusii were authoritarian and aggressive, and the children of each tribe were encouraged in their respective traditions. The importance of tradition, the emphasis on such socialization techniques as ritual, initiation, and the frequent stress on hierarchy and status found in primitive societies form an important link between them and modern societies. We have already seen that similar emphases are to be found in totalitarian societies, and this may be the result of the degree to which the social and the political are integrated, though these characteristics are also important in the socialization processes of developing societies in Asia, Africa and Latin America. In these societies we find the conjunction of the old and the new, the traditional and the modern.

POLITICAL SOCIALIZATION IN DEVELOPING SOCIETIES

The conjunction of the old and the new can be seen most clearly in those parts of the world which were formerly colonized by European powers. To varying degrees the colonial powers introduced Western political institutions, bureaucracy, culture and education. In the majority of cases these various manifestations of modern Western societies remained, if not intact, at least in

[1] See L. A. Fallers, 'Despotism, Status Culture and Social Mobility in an African Kingdom', in *Comparative Studies in Society and History*, **2**, 1959, pp. 11–32, and A. I. Richards, *East African Chiefs*, London, 1960, Chapter 2.

[2] Robert Le Vine, 'The Internalization of Political Values in Stateless Societies', *Human Organization*, **19**, 1960, pp. 51–8.

existence, invariably forming the vehicles of modernization in these societies. In juxtaposition to them, however, there remained the many manifestations of the traditional societies which had existed before colonization. During the struggle for independence, these traditional attitudes and influences tended to be submerged in the unity maintained by the common goal of national independence. Once independence was achieved the traditional pressures reasserted themselves, usually becoming the basis for interest groups and political parties. The result is a complex mixture of the traditional and the modern, consisting of a series of modern institutions resting (often precariously) on a traditional base which is continually under the impact of the increasing pressure of industrialization and urbanization. The traditional processes of socialization continue to shape the orientations and patterns of behaviour of the majority of the people, while the political leaders endeavour to break down those traditions which appear to be obstacles to 'progress'. Socialization becomes fragmented, however, partly because many developing countries consist of the amalgamation of several (often many) traditional societies, which often become competing power groups in new nations; and partly because the distinction between the social and the political becomes sharper. Specifically political institutions – executives, legislatures, judiciaries, political parties, interest groups – which are not integral parts of the traditional societies are created. These institutions have not evolved out of the traditional societies and the socialization processes of the latter may be ill-equipped for dealing with such institutions. The institutions are not, in other words, integrated into the social system and such legitimacy as they may possess is often precarious. Furthermore, the distinction between the institutions and those who hold office in them is blurred, and any failure of the individual office-holder, real or perceived, reflects on the institution.

This is clear from a study of political socialization in Colombia in which a questionnaire used in similar studies in the United States was replicated for comparative purposes. This study showed that whereas American children had increasingly favourable attitudes towards government and the political system as they proceeded through the various grades in school, Colombian children became increasingly critical. By the highest grade half of the Colombian children agreed with the statement, 'in the government there are some big, powerful men who run everything and don't care about the opinions of ordinary people', compared with only 6 per cent of U.S. children. Similarly, the *highest* proportion of U.S. children who said that they had no chance to express their opinions was 18 per cent, and this proportion fell steadily with grade, but among the Colombian children the *lowest* was 17 per cent and the highest 28 per cent, though the proportion fluctuated between grades.[1]

At the same time important similarities in socialization between developing countries and modern democracies may be found. Research on political socialization in Jamaica found strong party identity among school-children, especially among those who came from politically motivated families, and tendencies for children to conform to the dominant partisan pattern in their schools. Thus it is possible to detect patterns of reinforcement and cross-pressures of a type found in countries like Britain and the United States.[2] There is also evidence of class differences of the sort similar to those found in the latter countries. Upper class students in Panama, for example, were shown to be more anti-Communist than middle-class students, who showed greater concern with economic problems, were more likely to regard politics as dishonest and were more critical of the president and the National Assembly.[3] Similarly, Kenneth Langton, in the research cited above, found that working class Jamaican students were less committed to democracy, gave less support to civil liberties for minority groups, were less inclined to vote and generally less politically motivated than middle and upper class students.

Many new states have attempted to meet the problems created by the conflict of the traditional and the modern by means of political education. In 1964, for instance, the Kenyan government published an Education Commission Report describing the type of citizens that schools are expected to produce. Pupils are expected to have a commitment to national unity, tolerance of

[1] R. Reading, 'Political Socialization in Colombia and the United States', *Midwest Journal of Political Science*, **12**, 1968, pp. 352–81.

[2] Kenneth P. Langton, 'Political Partisanship and Political Socialization in Jamaica', *British Journal of Sociology*, **17**, 1966, pp. 419–29, and 'Peer Group and School and the Socialization Process', *American Political Science Review*, **61**, 1967, pp. 751–8.

[3] Daniel Goldrich and Edward W. Scott, 'Developing Political Orientations of Panamanian Students', *Journal of Politics*, **23**, 1961, pp. 84–105.

tribal, racial and religious differences, acceptance of social change and social equality. Similar aims may be found in Tanzania, and a survey of schoolchildren in these two countries found that majorities regarded the most important purpose of their schools as being to teach them to be 'good citizens'. The problem of the conflict between the traditional and the modern is illustrated, however, by the fact that the respondents in both Kenya and Tanzania exhibited overwhelming trust of their fathers, teachers and religious leaders (with no significant difference between primary and secondary levels), but trust of political leaders declined between these two levels from 72 per cent to 57 per cent in Kenya and from 89 per cent to 63 per cent in Tanzania. A similar result was found in Uganda.[1]

David Apter effectively summarises the problem of political socialization in developing societies when he suggests that the ideologies of many new nations take the form of a religion, not in a specifically spiritual sense but in that they are theocratic in practice. Leaders become deified and the state ideology is given the rank of a religion. Apter further suggests that although this process may assist the process of modernization and industrialization, it renders political change difficult – a change in politics may require a change of 'religion'.[2] The central problem of political socialization in developing societies is that of coping with change. This is well illustrated by the example of Turkey, where a systematic attempt was made both to effect and accommodate change following the First World War. Mustapha Kemal (Kemal Atatürk) sought to modernize Turkey not only materially but through the processes of socialization. Considerable stress was laid on the symbols of nationhood – the national flag and anthem, national holidays, monuments, military parades and the encouragement of Turkish language and history. Educational opportunities were increased and teachers were trained in methods of teaching the ideology of the Republican People's party (C.H.P.), the only official party. Adult socialization was achieved through 'People's Houses' in which political ideas stressing modernization,

---

[1] David Koff and George van der Muhl, 'Political Socialization in Kenya and Tanzania: A Comparative Analysis', *Journal of Modern African Studies*, 5, 1967, pp. 13–51.

[2] David E. Apter, 'Political Religion in the New Nations', in Geertz (ed.), *Old Societies and New States*, pp. 57–104.

secularism and nationalism were discussed and disseminated. Considerable changes were effected, and in 1945 Atatürk's successor, Ismet Inönu, called for the formation of other parties. These were formed and Turkey entered a period of competitive party politics. The system broke down, however, because the two main parties represented the main divisions in the nation – the traditional and the modern, the rural and the urban – while no agreement could be reached on an electoral system acceptable to both sides. The period ended with the military *coup* of 1960, and this has been followed by a further attempt to introduce a competitive party system based on free elections.[1]

Ghana provides a similar example, where, following a period of military rule which brought an end to the régime of Kwame Nkrumah in 1966, new elections were held in 1969 as a prelude to the resumption of civilian rule. The severe problems which face a developing country comprising a variety of groups and traditions can also be seen vividly in the history of Nigeria since its independence in 1960. Robert Le Vine has argued that political socialization in developing countries tends to be related more to local, tribal, ethnic and regional rather than national political systems. There are, he suggests, three important factors in the political socialization in such societies:

1. The growth of population in developing countries may outstrip their capacity to 'modernize' traditional family life through industrialization and education.
2. There is often an important disparity in education and traditional values between the sexes so that women may be more firmly attached to the latter, yet the mother may play an important role in the early socialization of the child.
3. It is likely that the influence of urbanization, which is invariably regarded as a powerful force in breaking down traditional values, is at least partially offset by the transference of traditional values into urban areas, especially by the establishment of tribal and ethnic communities in these areas.

Le Vine therefore concludes that it is misleading to regard traditional values as something which must be destroyed or replaced:

[1] Joseph S. Szyliowicz, 'Political Participation and Modernization in Turkey', *Western Political Quarterly*, **19**, 1966, pp. 266–84.

they need to be combined with the new institutions and patterns of behaviour.[1] The evidence available on political socialization suggests that some such process is necessary, possibly inevitable. No break with the past can be complete, and even though far-reaching and fundamental changes may be effected, an element of continuity remains. In the very act of seeking a break with its past a society is influenced by that past, however different the future may be. Political socialization is therefore closely involved in the process of change.

POLITICAL SOCIALIZATION AND CHANGE

It is clear that the nature of political socialization varies over time and according to the environment of which it is part and to which it contributes. Political socialization is therefore related to the nature of the polity and the degree and nature of change:

> The more stable the polity the more specified the major agencies of political socialization will be.
>
> Conversely, the greater the degree of change in a non-totalitarian polity, the more diffused the major agencies of political socialization will be. The more basic the degree of revolution in a polity, the more specified the major agencies of political socialization will be. (No revolutions are complete without setting up some specific agencies of political socialization in order to cut off the continuation of traditional values which are detrimental to the new régime.)
>
> The more totalitarian the nature of political change, the smaller and more specific the number of major agencies of political socialization will be.[2]

The more homogeneous a society and the longer it has persisted over time, the more likely it is that the process of socialization will become clearly defined and relatively unified, and a similar effect is likely in societies in which there is an overt attempt to control the process of socialization. Conversely, in heterogeneous societies and those subject to frequent and radical change, the process of socialization is likely to be fragmented and applicable to various groups in society rather than to society as a whole. At any given period in time, it is possible to posit for any given society a *political culture* which may be defined as the politically relevant

[1] Le Vine, 'Political Socialization and Culture Change', pp. 284–5.
[2] Kuroda, 'Agencies of Political Socialization and Political Change', p. 331.

values and attitudes of a society. The relationship between political culture and political socialization is crucial, since it is by means of the latter process that these politically relevant values and attitudes are transmitted from one generation to another. This does not mean, of course, that these values and attitudes are immutable, since the process of socialization is continuous and may effectively contribute to their change as well as their persistence.

In *The Civic Culture*, Almond and Verba presents the results of a cross-national survey of political culture. In their conclusions they suggest that each of the five nations they studied – the United States, Britain, West Germany, Italy and Mexico – has its own distinctive political culture. The United States and Britain were characterized by a general acceptance of the political system, by a fairly high degree of political participation and by a widespread feeling among respondents that they could influence affairs to some degree. Greater stress was laid on participation by Americans, whereas British respondents exhibited a greater deference towards their government. The political culture of West Germany was marked by a degree of detachment from the political system and a more passive attitude towards participation, but respondents nevertheless felt able to influence affairs. In contrast to these three countries, Italy showed widespread political alienation, involving low political interest, low participation and a feeling of an inability to influence affairs; while Mexico was a mixture of acceptance of the theory of politics and alienation from its substance.

A key factor in the concept of political culture is that of *legitimacy* – the extent to which a political system is accepted by society. As Weber pointed out, the basis of that legitimacy may vary. Furthermore, it is important to understand, as Lipset points out in *Political Man*, the basic legitimacy of a political system does not preclude conflict. Agreement may exist over the basic political framework, but within that framework conflict may continue over both means and ends. At the same time, if the conflict over means and ends becomes extensive, it may undermine any agreement over the political framework. Lipset argues that it is the existence of conflict within consensus that forms the basis of modern democracies. The concept of legitimacy is not, of course, limited to modern democracies – the political system in a totalitarian society may enjoy widespread legitimacy as a result of political socialization, just as the political system of a non-totalitarian society may be denied legitimacy. In another of the studies of Soviet refugees by Harvard University, Raymond Bauer found that younger respondents (i.e. those who grew up under the Soviet régime) had normally accepted the Soviet system initially and had seldom always been opposed to the régime. Moreover, these respondents generally retained important ideological commitments, such as support of the Welfare State and for the state ownership of various industries, and tended to blame the Soviet *leadership* rather than the *political system* for their disillusionment.[1] This evidence would suggest that Soviet political *system* enjoys (or enjoyed) a widespread degree of legitimacy. Conversely, the problems of the German Weimar Republic and the French Fourth Republic have been attributed in part to a loss of (or even a failure to acquire) legitimacy.

It is also important to understand that legitimacy may extend to many aspects of the political system or may be limited to a few. There is, for example, widespread evidence that most Americans accept their major political institutions – the presidency, Congress and the Supreme Court – but a distinction is drawn between the political institutions and the persons who wield power through them for a given period of time. At the end of that period of time they, or the party they represent, may win a further period of power or else their opponents may secure office. In either case, both those who seek power and those who choose between the rivals for office are normally prepared to abide by the results of electoral decision. Similarly, the right of the president or Congress to exercise their powers is not normally questioned, but the use to which those powers are put is subject to frequent criticism. Criticism of the political system in other countries may be much more fundamental, however, possibly to the extent of denying the system's legitimacy or subjecting it to severe strain. The expectation of violent change, for example, may differ substantially from one country to another: only 9 per cent of the respondents in an American opinion poll said that at some future date 'military leaders in the United States would try to take over the White House and rule the country (MINN, July 1966); whereas 46 per cent of respondents in an Argentine poll in 1966 expected the

---

[1] Raymond A. Bauer, 'Some Trends in Sources of Alienation from the Soviet System', *Public Opinion Quarterly*, **19**, 1955, pp. 279–91.

government to fall as a result of a *coup d'état* (EGA, Buenos Aires, March 1966).

The case of West Germany illustrates not only the extent to which a political system may be regarded as legitimate, but how this legitimacy may change over a period of time. Germany has suffered a series of drastic changes in its political system in the present century – changes which have been twice associated with military defeat and national humiliation, thus presenting severe problems of legitimacy. This would certainly appear to be true of the Weimar Republic, the impact of which on present-day West Germans appears to be limited: in 1966 no less than 53 per cent of the respondents said that they 'had no idea of the Weimar Republic' (EMNID, January 1966). It is not surprising, therefore, to find that the present Federal Republic lacked widespread legitimacy for a considerable period after its establishment in 1949, nor that the attitudes of West Germans towards Hitler, towards the first Chancellor of the Federal Republic and towards various ideas held strongly in other Western European countries, and towards the Federal Parliament, should have changed only slowly in the post-war period.

In 1951 only 32 per cent of the respondents in a West German poll were prepared to say that Germany was to blame for the outbreak of war in 1939; by 1956 this proportion had risen by 47 per cent; by 1964 to 51 per cent; and by 1967 to 62 per cent. (DMS, May 1967). Similarly and not surprisingly, no one was prepared in 1950 to say that Konrad Adenauer merited the accolade of the German who had 'made the most valuable achievement for Germany', compared with 10 per cent who nominated Hitler for this role; but by 1966 Adenauer's standing had risen to 44 per cent, Hitler's falling to 2 per cent (DMS, December 1966). In the same way, in 1953, 12 per cent of the respondents in a survey said they would vote for Hitler if he were still alive, compared with 67 per cent who said they would vote against him. Although a year later Hitler's opponents had swelled to 81 per cent, his supporters had actually risen to 15 per cent, though by 1967 this had dwindled to 4 per cent (EMNID, February 1967). Attitudes towards the basic ideology of the political system and the principal political institution of the Federal Republic tended to change equally slowly.

Table 9. *West German attitudes towards their political system*

(A) What are the most important 'freedoms'?

FREEDOM	1949	1954	1958	1962	1963	1964	1965	1967
Of religion	12	16	16	13	14	11	14	15
Of speech	26	32	44	47	56	48	54	52
From fear	17	17	10	8	10	10	8	10
From want	35	35	28	17	15	25	19	24
Don't know	10	–	2	15	5	6	5	5
	100	100	100	100	100	100	100	106*

SOURCE: EMNID, November 1967.   * Multiple response.

(B) What is your opinion of the Bonn Parliament?

OPINION	1951	1952	1953	1958	1963	1965	1967
Definitely good	7	3	9	6	4	3	5
Basically good	28	27	37	31	42	49	53
Moderate	31	35	31	41	36	34	28
Poor	9	13	10	16	7	4	4
No answer	25	22	13	6	11	11	10
Total	100	100	100	100	100	101	100

SOURCE: EMNID, August 1967.

The data presented in Table 9 suggests that the Federal German Republic and the political system of which it is part gained legitimacy only gradually in the postwar period. This same period was, of course, marked by Germany's reconstruction and economic recovery, and the figures in Section A of the table are consistent with the view that, as Germany again found her place among the Western nations (especially as part of the NATO alliance) and as economic prosperity increased, so the emphasis placed on 'freedom from fear' and 'freedom from want' tended to decrease, while the stress placed on the less material value of 'freedom of speech' increased. A number of writers, notably S. M. Lipset and James Coleman, have suggested that there are significant correlations between modernization and democracy,[1] but it is likely that the significance lies in delineating the conditions in which democracy is able to flourish, and this concept may be extended to posit the conditions under which legitimacy is likely to exist. It is possible, for example, that opinions of the Bonn Parliament in West Germany improved because the country became more

[1] Lipset, *Political Man*, pp. 45ff., and Almond and Coleman (eds.), *Politics of the Developing Areas*, pp. 538ff.

prosperous – the political system became more widely accepted as people became more satisfied with primarily non-political matters. The legitimacy of the political system becomes related to societal satisfaction.

Over a period of time, however, the situation may become complicated. It is likely that the various institutions which comprise the political system will become increasingly distinct from those who, at any given time, exercise power through them. The political institutions may thus acquire a legitimacy which was lacking in the early stages of their existence and it becomes increasingly possible for the members of a society to subject those who wield power to criticism without criticizing the political system itself. Ultimately, the political system may acquire a degree of legitimacy which enables it to withstand considerable strain caused by societal dissatisfaction. In the period following the 1966 election, for example, the British government found itself subject to increasing criticism and experienced growing unpopularity, and opinion poll evidence suggests that this was paralleled by widespread dissatisfaction with various aspects of the political system: 68 per cent of those interviewed said that they did not have 'enough say in the way the government runs the country'; 69 per cent agreed that important issues should be decided by referendum rather than left for the government to decide; 46 per cent favoured a coalition rather than government by either of the major parties; and 44 per cent said they were dissatisfied with the parliamentary system (soc, May, June and September 1968). How far is this evidence of a loss of legitimacy by the British political system?

The various proposed remedies which received widespread support from respondents – fixed terms of office for the government (63 per cent), the appointment of industrialists and businessmen as Ministers (61 per cent), committees of M.P.s to run government departments (56 per cent), the provision of offices and secretarial help for M.P.s (51 per cent), a reduction in the number of M.P.s (48 per cent), and the establishment of regional parliaments (47 per cent) – hardly suggest fundamental changes in the political system. This would suggest that where the system enjoys widespread legitimacy, the degree of dissatisfaction within society has to be considerable before a change of political system is likely or before the political system is seriously undermined.

Legitimacy may also be somewhat fragmentary – extended more fully to some aspects of the system than to others. The existence of a republic in France, for instance, probably enjoys very considerable legitimacy, so that a restoration of the monarchy has found little support there since the last serious attempt towards the end of the nineteenth century. Other French political institutions are less firmly established and no French constitution has achieved the inviolability of the American. Thus, in any given society, there may be overwhelming agreement on certain fundamentals, such as the holding of periodic elections, the maintenance of a particular form of executive, legislature and judiciary, the creation of a neutral bureaucracy, and so on, but other aspects of the political system may be the subject of conflict. An agreement to hold periodic elections does not constitute agreement on the actual electoral machinery; agreement on a particular form of executive, legislature and judiciary does not constitute agreement on the use to which these institutions are to be put; and agreement on the desirability of creating a neutral bureaucracy does not constitute agreement that the bureaucracy is neutral.

Political socialization is the process by which individuals acquire knowledge, values and attitudes about the political system of their society. It does not assure that society legitimacy for its political system, though that may be the result. It may equally result in the denial of legitimacy, but whether this leads to stasis or change will depend on the circumstances of that denial. Where lack of legitimacy is accompanied by active hostility to the political system, then change is likely, but where it is accompanied by apathy towards the political system, the result is stasis. Through his experiences the individual acquires political orientations and patterns of behaviour which 'may contribute to the maintenance or replication of a given system, to its transformation or to its total destruction.'[1]

---

[1] Easton and Dennis, *Children in the Political System*, p. 66.

3 · Political Participation

We have already seen how the process of political socialization provides the individual with a perceptual screen through which he receives political stimuli. We now have to deal with the effects of these stimuli as they are seen in the process of political participation, the extent to which individuals are involved at various levels in the political system. Political participation may be considered from four points of view:

1 What are the types or forms of political participation?
2 What is the extent of political participation?
3 Who participates?
4 Why do they participate?

FORMS OF POLITICAL PARTICIPATION

There is little difficulty in suggesting the various forms of political participation, regardless of the type of political system concerned: the roles of the professional politician, the voter, the party activists, and the demonstrator immediately spring to mind. It is important, however, to posit the full range of political activities and to see whether there is some sort of hierarchical relationship between them. The simplest and most meaningful hierarchy is probably one based on the degree or extent of participation.

holding political or administrative **office**
seeking political or administrative **office**
active membership of a **political** organisation
passive membership of a **political** organisation
active membership of a **quasi-political** organisation
passive membership of a **quasi-political** organisation
participation in **public** meetings, demonstrations, etc
participation in **informal** political discussion
general interest in politics
voting

total apathy

Figure 2. A hierarchy of political participation

The hierarchy suggested in Figure 2 is intended to cover the whole range of political participation and to be applicable to all types of political systems. The significance of the various levels is, of course, likely to vary from one political system to another, and particular levels may be of great consequence in one system and of little or no consequence in another.

It is also important to appreciate that participation at one level of the hierarchy is not necessarily a precondition of participation at a higher level, though this may be true for certain types of participation.

At the top of the hierarchy there are those who hold various types of office within the political system, including both holders of political office and members of the bureaucracy at various levels. They are distinguished from other political participants in that, to varying degrees, they are concerned with the exercise of formal political power. This does not exclude the actual exercise of power, nor the exercise of influence, by other individuals or groups in the political system. Power may or may not reside among the office-holders, but they remain important because normally they are the formal repositories of power. Any consideration of the office-holders must also include some consideration of those who aspire to and seek the offices concerned. The roles of office-holders and potential office-holders, however, will be dealt with in Chapter 4, where political recruitment is considered.

Below those who hold or seek office in the political system, there are those who are members of various types of political or quasi-political organizations. These include all types of political parties and interest (or pressure) groups. From the point of view of the political system, <u>political parties and interest groups may be defined</u> as *agents of political mobilization*. They are organizations through which individual members of society may participate in certain types of political activity involving the defence or promotion of particular ideas, positions, situations, persons or groups through the political system.

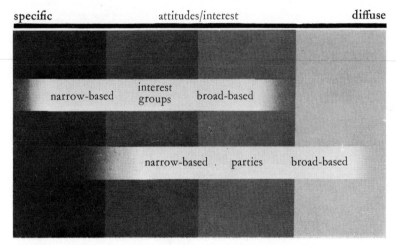

Figure 3. The relationship between political parties and interest groups

Figure 3 looks at the relationship between political parties and interest groups. The basic distinction between the two lies in their attitudes. <u>Interest groups are those organizations which seek to promote, defend or represent limited or specific attitudes, whereas political parties seek to promote, defend or represent a broader spectrum of attitudes.</u> The support that interest groups and political parties receive, however, may be specific or diffuse, stemming, that is, from only a few individuals or groups in society, or from a diverse and large number of individuals or groups. Thus an interest group has <u>limited objectives</u>, such as the introduction, repeal or modification of certain laws or regulations, the protection of the interests of a particular group in society, or the promotion of particular ideologies, beliefs, principles or ideas. In some cases the objective is especially limited – the abolition of capital punishment or opposition to the siting of an airport, for instance – and the interest group ceases to operate once its objective has been achieved (or defeated). In other cases the objective is of a continuing nature – the protection or extension of civil rights and liberties or the defence of various economic interests, for example – in which case the interest group concerned has an indefinite existence. The range of matters which may give rise to interest groups is obviously legion, but it is clear that some of these groups will attract only limited, others widespread, support. Trade unions, for instance, may fall into either category according to the size and nature of the industry in which they operate. Similarly, the extent to which groups are involved in *political* activity varies considerably, from the group operating entirely within the political sphere to the group which does so only occasionally. A group like the Campaign for Nuclear Disarmament, for example, operates for the most part as a specifically political interest group, whereas groups like the Automobile Association are not concerned solely with providing motorists with a political voice. In Figure 2, therefore, the term 'political organization' is intended to include both political parties and those interest groups whose *raison d'être* is primarily political, and the term 'quasi-political organization' to include those interest groups whose function is only partly political.

Political parties, like interest groups, may enjoy diffuse or specific support, but differ from interest groups in that they have diffuse rather than specific attitudes. Their objectives range over the whole spectrum of problems with which society is faced, although a particular party may place greater emphasis on some problems or aspects of problems than others. Some political parties, however, have a broad support base, others a narrow support base. The pragmatic, bargaining mass parties of modern democracies and the totalitarian mass parties of Nazi Germany and various Communist states are examples of broad-based parties, while the regional, religious, ethnic and élitist parties found in many parts of the world are examples of narrow-based parties.

Participation in political parties and interest groups may take an active or passive form, ranging from holding office in such an organization to the provision of financial support through the payment of subscriptions or membership dues. No sharp distinction between active and passive membership is intended and the individual may move from one to the other as circumstances vary. There remains, nevertheless, a basic commitment to the organization through membership, which may have some political significance, both for the organization and the individual, by strengthening the bargaining position of the organization and influencing the political behaviour of the individual.

For various reasons individuals may not belong to any political or quasi-political organizations, but they may be persuaded to participate in some form of public meeting or demonstration. This form of participation may be spontaneous, but it is far more likely to have been organized by political parties or interest groups as part of their political activity. Many, perhaps in some cases all, of the participants will be members of the organizing bodies, but not necessarily, and non-members may be persuaded to support the objects of the meeting or demonstration. Such activity is, however, intermittent and does not have the continuous nature of even the minimal commitment of membership of a political or quasi-political organization.

Another intermittent form of political participation is that of informal political discussion by individuals in their families, at work or among friends. Obviously the incidence of such discussions varies both among individuals and in relation to events. More discussion is likely during election campaigns or at times of political crisis, while discussion may be inhibited or encouraged by the attitudes of the family, fellow-workers or friends.

Some people may not discuss politics with anyone, however, but may, none the less, have some interest in political matters and maintain that interest through the mass media. They will be able to keep themselves informed about what is happening and form opinions about the course of events, but they will tend to limit their participation to this and, possibly, to voting.

The act of voting may be regarded as the least active form of political participation since it requires a minimal commitment which may cease once the vote is cast. Furthermore, regardless of other restrictions which may exist, the act of voting is inevitably restricted by the frequency of elections.

In considering political participation, however limited it may be, some attention should be paid to those who do not participate at all in the political process. Whether this is by choice or because of factors beyond the control of the individual remains to be seen, but whichever it is, such individuals may be described as totally apathetic.

Two matters have deliberately been excluded from the hierarchy in Figure 2: alienation and violence. This is because neither can be properly considered in a hierarchical sense. It will later be argued that alienation may result in participation or non-participation: an individual who feels hostile towards society in general or the political system in particular may withdraw from all types of participation and join the ranks of the totally apathetic, or he may become active at various levels of participation. Participation does not necessarily involve acceptance of the political system and alienation may be expressed by political activity as well as inactivity.

Similarly, violence may manifest itself at various levels in the hierarchy, not only in the form of demonstrations or riots, but also through various political and quasi-political organizations, some of which may regard violence as an effective means of achieving their ends.

THE EXTENT OF POLITICAL PARTICIPATION

Having outlined the various forms of political participation it is obvious that their importance will vary from one political system to another. Moreover, they will vary within a system over time. Various limitations on political participation will therefore exist. Some of these limitations will be formal in nature, others will be informal.

In primitive societies, where politics tends to be closely integrated with societal activity in general, participation is likely to be high and may be difficult to distinguish from other activities. In developing societies, however, with their combination of modern and traditional institutions and influences, participation may be limited by such factors as the level of literacy and the general problem of communication. Contrasting with this, political participation in totalitarian societies may, for some forms of participation, be very high and for others very low, while by definition one of the most important characteristics of totalitarian societies is that they seek to control participation in the political process at all levels. The greatest degree of variation is likely to be found in modern democracies, which, while usually encouraging participation by various means, generally leave it to find its own level.

It is useful to consider political participation in a hierarchical sense, but it should also be borne in mind that some levels of participation may be absent from some political systems. Not all political systems have elections or any form of voting; some systems severely restrict or ban public meetings and demonstrations, while others forbid the formation of political parties and other types of political or quasi-political organizations, and so on. Furthermore, apathy, alienation and the use of violence clearly vary considerably from system to system, but remain important factors in any examination of political participation. Even where participation occurs at the same level in different political systems, however, its nature and significance may vary. This is clearly shown by a brief perusal of voting in different political systems.

The purpose of voting, for example, may be to elect (directly or indirectly) a government, or various officials, or members of a legislature, or to approve or disapprove of certain proposals by means of a referendum or plebiscite, or to enforce legislative responsibility through the device of 'recall' (which enables an electorate to call its representative to account). The voter in the United States is faced with as many as forty choices at some election times: he is called upon to choose a president, a senator, and a member of the House of Representatives (all at federal level), a governor, members of the state legislature and various officials (all at state level), various local government officials (at county and, possibly, municipal level), members of bodies like school boards, and, not infrequently, to participate in a referendum and, more rarely, in a 'recall'. Even in those years when no federal offices and fewer state offices are at stake, the choice remains formidable, and it is as well to remember that presidential elections occur every four years and congressional elections every two. Compared with this the demands made upon the British voter are mild: general elections must take place at least once every five years, but in practice occur on average about once every three years; there is also the occasional by-election, but these are infrequent for any particular constituency; at local level elections may occur annually or at three-year intervals, and some electors are called upon to elect representatives to more than one local government body, and again by-elections may occur from time to time; and finally, but very rarely, a referendum may be used at local level to decide a particular issue. At the very most, therefore, the British voter could be faced with seven choices (assuming the occurrence of a general election, national and local by-elections, and a referendum) in one *year*, though not at one time, while his American counterpart is faced with nearly six times this number.

The significance of voting also differs according to the purpose of the elections: national elections are usually regarded as more important than local elections, while the election of a chief executive is normally more important than the election of a member of a legislature. Other factors, such as the extent of the franchise, may also affect the significance of voting. In some political systems voting may play a very important role, such as deciding which party or persons will hold political power for a certain period, but in other systems voting may be little more than a ritual by which those in power seek to confer legitimacy on their rule. Whatever the purpose of voting, however, there is little doubt that it varies considerably from one political system to another, and, moreover, that the number of people who vote also varies considerably.

Table 10. *Comparison of voting turnout in different types of societies*

STAGE OF ECONOMIC AND SOCIAL DEVELOPMENT	Votes as to % of voting age population
(1) 'Traditional primitive' societies	30
(2) 'Traditional civilizations'	49
(3) 'Transitional 'societies	41
(4) 'Industrial revolution' societies	69
(5) 'High mass consumption' societies	78

SOURCE: Bruce M. Russett, Hayward R. Alker Jr, Karl W. Deutsch and Harold D. Lasswell, *World Handbook of Political and Social Indicators*, New Haven, Conn., 1964, p. 294. For definitions of each type of society, see ibid., pp. 293–303.

The figures in Table 10 illustrate vividly the extent to which voting turnout differs from one type of society to another. The possible reasons for these variations do not concern us for the moment, but it is important to appreciate how variable the lowest form of political participation can be. The percentages shown in the table are the means for each category, and these have a range of 30 to 78 per cent, but the lowest voting turnout found by Russett and his colleagues was 1·9 per cent (Rhodesia and Nyasaland), and the highest 99·6 per cent (Soviet Union), so that the actual range is very large indeed. It does not, of course, follow that, because there is a high voting turnout, other types of participation will also be relatively high. Much depends on the reasons for a high or low turnout. Thus there is a considerable contrast between voting turnout and the extent to which people are interested in politics, some idea of which can be seen from the results of opinion polls in various countries (Table 11).

Table 11. *Levels of interest in politics in the United States, Britain and West Germany*

(A) United States and Britain

LEVEL OF INTEREST	United States	Britain
	%	%
Great deal of interest/Very interested	19	15
Some interest/Interested	47	37
Not very much/Not really interested	29	33
None/Not at all interested	5	15
Total	100	100

(B) West Germany

LEVEL OF INTEREST	
	%
Very deeply/Deeply interested	11
Rather interested	20
Somewhat interested	25
Hardly interested	19
Not at all interested	25
Total	100

SOURCES: United States: MINN, February 1966.
Britain: Mark Abrams, 'Social Trends and Electoral Behaviour', *British Journal of Sociology*, **13**, 1962, p. 233.
West Germany: DIVO, March 1966.

Although the terms used in these surveys are not identical, they are sufficiently similar to allow comparison. It is clear from the table that interest in political affairs is highest in the United States and lowest in West Germany. Nevertheless, the differences are not great, especially among those who claim the most interest.

It is also interesting to compare voting turnout with interest in politics. In spite of the fact that the United States respondents showed the greatest interest in politics, turnout is normally higher in Britain, though lower in West Germany. It is therefore misleading to expect the relationship between voting turnout and other forms of participation to have any exact relationship or ratio, although it is possible to speak of political systems as having a high or low rate of political participation in general. What is clear is that a basic hierarchical pattern remains, and it is to be expected that fewer people say that they are very interested in politics than actually vote, and that fewer people *discuss* politics than say they are at all interested in it.

Table 12. *Frequency of discussing politics with other people in the United States, Britain and West Germany*

FREQUENCY	United States	Britain	West Germany
	%	%	%
Sometimes	76	70	60
Never	24	29	39
Other and don't know	–	–	1
Totals	100	99	100

SOURCE: Almond and Verba, *The Civic Culture*, p. 79.

If the figures in Tables 11 and 12 are compared, it is clear that this is in fact the case: in each country more people say they are to some degree interested in politics than actually discuss it, and the proportion who discuss politics frequently is, of course, much smaller, as another West German survey shows. The respondents were asked how often they discussed politics with their fellow-workers: 16 per cent replied 'often', 52 per cent replied 'sometimes', 22 per cent replied 'never', with the remaining 10 per cent giving no answer (INFAS, October–November 1967).

There is very little data available on the extent to which people participate in demonstrations, public meetings and other intermittent forms of participation, but a fragmentary picture does emerge. A Danish poll suggests that the number of people who participate in any sort of demonstration is fairly small: only 8 per cent of the respondents said that they had *ever* done so (GMA, February 1968). Compared with this, 57 per cent of the respondents in a Norwegian poll said that they had spoken at a meeting, but only 18 per cent had ever written to a newspaper to promote a point of view (PRIO, November-December 1964). Similarly, in the United States a survey found that 13 per cent of the respondents had written to their Congressman or some other public official, and 15 per cent had spoken to a public official 'within the past year' (POSU, June–July 196₅). Another poll in the United States found that only 11 per cent of the respondents said that it was likely that they would attend a forthcoming precinct caucus meeting (MINN, February 1966).

With the exception of the fairly high proportion of Norwegian respondents who said that they had spoken at a meeting (although they, too, were asked whether they had *ever* done so), these are not especially high levels of participation. It is possible, however, that the specifically political nature of an election campaign might produce increased levels of participation.

Table 13. *Levels of participation in election campaigns in the United States and Britain*

(A) United States (recent election campaigns)

ACTIVITY	Proportion participating %
Talked to someone and tried to show them why they should vote for a particular party or candidate	30
Attended party meetings, rallies, or dinners, etc.	13
Gave money to help the campaign of one of the parties or candidates	14
Distributed campaign literature, etc.	7

(B) Britain (1966)

ACTIVITY	Proportion participating %
Watched a Conservative broadcast on TV	78
Watched a Labour broadcast on TV	78
Watched a Liberal broadcast on TV	69
Listened to any party broadcast on the radio	21
Read an election address	49
Heard a local candidate at a meeting	10
Canvassed for a candidate	2
Other work for a candidate	2

SOURCES: United States: POSU, June–July 1965.
Britain: SOC, April 1966.

As with levels of interest in politics, there are problems of comparability between the figures in the two sections of Table 13, but this has little significance since they are sufficient to demonstrate that there is little increase in participation during election campaigns, apart from that which can be associated with increased political communication in Section B.

Much more data is available on the membership of voluntary organizations, which include both political and quasi-political organizations, although the majority probably fall into the second category.

Table 14. *Membership of voluntary organizations in various countries*

NUMBER OF ORGANIZATIONS	United States	Britain	Germany	Italy	France	Mexico
	%	%	%	%	%	%
At least one	57	47	44	29	20	25
More than one	32	16	12	6	6	2

SOURCES: United States, Britain, West Germany, Italy and Mexico: Almond and Verba, *The Civic Culture*, pp. 246 and 264. France: IFOP, March–April 1966.

Membership of voluntary organizations varies considerably from one country to another, as the figures in Table 14 show. Furthermore, the extent to which these organizations may be regarded as 'political' varies. With the exception of the Italian respondents, Almond and Verba found that approximately two-fifths of those who were members of voluntary organizations believed that one or more of the organizations to which they belonged were involved in political affairs; the proportion for the Italian repondents was one-fifth.[1] It none the less remains difficult to assess the significance of membership of voluntary organizations on a comparative basis, partly because the nature of membership varies considerably from one country to another, and partly because of the problem of assessing the respective levels of active and passive membership.

The membership of political parties provides a useful example of the first problem. Maurice Duverger has shown clearly how political parties may be based on various types of membership. He posits three types: (1) 'cadre' parties, where membership is based on a limited élite group of important individuals (typified by the

[1] Almond and Verba, *The Civic Culture*, p. 251.

British Conservative and Liberal parties prior to the rise of the Labour party); (2) 'cell' and 'militia' parties, where membership is based on a centralized hierarchy directly responsible to the leadership (typified by Communist and Fascist parties respectively); and (3) mass-membership parties, based on a dues-paying membership to which the leadership is to varying degrees constitutionally responsible (typified by many European Socialist parties).[1] There is often, as Duverger points out, a further complication in some mass-membership parties in that a number have indirect or affiliated members, that is, members who belong to the party by virtue of their membership of some other organization (in most cases a trade union) which is affiliated to the party. Since the number of members that these organizations choose to affiiliate often represents what they are prepared or can afford to pay to the party in dues rather than the actual number of members who wish to be associated with it, the affiliation of an organization to the party is of greater significance than the association of the individual members. Thus the British Labour party has some six million affiliated members, but rather less than a million individual members. The British Conservative party, on the other hand, has no affiliated members and an individual membership of more than two million. This presents the problem of comparing like with like. Until 1965, for example, members of the ruling bodies of constituency Labour parties did not have to be *individual* members of the Labour party, while membership of the Conservative party is not necessarily a prerequisite of selection as a Conservative candidate.[2] A more difficult comparison exists between American and British parties, since, as Leon Epstein notes:

> Dues-paying is still unusual in major American political parties – so much so that a recent text was not far wrong in asserting that 'there are no card-carrying Republicans or Democrats'. For the national parties, as such, the statement is entirely correct. And in state parties little is known of regular dues-paying by members outside of California and Wisconsin. Locally, however, there are dues-paying clubs – like those in New York and Chicago.[3]

[1] Maurice Duverger, *Political Parties*, translated by Barbara and Robert North, London, 1954, Book I.

[2] Michael Rush, *The Selection of Parliamentary Candidates*, London, 1969, pp. 56 and 153n.

[3] Leon Epstein, *Political Parties in Western Democracies*, New York, 1967, p. 123.

It is clearly important to take into account the particular environment in which various political organizations have to work. It is also important, however, to take account of the second problem mentioned above – the extent to which membership of voluntary organizations is active or passive. Almond and Verba found that the proportion of their respondents who were members of voluntary organizations and had held office tended to vary (Table 15).

Table 15. *Holding office in voluntary organizations*

COUNTRY	Proportion of members who have held office
	%
United States	46
Britain	29
West Germany	16
Italy	23
Mexico	34

SOURCE: Almond and Verba, *The Civic Culture*, p. 257.

As might be expected, the majority of people (in four of the five countries listed in Table 15) the overwhelming majority are passive rather than active members of the voluntary organizations to which they belong. If these proportions are expressed as percentages of the total number of respondents in the five-nation study, they are, of course, much lower: 26 per cent for the United States, 13 per cent for Britain, 7 per cent for Germany and Italy and 8 per cent for Mexico. In most voluntary organizations, however, the *most* active individuals – those who exercise the most influence and take the crucial decisions – constitute a much smaller proportion of the membership than those who hold some sort of office. It is doubtful, for example, whether more than 5 per cent of the individual and affiliated members of Constituency Labour parties and only 1 per cent of the members of local Conservative associations in Britain (largely because Conservative associations tend to have larger memberships) are in any way associated with the selection of their parliamentary candidates, yet this is one of the most important roles of local parties.[1]

Once again, we can see that the higher we ascend up the hierarchy the fewer the number of people who participate. Lester Milbrath has summed up the situation in the United States as follows:

[1] Rush, *The Selection of Parliamentary Candidates*, pp. 35, 164, 276 and 279.

Probably less than 1 per cent of the American adult population engage in the top two or three behaviours [i.e. holding public and party office, being a candidate for office and soliciting political funds]. Only about 4 or 5 per cent are active in a party campaign, and attend meetings. About 10 per cent make monetary contributions, about 13 per cent contact public officials, and about 15 per cent display a button or sticker. Around 25 or 30 per cent try to proselyte others to vote a certain way, and from 40 to 70 per cent perceive political messages and vote in any given election.[1]

Similarly, Richard Rose has summarized the position in Britain:

Table 16. *Hierarchy of political participation in Britain*

ACTIVITY	Proportion of electorate involved
	%
M.P.s, senior civil servants	0·01
Local party activists	0·4
Individual party members	10
Organization officers (past and present)	14
Very interested in politics	15
Informed (name six major politicians)	16
Party members (all categories)	25
Organization members	47
Voters (1964)	77

SOURCE: Richard Rose, *Politics in England*, London, 1965, p. 94.

The evidence on the extent of political participation is clear enough, even if it is somewhat fragmentary, nor is it difficult to discover *who* participates. What *is* difficult, however, is finding out *why* they participate, and since the problem of who participates may throw light on why they do so, it is to these two questions that we now turn.

WHO PARTICIPATES AND WHY

Thus far we have only touched upon the question of apathy, but in examining the reasons for participation it is inevitable that we should ask why some people shun all forms of political participation, or participate only at the lowest level. This is all the more important in view of the fact that those who do participate in most forms of political activity constitute a minority (often a very small minority) of the members of any society.

[1] Milbrath, *Political Participation*, p. 19.

A variety of terms are assigned to these non-participants, and they are variously described as *apathetic, cynical, alienated* or *anomic*. Quite obviously these terms are by no means synonymous, although they may be related to one another and possibly have some characteristics in common. It is therefore important to distinguish between the four terms and examine how they have been applied to studies of political participation.

Apathy may be defined very simply as a lack of interest in or lack of concern for persons, situations or phenomena in general or particular. From a sociological point of view, it may apply to society in general or merely to certain aspects of society. Like many behaviour patterns it is often linked to a particular personality syndrome:

> The apathetic's characteristics – inability to recognize personal responsibility or to examine – or even to accept – his own emotions and feelings; vague, incomprehensible feelings of worry, insecurity, and threat; complete, unchallenging acceptance of constituted authority (social codes, parents, religion) and conventional values – form a self-consistent pattern which, in a clinical situation, would be labelled *passivity*.[1]

These characteristics are contrasted by the same authors with those of the active individual, which comprise:

> an emphasis on strivings for ego-satisfaction, independence, maturity, and personal happiness . . . active attempts to achieve self-understanding . . . sensitivity to others' feelings, emotions and conflicts . . . great social consciousness and emphasis on social contribution and love-giving.[2]

As far as political participation is concerned, therefore, the most important trait of the apathetic individual is his passivity or abstention from political activity. It is nevertheless important to consider whether the term apathy should be limited to those who refrain from all types of political participation (including voting), or whether it should be used more widely to apply to those who refrain from more active participation, especially those who shun activity through political or quasi-political organizations. The hierarchy shown in Figure 2 referred only to the totally apathetic, to those who refrain from all types of participation, but to assume that apathy is in no sense applicable to other levels in the hier-

[1] Paul H. Mussen and Anne B. Wyszynski, 'Personality and Political Participation', *Human Relations*, 5, 1952, pp. 78–9. (Original italics.)
[2] ibid.

archy is to be less than realistic. Thus, while apathy may be total, it should be recognized that there may be <u>degrees of apathy</u>. In other words, one explanation of non-participation at various levels of the hierarchy may simply be that of apathy.

Morris Rosenberg[1] has suggested three major reasons for political apathy. His conclusions were based on a series of unstructured interviews in depth. The first reason is the perceived consequence of political activity. This may take several forms: the individual may feel that political activity is a threat to various aspects of his life. He may, for example, believe that it will alienate his friends and neighbours, or even members of his family – his social position may, he feels, be disturbed or undermined; or political activity may threaten his occupational position by identifying him too closely with a particular party or point of view; or he may feel that political activity would threaten or undermine his self-esteem by exposing what he regards as his own ignorance, inadequacies and incompetence. In general, therefore, <u>where the individual is faced with controversy or cross-pressures, he may find political inactivity more congenial than activity.</u>

Rosenberg's second reason is that the <u>individual may regard political activity as futile</u>. As a single individual, he may feel that he is totally unable to influence the course of events and that the political forces he perceives are in any case beyond the control of the individual. Moreover, he may regard the results of political activity as a foregone conclusion and feel that even combining with others to achieve some political aim is useless. Finally, he may perceive a gulf between his ideals and political reality, a gulf of such proportions that no amount of political activity seems likely to bridge it.

Third, like Milbrath,[2] Rosenberg regards 'spurs to action' or political stimuli as important factors in encouraging political activity, and the <u>absence of such stimuli may contribute to feelings of apathy</u>. The individual may feel that the subject-matter of politics is not very interesting and may even divorce many actions from the political sphere because he perceived them as personal rather than political. Furthermore, he may feel that political

[1] Morris Rosenberg, 'Some Determinants of Political Apathy', *Public Opinion Quarterly*, **18**, 1954, pp. 34–66.
[2] *Political Participation*, Chapter 2.

activity provides little or no immediate satisfaction and few direct results. In sum, political participation is perceived as utterly inappropriate to the personal and material needs of the individual.

Cynicism, as against apathy, which involves relative passivity and inactivity, is an attitude applicable to either activity or inactivity. Robert Agger and his colleagues define cynicism as being 'contemptuously distrustful of human nature', and by means of an attitude scale designed to measure the degree to which their respondents were cynical, both personally and politically, they sought to relate cynicism to various aspects of political behaviour.[1] They found that Democratic party supporters tended to be slightly more cynical than Republicans, and that the latter were considerably more trusting, although this may have been linked with Republican control of the White House at the time the survey was conducted. This did not, however, appear to constitute a complete explanation, since Agger and his colleagues found clear links between cynicism and other variables. They found, for instance, that political cynicism tended to decrease with higher education and, to a lesser extent, with higher income. Of greater significance for political participation, however, was their finding that the more cynical their respondents the less they felt able to influence events, and that in general political participation decreased with cynicism.

Cynicism, then, is a feeling that the actions and motives of others are to be regarded with suspicion, that pessimism is more realistic than optimism, and that the individual must look after his own interests because society is basically self-centred. Politically cynicism manifests itself in a variety of ways: the feeling that politics is 'a dirty business', that politicians are not to be trusted, that the individual is at the mercy of manipulating groups, that the 'real' power is exercised by 'faceless men', and so on. It should be recognized, however, that cynicism may be extensive, even where a political system is generally regarded as enjoying widespread legitimacy (Table 17).

[1] Robert E. Agger, Marshal N. Goldstein and Stanley A. Pearl, 'Political Cynicism: Measurement and Meaning', *Journal of Politics*, **23**, 1961, pp. 477–506. See also Edgar Litt, 'Political Cynicism and Political Futility', *Journal of Politics*, **25**, 1963, pp. 312–23.

Table 17. *Evidence of cynical political attitudes in Britain*

ATTITUDE	Proportion agreeing
	%
Most politicians will promise anything to get votes	78
Most politicians care more about their party than the country	66
Politicians are all talk and no action	59
Most politicians are in it for what they can get	57
Once they become M.P.s they forget about the voters	55

SOURCE: NOP, February 1968.

Each of the cynical attitudes about British politics and politicians shown in Table 17 had the support of a majority of the respondents, in several cases very substantial support. Much depends, of course, on how strongly opinions are held, but it is significant that they are widely held and suggests that, like apathy, cynicism should be regarded as a matter of degree. A person who is extremely cynical may well feel that political participation in any form is futile and thus join the ranks of the totally apathetic, but for others their cynicism may simply limit their participation or merely be regarded as 'the only realistic way of looking at things'. Cynicism may not, therefore, preclude participation at any level of the hierarchy, although it may provide an explanation of non-participation by particular individuals at particular levels.

Alienation suggests actual hostility, where cynicism suggests a certain distaste for politics and politicians. Robert Lane defines political alienation as 'a person's sense of estrangement from the politics and government of his society . . . (and) . . . the tendency to think of the government and politics of the nation as run *by* others *for* others according to an unfair set of rules'.[1] Clearly such an attitude goes far beyond cynicism, and Lane suggests that, as far as the United States is concerned, it is misleading to speak of widespread alienation and more meaningful to think in terms of those who are 'politically divorced'.[2] The latter are those who regard the government as being of little or no consequence for them. Such an attitude may be quite widely held, as Almond and Verba found in their five-nation study (Table 18).

[1] Lane, *Political Ideology*, pp. 161 and 177.
[2] ibid., p. 173.

Table 18. *Proportion of 'politically divorced' individuals in the United States, Britain, West Germany, Italy and Mexico*

	National government		Local government	
COUNTRY	No effect	Don't know	No effect	Don't know
	%	%	%	%
United States	11	4	10	2
Britain	23	4	23	3
West Germany	17	12	18	8
Italy	19	24	22	18
Mexico	66	3	67	3

SOURCE: Almond and Verba, *The Civic Culture*, pp. 46 and 47.

As the table shows, only a small proportion of respondents in the United States felt that neither national nor local government had an effect on their daily lives, but in the other four countries higher proportions expressed this view – as many as two-thirds in the case of the Mexican respondents. With Germany and Italy, especially the latter, the proportion who replied 'don't know' is higher than in the other three countries, and the sense of being politically divorced may be somewhat higher than Almond and Verba's actual figures suggest. If account is taken of the 'don't knows' (though in what proportion remains a matter of judgement), then the proportion of British and German respondents believing that the government is of little or no consequence to them personally would probably be similar, while the proportion of Italian respondents would be substantially higher.

Anomie: whether those who adopt an attitude of alienation should be described as 'politically divorced' or 'alienated' is a matter of opinion, but the attitude is also consistent with the fourth term mentioned above – 'anomie'. This was devised by Durkheim in his famous study of suicide,[1] and is described by Lane as 'a sense of value loss and lack of direction' in which the individual experiences a feeling of ineffectiveness and that authority 'doesn't care', resulting in the devaluation of his goals and the loss of urgency to act.[2] Leo Srole has developed an anomie scale which has been used in a number of studies. Using this attitude scale, Srole found

[1] Emil Durkheim, *Suicide*, translated by John A. Spaulding and George Simpson, and edited by George Simpson, London, 1952.

[2] Lane, *Political Life: Why People Get Involved in Politics*, Glencoe, Illinois, 1959, pp. 166–9.

a close relationship between anomie (which he regards as syony-
mous with alienation) and the authoritarian personality.[1] Other
studies, however, have sought to use the Srole scale to measure
degrees of anomie (alienation) among various groups in society.
Using a sample of respondents from Detroit in 1958, for instance,
Marvin Olsen found considerable variation in levels of anomie
according to race, income and education (Table 19).

Table 19. *Levels of anomie in the United States (Detroit)*

CHARACTERISTIC	Proportion with a high score on the Srole Scale
	%
Negroes	53
Whites	30
High-income white collar ⎫ Low-income white collar ⎭	22
High-income blue collar	30
Low-income blue collar	47
Unemployed	54
Some college education	18
High school education	35
Less education	45

SOURCE: Marvin E. Olsen, 'Alienation and Political Opinions', *Public Opinion
Quarterly*, 29, 1965, pp. 200–12.

With the exception of the difference between white persons and
Negroes, Olsen found that levels of anomie were closely associated
with occupation, a finding supported by Lipsitz's study of skilled
and unskilled auto-workers in Detroit and the relationship
between job satisfaction and political attitudes.[2] Olsen's study
suggests that anomie not only varies between groups, as might
be expected, but that it is a fairly widespread, at least in Detroit.
In addition to measuring levels of anomie, he also found that
respondents with high scores on the Srole scale favoured more
government action in domestic affairs and a decrease in foreign
aid, and that they were more likely to favour limits on the freedom
of speech. These findings are important for our purposes in so far
as they provide evidence of the political opinions held by those
whom Olsen regards as 'alienated'. Further evidence of this is

[1] Leo Srole, 'Social Integration and Certain Corrollaries: An Exploratory
Study', *American Sociological Review*, 21, 1956, pp. 709–16.
[2] See Chapter 2, p. 46 above.

provided by Frederic Templeton, who, using the Srole Scale on a sample of respondents in California, tested the relationship between anomie and political interest and knowledge, and political participation as measured by voting (Table 20).

Table 20. *Relationship between anomie (Srole Scale) and political interest, knowledge and participation*

LEVELS OF INTEREST, KNOWLEDGE AND PARTICIPATION	Manual workers (anomie score)		Non-manual workers (anomie score)	
	Low	High	Low	High
	%	%	%	%
High political interest	44	29	52	39
High political knowledge	44	12	52	18
Constant party voter	75	54	66	45

SOURCE: Frederic Templeton, 'Alienation and Political Participation: Some Research Findings', *Public Opinion Quarterly*, 30, 1966, pp. 249–61.

In each case, Templeton found that those respondents who had a high anomie score had lower levels of political interest, knowledge and participation than those with a low anomie score. He also found that those with a high anomie score were more likely to alter their voting behaviour from one election to another.

There is little doubt that apathy may be explained by cynicism, alienation or anomie, yet it is doubtful whether single or collectively they provide a complete explanation. What does seem clear is that political apathy is closely linked to general apathy: Lane, for instance, found that those of his respondents who were politically alienated were also alienated to varying degrees from society;[1] while Agger and his colleagues found that political cynicism was linked to personal cynicism. Moreover, the concept of anomie and the anomie scale evolved by Srole are based on social rather than political attitudes. Political behaviour is, as the process of political socialization suggests, an integral part of social behaviour. The more an individual is involved in social activities generally, the more likely he is to participate in the political sphere. William Erbe, for example, in a replication of various studies of political participation, found that organizational involvement was a major antecedent of political participa-

[1] Lane, *Political Ideology*, Chapter 11.

tion, at all levels.[1] Similarly, a comparison of group leaders with a sample of the general population in the United States found that the group leaders were more socially integrated than the general population.[2]

It is important, however, to make the distinction between apathy, cynicism, alienation and anomie clear. Defined simply, apathy is a lack of interest, cynicism is an attitude of distaste and disenchantment, while alienation and anomie both involve a feeling of estrangement or divorce from society, but where alienation is characterized by hostility, anomie is characterized by bewilderment. The available evidence suggests that the totally apathetic are, at the very least, cynical and more often alienated or anomic. Apathy, cynicism, alienation and anomie, however, are all matters of degree and may therefore affect not only those who shun all forms of participation, but those who are involved in political activity. Relative degrees of apathy, cynicism, alienation and anomie may account for non-participation at the higher levels of political participation while not precluding activity at lower levels of the hierarchy. Moreover, alienation, far from taking a passive form, may result in considerable political activity, particularly that involving violent political action.

For example, following its establishment in 1948, the Communist régime in Hungary systematically sought to undermine the social and economic position of the upper and middle classes, and this was combined with a programme of 'Russification', all of which resulted in social, economic, cultural and political alienation among members of these classes. A study based on intensive interviews with refugees from Hungary, following the revolt of 1956, found that those who had suffered a loss of socio-economic status were more hostile and more uncompromising in their attitudes towards the Communist régime than those who had suffered no such loss. Furthermore, these respondents were also more active in the revolt *before* the Russian intervention than those who had suffered no loss of status.[3] It would appear that

[1] William Erbe, 'Social Involvement and Political Activity', *American Sociological Review*, **29**, 1964, pp. 198–215.

[2] Arnold M. Rose, 'Alienation and Participation: A Comparison of Group Leaders and the "Mass",' *American Sociological Review*, **27**, 1962, pp. 834–8.

[3] Henry Gleitman and Joseph T. Greenbaum, 'Hungarian Socio-Political Attitudes and Revolutionary Action', *Public Opinion Quarterly*, **24**, 1960, pp. 62–76.

the more alienated sections of Hungarian society were, under certain conditions, not only more likely to express their hostility in an active rather than passive form, but that under those conditions violence was an acceptable form of political participation. The less alienated sections of society tended to participate in the revolt only *after* the Russian forces had invaded the country and thus provided them with a stimulus to action.

It is therefore important to link alienation with the expression of extreme hostility, including the use of violence. In those societies in which alienation is widespread and in which the political system has only limited legitimacy, various forms of hostility to the political system in particular and the social system in general are likely to be manifested. The extent to which such hostility will include the use of violence depends on a variety of factors, some practical, some material, some traditional, some ideological. The use of violence may, for example, depend on the extent to which it is regarded as a viable means of securing particular ends – if it is thought that the assassination of a public figure, or a *coup d'état*, or armed insurrection, or mob violence is likely to effect the changes desired, then violence is more likely, but its use also depends on other factors. Thus while violence is often the last resort of those whose situation is desperate, the more sophisticated forms of violence depend upon the availability of material means. The availability of arms, efficient means of communication and effective leadership are, for instance, usually found in the successful *coup d'état* or armed insurrection. The availability of the means to effect violence may be offset, however, by traditions or ideologies which militate against the use of violence as an instrument of political policy.

In the United States, for instance, the traditional right to bear arms, legally recognized in the Second Amendment to the Constitution, has been associated with the levels of social violence in America and with the fact that four presidents have been assassinated, yet, as we have already seen, the expectation of a military *coup d'état* is very low and ideological norms militate against this form of political violence. In many countries the armed forces have the means of political violence at their disposal, but lack the will to use them for political ends. In other countries it is widely expected, though not necessarily accepted, that the armed forces will intervene with force in political affairs from time to time, and such traditions are often difficult to break down, as the United States found in Nicaragua in the 1920s and 1930s. During a period of military intervention in Nicaraguan affairs, the United States government sought to establish and train a National Guard which would remain politically neutral once independence had been restored to the country, but this did not prevent the National Guard from being involved in the assassination of a prominent guerrilla leader, Augusto Sandino, in 1934, nor did it prevent the guard's commander, General Anastasio Somoza, from assuming the presidency in 1937 and effectively establishing a dynasty whose power depended on its control of the National Guard.

Similarly, the widespread use of assassination and terror may stem from the ideological acceptance of violence as a legitimate political instrument. The ideological acceptance of violence is thus characteristic of various groups (such as the nineteenth-century Russian Anarchists, Lenin's Bolsheviks, the Resistance groups in German-occupied countries during the Second World War, the E.O.K.A. organization in Cyprus, the Mau-Mau in Kenya, or the Vietcong in Vietnam) which seek to overthrow existing political régimes. Russett and his colleagues devised an index of violence (although it should be noted that the index referred to social violence generally rather than exclusively political violence) based on the number of violent deaths per million population. They found that a low level of violence was associated with those countries that had either high or low levels of income, whereas a higher level of violence was found in those countries in the middle-income range. They associated violence with development and suggested that countries undergoing extensive social, economic and political change were more likely to experience violence.[1] Certainly it is reasonable to suggest, as in the case of political socialization, that the conflict between the traditional and modernizing influences is an important factor; and in the case of political participation such conflict may take the form of violence.

The use of violence for political ends may be regarded as one, but only one, manifestation of political alienation. Obviously, hostility to a particular régime or even to a particular social system need not take a violent form. Socialist groups in many countries have, for example, sought fundamental changes in the

[1] Russett *et al.*, *World Handbook of Political and Social Indicators*, pp. 306–7.

social system and yet have shunned violence as a means of effecting those changes. Alienation may therefore stimulate a variety of forms of political participation or result in abstention from such activity.

Since the use of violence for political ends may be regarded as a manifestation of political alienation, it is misleading to associate the latter solely with political inactivity. Furthermore, it is also clear that many of those politically active at some levels may, none the less, be cynical about political phenomena and apathetic about other types of participation. Whether individuals are described as apathetic, cynical, alienated or anomic, they remain in effect part of a *satisfaction-dissatisfaction* syndrome. It is also possible, of course, that those who are politically apathetic are satisfied rather than dissatisfied, but this is a subject on which little or no research has been done. As already noted, the available evidence on those who are totally apathetic suggests that they are, to varying degrees cynical, alienated or anomic, but it may well be that those who are apathetic about the higher levels of political participation are satisfied rather than dissatisfied. Conversely, apart from those who are alienated in a way that encourages them to be politically active rather than inactive, there is evidence to link satisfaction rather than dissatisfaction with increased political participation.

Using a national sample survey in the United States, Frank Lindenfeld found that those respondents who expressed *financial satisfaction* were more involved in political life.[1] Levels of involvement was measured in terms of interest in politics, feelings of political competence or efficacy, and actual participation in political activities. Lindenfeld also found that among respondents of low socio-economic status, financial dissatisfaction was related to feelings of political alienation and apathy, but this is not the case between medium- and high-status respondents who were financially dissatisfied. We have already seen in Table 19 that scores on the Srole anomie scale vary considerably from one demographic group to another, and it is instructive to compare two of these groups on levels of satisfaction (Table 21). While it should be noted that the figures in Tables 19 and 21 are based on different surveys at different times, and therefore too much stress should not be laid on the actual details, it is notable that Negro

[1] Frank Lindenfeld, 'Economic Interest and Political Involvement', *Public Opinion Quarterly*, **28**, 1964, pp. 104–11.

Table 21. *Levels of dissatisfaction among whites and Negroes in the United States*

AREA	Proportion dissatisfied	
	Whites	Negroes
	%	%
Work	8	18
Education	16	23
Housing	19	44
Income	29	49

SOURCE: AIPO, November 1966.

respondents showed a much higher proportion with a high score on the anomie scale and much higher levels of dissatisfaction than white respondents, especially over housing and income. All the various studies of cynicism, alienation and anomie that have been cited in this chapter have found that the levels of these phenomena have varied according to such factors as education, income, occupation and from country to country, and this is common to all levels of political participation. Although there is insufficient data available on every level of participation to demonstrate the importance of all these factors, there is enough to show that it is likely that their importance is widespread.

A number of electoral studies in various countries have shown that voting turnout varies considerably from one group of voters to another, and these studies have been summarized by S. M. Lipset (Table 22). He also suggests that a number of environmental factors influence turnout: whether the election is taking place at a time of crisis; the extent to which the policies of the government are relevant to the individual; the extent to which the individual has access to relevant information; the extent to which the individual is subjected to group pressures to vote; and the extent to which the individual is subjected to cross-pressures.[1]

A similar pattern is found with levels of political interest (Table 23). The West German survey (Section B) also showed that political interest increased with age, income and occupational status, and was higher in urban areas and certain regions. Another West German survey found that women discuss politics less than

[1] Lipset, *Political Man*, pp. 185–216.

Table 22. *Social characteristics correlated with voting turnout*

HIGHER TURNOUT	LOWER TURNOUT
High income	Low income
High education	Low education
Occupational groups:	Occupational groups:
Businessmen	Unskilled workers
White-collar employees	Servants
Government employees	Service workers
Commercial crop farmers	Peasants, subsistence farmers
Miners	
Whites	Negroes
Men	Women
Middle-aged people (35–55)	Young people (under 35)
Older people (over 55)	
Old residents in the community	Newcomers in the community
Workers in Western Europe	Workers in the United States
Married people	Single people
Members of organizations	Isolated individuals

SOURCE: Lipset, *Political Man*, p. 184.

Table 23. *Social characteristics correlated with political interest in Britain and West Germany*

(A) Britain

LEVEL OF INTEREST	Men	Women	Working class	Middle class	Left school Under 16	Left school 16 or over
	%	%	%	%	%	%
Very interested	21	8	14	17	14	19
Interested	39	35	30	52	32	53
Not really interested	29	38	38	22	37	22
Not at all interested	11	19	18	9	17	6

(B) West Germany

LEVEL OF INTEREST	Men	Women	Primary education No vocational training	Primary education Vocational training	Secondary education Lower grade	Secondary education Completed higher grade
	%	%	%	%	%	%
Very deeply/deeply	16	8	6	13	19	26
Rather interested	28	14	11	23	29	43
Somewhat interested	28	21	22	27	25	12
Hardly interested	17	20	21	20	13	14
Not at all interested	11	37	40	17	14	5

SOURCES: Britain: Abrams, 'Social Trends and Electoral Behaviour', p. 233.
West Germany: DIVO, March 1966.

men: only 6 per cent of the women respondents said that they *often* discuss politics, compared with 19 per cent of the men, while 37 per cent said they *never* discuss politics compared with 17 per cent of the men (INFAS, October-November 1967). Almond and Verba found that

> talking politics . . . [is] closely related to educational attainment. The frequency of talking politics rises sharply from primary to secondary to the university levels in all five countries. But the difference between educational levels are not as sharp in the United States and Britain as in the other three countries.[1]

Although the information on participation in demonstrations is very limited, the Danish poll cited earlier (p. 84) found differences in participation between men and women, and between members of different parties. Only 5 per cent of the women respondents had ever taken part in a demonstration, compared with 11 per cent of the men; and members of left-wing parties were far more likely to have taken part in demonstrations than members of other parties (GMA, February 1968).

The likelihood of members of the public writing to M.P.s, Congressmen or other legislative representatives also increases with education and occupational status,[2] while a survey in Minnesota found that participation in party meetings increased markedly among those with a college education: of those respondents who had been to grade school or high school, 16 per cent said it was likely that they would attend a forthcoming precinct caucus meeting, compared with 30 per cent of those with a college education (MINN, February 1966).

A similar pattern was found by Almond and Verba in participation in voluntary organizations. The data in Table 24 confirm the pattern that is characteristic of other forms of participation: men are more likely to be members of voluntary organizations than women, and participation increases with education. Almond and Verba also note that 'higher occupational status generally involves more frequent voluntary association membership, though the relationship is not as close as that between education and

[1] Almond and Verba, *The Civic Culture*, p. 83.
[2] See Hedley Cantril (ed.), *Public Opinion 1935–46*, Princeton, N.J., 1951, p. 703.

Table 24. *Membership of voluntary organizations by sex and education*

CHARACTERISTIC	United States	Britain	Germany	Italy	Mexico
	%	%	%	%	%
Men	68	66	66	41	43
Women	47	30	24	19	15
Primary education, or less	46	41	41	25	21
Some secondary education	55	55	63	37	39
Some university education	80	92	62	46	68

SOURCE: Almond and Verba, *The Civic Culture*, pp. 247 and 249. In assessing membership of voluntary organizations Almond and Verba have excluded *church* membership and confined religious organizations to 'church-related organizations' rather than recording church affiliation. If the latter were included, female membership of voluntary organizations would be higher, especially in such Catholic countries as Italy and Mexico.

affiliation'.[1] Moreover, the five-nation study also found that activity *within* voluntary organizations, as measured by having held office, was greater among men than women and again increased with education. The major exception to this was that more women than men (52 per cent compared with 41 per cent) had been officers of voluntary organizations in the United States, and the authors suggest that this may be because women's organizations tend to be smaller, thus providing a greater opportunity for their members to hold office.

Although the data presented on the variations in political participation is both fragmentary and not always directly comparable, it is sufficient to demonstrate that participation does vary in relation to a number of important social characteristics and that these variations are not confined to particular countries, but are found in different countries with varying social and political systems. There are, of course, differences between various countries, but the basic patterns are similar. Milbrath suggests that political participation varies in relation to four major factors: (1) the extent to which the individual receives political stimuli; (2) the individual's personal characteristics; (3) the individual's social characteristics; and (4) the political setting or environment in which the individual finds himself.[2]

[1] Almond and Verba, *The Civic Culture*, p. 249n.
[2] See Milbrath, *Political Participation*, passim.

The more the individual is exposed to political stimuli through personal and organizational contacts and through the mass media, the more is he likely to engage in political activity. Obviously this exposure is likely to vary from individual to individual, and it is after all part of the process of political socialization. Someone who belongs to a family which frequently discusses politics, or to an organization which encourages political activity, is likely to be stimulated into political activity. Similarly, exposure to the mass media may stimulate and maintain the individual's interest in political affairs and increase the likelihood of his participation in those affairs. At the same time, the individual has a measure of control over his exposure to political stimuli and may choose to avoid personal and organizational contacts, either generally or merely those which are specifically political. Thus those who are interested in politics are likely to welcome the opportunity to participate in the political process or may feel that they have some obligation, moral or otherwise, to do so. By means of the perceptual screen outlined in Chapter 2 (p. 30), the individual limits the stimuli which surround him, some consciously, others subconsciously. His knowledge, values and attitudes, his experience and his personality, affect his response to these stimuli and thus the extent to which he engages in political activity. An individual who lacks knowledge or information about a political problem or situation is less likely to feel competent to participate in any effort to resolve that problem or change that situation; political competence or efficacy increases with knowledge. Similarly, the individual's values and attitudes may militate against participation to the extent that he is cynical, alienated or anomic, or they may encourage political activity because they fulfil feelings of duty, obligation or achievement. Or again, experience of political participation, or lack of it, is likely to influence the individual's attitude towards future participation, while the nature of his personality is likely to be important. Sociable, dominant and extravert personalities, for instance, would be more likely to engage in political activity, whereas less sociable, submissive and introvert personalities would not.

A person's social characteristics, such as his socio-economic status, his racial or ethnic group, his age, sex and religion, whether he lives in a rural or urban area, whether he belongs to voluntary organizations, and so on, are all likely to influence his political participation, as we have already seen in a number of instances.

Although the receiving of political stimuli and the nature of the individual's personal and social characteristics are crucial in influencing the extent to which he is politically active, it is important to take into account the political environment or setting. This applies as much to the constitutional and institutional arrangements found in a particular political system as it does to its less formal aspects, such as the nature of the party system, or regional differences, or factors affecting particular events, such as elections. The separation of powers in the United States, for instance, affects political participation in important areas like interest group activity. Thus American interest groups pay a great deal of attention to Congress because it has considerable independence in the exercise of its legislative powers. Conversely, in Britain, the attention of interest groups tends to be concentrated more upon ministers and upon the bureaucracy because Parliament does not normally act independently of the executive.

In the same way, the legal requirements of an electoral system may influence political participation. An obvious example is that of compulsory voting: Russett and his colleagues report that seven countries require members of their electorates to vote, and with one exception the level of voting is higher than the mean for countries at a similar stage of development.[1]

Other factors, such as the nature of the party system, are also important. For example, societies characterized by fairly rigid class divisions are more likely to give rise to class-based parties, and the existence of such parties usually increases participation among the lower classes. This is the case in Britain and a number of other Western European countries, which, compared with the United States, where there is no party based on the working class, have powerful Socialist parties to provide vehicles for working-class participation. A variation of this theme may be seen in Canada, where the presence of the New Democratic party (and its predecessor, the Co-operative Commonwealth Federation) marks a departure from the broadly-based, loosely-organized pragmatic parties common to North America by seeking an electoral base of working-class support.[2]

[1] Russett *et al.*, *World Handbook of Political and Social Indicators*, pp. 84–6 and 294.

[2] See Gad Horowitz, *Canadian Labour in Politics*, Toronto, 1968.

Regional differences provide yet another type of environmental factor, often forming the basis of variations in electoral behaviour and other forms of political participation. For instance, the long association between the Democratic party and the American South, the presence of Quebec within the Canadian federal system, the tribal divisions in Nigeria, the physical separateness of the component parts of Indonesia, all contribute to the patterns of political participation in their respective countries.

Beyond specific examples, however, by far the most significant differences in political environment are those which mark off a political system as belonging to a particular 'type' or 'group'. Clearly there are differences in political environment between countries like Britain and the United States, or Ghana and Nigeria, or the Soviet Union and Hungary, but more fundamental differences are found between, say Britain, Nigeria and the Soviet Union, between modern democracies, developing countries and totalitarian states.

There is every reason to believe that the personal and social characteristics of the individual are important in all types of political systems, although the particular characteristics which are important will vary from system to system. Socio-economic status is undoubtedly important in Britain, for instance, as are tribal groupings in Nigeria and ethnic differences in the Soviet Union. The U.S.S.R., in fact, provides an excellent example of how social characteristics are just as important in a totalitarian society as they are in other types of political system in the field of political participation.

This is especially clear from the data available on the membership of the Communist Party of the Soviet Union (C.P.S.U.), which has been subject to important changes in its social composition since the Revolution of 1917.[1] We have already seen that in countries like the United States, Britain and West Germany, women tend to be less active in politics than men, and the same is true of the Soviet Union: in 1924, 8 per cent of the members of the C.P.S.U. were women, and by 1961 this figure had risen to approximately 20 per cent. Similarly, 7 per cent of the voting delegates at the Seventeenth Party Congress in 1934 were women, compared with 22 per cent at the Twenty-Second Congress in

[1] The data that follows is taken from Fainsod, *How Russia is Ruled*, Chapter 8.

1961, while it was not until 1957 that Madame Furtseva became the first woman to be elected a full member of the party Presidium. The proportion of party members with a higher education has also increased from less than 1 per cent in 1922 to more than 6 per cent in 1947, but of much greater significance is the increase among delegates to the party congresses from approximately 10 per cent in 1934 to 52 per cent in 1961, although the proportion was as high as 59 per cent in 1952. Changes have also taken place in the occupational backgrounds and social origins of party members. Prior to the Revolution, three-fifths of the party members were workers by social origin, a third were middle class (or non-manual) and less than 5 per cent of peasant origin. By 1929 the proportion of party members of peasant origin had risen to a fifth, those of non-manual origin had fallen to a sixth, while those of worker origin remained at three-fifths – although in the intervening period the proportion of peasants had risen to more than a quarter and the proportion of workers to two-fifths. What was of greater significance, however, as Fainsod points out in commenting on the party at the end of this period, was the fact that,

> In terms of social origin, its membership was predominantly working class. In terms of occupation, workers at the bench only slightly exceeded those performing administrative or other non-manual work.[1]

Furthermore, as the data on the proportion of party members of peasant origin suggests, the membership of the C.P.S.U. is predominantly urban rather than rural in character. In 1927 the ratio of party members within the population was 319 : 10,000 in cities and 25 : 10,000 in villages, and by 1947 approximately 27 per cent of party members lived in rural areas. Yet, according to the official census data in 1926, the rural population of the Soviet Union constituted 82 per cent of the total population and, in 1939, 67 per cent. Similarly, the distribution of national-ethnic groups in the C.P.S.U. does not entirely reflect their distribution within the population generally. Russians, Georgians and Armenians, for instance, are over-represented, while a number of other groups are under-represented.

In the field of party membership, the party seeks to control the composition of that membership to a much greater extent than any non-totalitarian political party. Entry to the party is carefully

[1] ibid., p. 259.

controlled: would-be members must first serve a probationary period as candidates for membership, and their applications must provide detailed information about their backgrounds and qualifications and be supported by three party members. The C.P.S.U. · is not intended to be a mass organization to which all supporters of the régime and party belong, but a body which provides political leadership and acts as a focal point of political power. The membership of the C.P.S.U. has never been more than a small proportion of the population of the U.S.S.R. – in 1961 the total number of party members and candidates constituted less than 5 per cent of the Russian population.[1] Furthermore, from time to time the party leadership has sought to exclude certain groups from party membership and to encourage other groups to join the party. The various purges that have occurred since the inception of the Communist régime in Russia have usually resulted in a reduction of the number of party members, and these have often affected particular social groups. Similarly, the qualifications for party membership have varied, often excluding specific groups as a matter of policy. Conversely, strenuous efforts have been made at various times to recruit particular groups, but these efforts have hardly, as Fainsod points out, resulted in a party which is a microcosm of the Russian population:

> In enlisting the new technical and administrative intelligentsia as its primary cadre beginning in the late thirties, the party's position among rank-and-file workers tended to weaken, and it risked increasing isolation from the production line. The recent emphasis on the recruitment of leading workers and collective farmers represents an effort to redress the balance. . . . Party membership among rank-and-file workers and farmers remains thin, and the ordinary collective farmer, even more than the factory worker falls outside the circle of the party élite. Although the party has strengthened its position among women . . . they continue to be largely inactive in party affairs. The nationality weaknesses of the party offset its great Russian, Georgian and Armenian strength . . . [and reflect] the slowness of Communist penetration in the rural sections of the areas acquired since World War II.[2]

It is clear from the data presented above that social characteristics are significant factors in determining the membership of the C.P.S.U., although it is difficult to judge how far its composition is a reflection of supply and how far it is a reflection of demand. None the less, political participation in the Soviet Union is subject

---

[1] ibid., pp. 232 and 280.   [2] ibid., pp. 281–2.

to conditions not present in non-totalitarian societies. In the latter, participation through such organizations as political parties is invariably encouraged, but the state does not normally seek to control the whole process of political participation in the way it does in totalitarian societies. Elections in the U.S.S.R., for example, are not a means of choosing between alternative sets of leaders, but, in the words of a former Soviet politician:

> '. . . a mighty instrument for further educating and organizing the masses politically, for further strengthening the bond between the state mechanism and the masses, and for improving the state mechanism and grubbing out the remnants of bureaucratism . . . [Elections show] that the entire population of the land of the Soviets are completely united in spirit.'[1]

or, as Fainsod himself describes them, 'Soviet elections serve as a form of national mobilization.'[2] Thus elections in which over 99 per cent of the electorate actually votes, and in which a similar proportion supports candidates of the 'Communist and non-Party bloc', are intended to serve as demonstrations of political mobilization and are probably the C.P.S.U.'s least important role in the process of political participation.

The various party organizations in the Soviet Union are the major vehicles of political participation. The role of the primary party units, for instance, is to recruit and admit new party members, to organize ideological instruction and maintain the ideological commitment of party members, to implement the policies and achieve the aims of the state, to act as a check on administrative efficiency, and to conduct mass agitation and propaganda. Obviously, several of these functions are performed by political parties in modern democracies, but two characteristics distinguish the C.P.S.U. from the latter: first, it is the only party which is allowed to exist in the U.S.S.R., and secondly, the informal power links between party and governmental officials and the parallel organizations of the party and the government place the C.P.S.U. in a position of political dominance unequalled by any party in a competitive party system. Furthermore, the C.P.S.U. is not simply one means of political mobilization, nor is it one of several vehicles of political recruitment, nor one of many channels of political communication: in each case it is either by far

[1] A. Vyshinsky, quoted in ibid., p. 238.
[2] ibid., p. 382.

the most important or the sole instrument by which these political processes are effected.[1]

A very similar situation is found in Communist China, although there are some differences resulting from the Chinese social and political environment. For instance, turnout at elections is not as high in China: in local elections in 1953-4 and 1956 the turnout was 86 per cent, which, according to one observer, 'represents a substantial achievement in view of the traditional political and cultural obstacles to political participation in China.'[2] Neverthe-less, elections serve a similar purpose to those in the Soviet Union. According to the party press, elections are a means of raising mass political consciousness, of stimulating increases in production, of strengthening unity, of democratic education for the masses and of teaching the party cadres about the structure of the state and making them aware of their political rights and duties, as well as being a means for securing demographic and political information.[3] Moreover,

> In the Chinese political system, popular political activities constitute one of the primary structures through which the C.C.P. [Chinese Communist Party] executes its policies. The party also relies on mass political partici-pation for the political education of the people, the recruitment of new party members and other activists, the creation and maintenance of popular identification with the present régime, and informing the party about popular moods and demands.[4]

The form and nature of political participation clearly varies from one type of political system to another, even where ostensibly similar political institutions, such as elections or political parties, exist. In spite of such differences, however, all political systems appear to exhibit some sort of relationship between political participation and the personal and social characteristics of those who are politically active. The nature of this relationship depends upon the social and political environment of each political system. Most modern democracies have a social environment character-ized by an extensive but relatively flexible system of social stratification, and a political environment which ideologically seeks to encourage political participation. Primitive societies provide an integrated social and political environment in which

[1] See ibid., Chapter 7.
[2] Townsend, *Political Participation in Communist China*, p. 119.
[3] ibid., pp. 135-6.   [4] ibid., p. 211.

the differentiation between political and other sorts of activity is less marked than in more developed societies. Totalitarian societies are also characterized by the integration of social and political activity, but, unlike primitive societies, the political environment takes ideological precedence over the social environment. Developing societies tend to have fragmented social and political environments: the social environment is frequently based on a relatively rigid system of traditional social stratification which modernizing forces are trying to break down, and this forms the basis of a political environment in which largely modern institutions co-exist, political behaviour being determined by essentially traditional forces.

Explanations of the political behaviour of individuals in general, and political participation, in particular, are not especially difficult to suggest. S. M. Lipset, for example, drawing upon a wide range of studies and data, has offered explanations of various aspects of electoral behaviour, including turnout, the direction of voting and support for extremist movements.[1] Similarly, exhaustive voting studies in a number of countries offer strong evidence to support a wide range of hypotheses.[2] In particular, the association between socio-economic status and electoral behaviour has been widely documented,[3] and a great deal of attention has been paid to those individuals who 'deviate' from the norm of 'class voting'.[4] These studies suggest that the political behaviour of the individual is determined by the <u>interaction of the individual's</u>

[1] Lipset, *Political Man*, Chapters 4–9.

[2] See, for example, the various studies of American presidential elections: Paul F. Lazarsfeld, Bernard R. Berelson and Hazel Gaudet, *The People's Choice*, New York, 1948; Bernard R. Berelson, Paul F. Lazarsfeld and William N. McPhee, *Voting: A Study of Opinion Formation in a Presidential Campaign*, Chicago, 1954; Angus Campbell, Gerald Gurin and Warren E. Miller, *The Voter Decides*, Evanston, Ill., 1954; and Angus Campbell, Philip E. Converse, Warren E. Miller and Donald E. Stokes, *The American Voter*, New York, 1960. See also, S. M. Lipset, Paul F. Lazarsfeld, Allen H. Barton and Juan Linz, 'The Psychology of Voting: An Analysis of Political Behaviour', in G. Lindzey (ed.), *Handbook of Social Psychology*, Vol. 2, pp. 1124–75.

[3] For useful comparative material, see Robert R. Alford, *Party and Society*, Chicago, 1963, and S. M. Lipset and Stein Rokkan, *Party Systems and Voter Alignments*, New York, 1967.

[4] For a discussion of working-class support for the British Conservative party, see Robert T. McKenzie and Allan Silver, *Angels in Marble*, London, 1968, and Eric Nordlinger, *Working Class Tories*, London, 1967.

basic social and political attitudes and the specific situations with which he is faced. The association between various personal and social characteristics (such as socio-economic status) and political behaviour may be the result of conscious or unconscious motivation, or, what is more likely, some combination of the two. This association does not, however, constitute an explanation, nor does it establish a causal relationship, even though the association of, say, those of lower socio-economic status with parties of the left and those of higher status with parties of the right surprises no one.

Rudolf Herbele suggests that there are four problems which make studying the motives for social and political behaviour difficult. Firstly, the real motives may be deliberately concealed by the individual and the observer is consequently misled by what appears to be accurate information. Secondly, the real motives may not, in fact, be apparent to the individual and he may have rationalized his action before, after or during the event. Thirdly, the real motives may be unapparent not only to the individual whose action is being investigated, but to others who have influenced his action. Finally, motives are invariably complex and difficult to measure accurately.[1]

The difficulties of studying motivation do not, of course, preclude attempts to analyse the range of possible motives for action. Weber, for example, suggested that there are four types of motives:

1 The *value-rational,* based on the rational acceptance of the values of a group or movement.
2 The *emotional-affectual,* based on resentment of or enthusiasm for an idea, organization or individual.
3 The *traditional,* based on the acceptance of the behavioural norms of a social group to which the individual belongs.
4 The *purposive-rational,* based on personal advantage.[2]

Similarly, Robert Lane in his study of political involvement, argues that political participation fulfils four functions. First, as

[1] Rudolf Herbele, *Social Movements: An Introduction to Political Sociology* New York, 1951, pp. 94–5.
[2] See Max Weber, *Theory of Social and Economic Organization,* translated and edited by A. M. Henderson and Talcott Parsons, New York, 1947, pp. 115–18.

a means of pursuing economic needs; secondly, as a means of satisfying a need for social adjustment; thirdly, as a means of pursuing particular values; and fourthly, as a means of meeting subconscious and psychological needs.[1] There is, in fact, a basic similarity between Weber's typology of motivation and Lane's functions of political participation. If Weber and Lane are correct, then political participation is determined by the basic social and political attitudes of the individual, which are closely associated with his personal and social characteristics as well as with the social and political environment which forms the context of his political behaviour. Because this social and political environment varies from one society to another, political participation varies from one political system to another.

The individual acquires his political orientations and pattern of political behaviour through the process of political socialization, and his experience of social and political phenomena, through various levels and types of political participation (or through abstention from such participation), is part of a continuing process of socialization and a crucial factor in influencing his future participation. Furthermore, the individual is not faced with un-changing social and political phenomena, since these are subject to changes of problems, personnel and time – to the *uniqueness* of any given political event. It is likely, moreover, that the higher the level of political participation the more crucial these factors become, so that the process of political recruitment becomes an area of particular interest to the political sociologist.

---

[1] Lane, *Political Life*, pp. 102 and 114, and Chapters 9 and 10.

4 · Political Recruitment

The proportion of individuals in any given society who are active at the highest level of political participation – those who hold political and administrative offices – constitute only a tiny minority of the total population. Moreover, this proportion is scarcely increased to any significant extent if those who *seek* political and administrative office are included, as indeed they must be if effective assessment of political recruitment is to be made. The fact that those who are most active politically constitute a minority in society is of significance for two reasons: firstly, because it is a major feature of all political systems, with the possible exception of those in some primitive societies; and secondly, because it forms the basis of a number of important theories which seek to explain the working of political systems in terms of oligarchies, élites and classes.

Whatever the validity of these theories, however, one of the major concerns of political sociology is to examine and account for the recruitment of those who exercise political power, whether this is through the holding of political offices, such as prime minister or president, cabinet member or state governor, local councillor or mayor, or through being a member of the national or local bureaucracy and being a civil servant, state administrator or local government officer. Similarly, this concern extends to the personnel of the ruling party and governmental hierarchy in totalitarian societies.

It is important to examine recruitment to the bureaucracy, not only because the distinction between the *politician* and the *administrator* is inevitably blurred in the totalitarian societies of the Soviet Union, Eastern Europe and Communist China, but also because the distinction between *policy* and *administration* becomes increasingly meaningless as one moves from the periphery to the centre of the political system. The relationship between politicians and senior members of the administrative machine is such that the impact of politicians on administration and of administrators on policy is invariably profound. This is not to say that the impact of one is always greater than the impact of the other, nor to suggest some sort of equilibrium or counter-balancing forces: the relationship between the two will, of course, vary from one political system to another, and in some instances they will constitute opposing forces, in others complementary forces, and often a mixture of the two.

For example, a number of political systems endeavour to separate political and bureaucratic offices by instituting a doctrine of political neutrality for administrators. This is the case in Britain, for example, where civil servants are recruited through politically neutral machinery and, once appointed, are expected to maintain their political neutrality by refraining from the higher levels of political activity and by serving impartially each government no matter what its political complexion may be. Thus governments may come and go, different parties may hold political power, but the civil servant remains in office. Such a system may be contrasted with that found in the United States, where the party in power institutes extensive changes of personnel in the higher echelons of the civil service on assuming office. This system involving the extension of direct party control from political to administrative offices stems partly from the belief that direct control of these administrative offices is necessary, partly from the historical belief that such a turnover of personnel is administratively beneficial and partly from the long-established tradition that administrative office is a legitimate means of rewarding the party faithful, hence the term 'spoils' system. This close relationship between the ruling party and the holders of administrative office is, however, most clearly seen in totalitarian political systems, where the doctrine of a political neutral bureaucracy is not only anathema, but a contradiction in terms. This does not exclude the possibility of a turnover of personnel, particularly as a result of purges, but in a totalitarian system there are no alternative groups waiting to assume office.

The institutional arrangements of each political system are

another relevant factor in political recruitment. Whether a political system has unitary or federal institutional arrangements, or the extent to which there is a fusion or separation of powers, for instance, will provide important environmental variations. Furthermore, the working characteristics of the political system are also important. Canada provides another example of a political system in which the doctrine of a politically neutral civil service is accepted, but also illustrates a deviation from this doctrine to the extent that a number of prominent politicians, among them Mackenzie King and Lester Pearson, have entered politics through the civil service, so that there exists a certain amount of cross-recruitment between politicians and administrators, although it is mainly a matter of administrators becoming politicians rather than vice versa. Or again, as Alfred Diament has argued in the case of France under the Fourth Republic, where there is

> a weak political consensus the administrative machinery necessary for a modern style will develop its own rules and procedures. It will create a system of internal controls to supplement, or even take the place of, the external control mechanisms. Ultimately the system will develop procedures for operating without any political direction whatsoever.[1]

THE MACHINERY OF POLITICAL RECRUITMENT

The machinery of political recruitment is naturally subject to infinite variation, although two particular devices – those of elections and formal examinations and training – may be regarded as the most important. Even these two devices are, of course, subject to considerable variations, many of which have important implications for political recruitment. Before considering the most important devices, however, some mention should be made of other methods that have been used from time to time and which, in some cases, are still important in various political systems. One of the oldest methods used to secure political leaders was that of sortition, or the drawing of lots: this method was used in ancient Greece. A similar method, which is designed to prevent the domination of office and positions of power by a particular individual or group of individuals, is that of rotation.

---

[1] Alfred Diament, 'A Case-Study of Administrative Autonomy: Controls and Tensions in French Administration', *Political Studies*, 6, 1958, p. 147.

The 'spoils' system of the United States is, in effect, a rotational system of recruitment, while a number of countries have constitutional provisions which are designed to ensure some degree of rotation of executive personnel. The president and vice-president of the Swiss Federal Council, for example, serve only for a year and may not be immediately re-elected for a further term of office. Similarly, the 24th Amendment to the United States Constitution stipulates that no president may be elected for more than two terms of office; in seventeen Latin American states, no incumbent president may immediately succeed himself, while in Mexico no president may *ever* be re-elected to office.

Another long-standing method of recruitment, common to many political systems, is that of seizing office by the use or threat of force. The violent overthrowal of a political régime, whether by *coup d'état*, revolution, military intervention from outside, assassination or mob violence, is often, though not necessarily, instrumental in effecting radical changes of personnel at the higher levels of political participation. The most immediate and obvious result of such methods is the replacement of political office-holders, but changes in bureaucratic personnel are usually brought about more slowly, especially in complex and highly-developed societies.

Just as there are recruiting devices which are normally associated with extensive changes of personnel, so there are others which are associated more often with the continued recruitment of the same type of personnel. One such device is that of patronage, a system which was very common in earlier times in the United States and Britain, and which remains important in many developing countries. Prior to the reforms of the nineteenth century, for instance, patronage was part of an elaborate system of bribery and corruption which pervaded many areas of public life in Britain. This system was partly a well-established method of influencing the exercise of political power by varying degrees of control over the results of general elections and of support in Parliament *between* elections, and partly a means of political recruitment, since entry to Parliament and the embryonic civil service was secured almost totally through the patronage system. It is, however, misleading to regard patronage as specifically designed to secure and maintain political control, since the system as it existed in the eighteenth century was merely a development of long-standing practices whose purposes varied considerably from patron to patron, while it was far from a guarantee of a subservient House of Commons.[1] It was, moreover, a system in which preferment could be *purchased* by an individual seeking office, as well as one in which individuals could be persuaded to act in a particular way in return for 'favours'. As a system of political recruitment, therefore, it did not necessarily secure office-holders who were 'suitable', either politically or in terms of ability.

Differing from the system of patronage, but also tending towards the perpetuation of particular types of personnel, is a device which may best be described as 'the emergence of natural leaders'. In the past this has served as a rather crude justification for aristocratic rule, and it remains in most political systems as a vital contextual factor. Thus even though it can now be argued that the leader of the Conservative party in Britain no longer 'emerges', since he is elected by a ballot of Conservative M.P.s, the political system imposes a number of contextual limitations which severely reduces the number of potential Conservative leaders from which the choice is made. In other words, quite apart from the convention that he must normally be an M.P., a Conservative leader must also exhibit various abilities which enable him to fulfil the demands of a parliamentary and cabinet system of government: the ability to conduct an effective election campaign, the ability to meet the demands of parliamentary debate, the ability to shoulder the responsibilities of high office, and so on.

Clearly, such demands are made of all party leaders who aspire to high political office in Britain, although their parties are likely to make further specific demands related to the exigencies of the time and the nature of the party concerned. It can thus be argued that the environmental or contextual conditions that a particular political system imposes tend to favour the emergence of particular types of leader and to exclude or limit the emergence of other types. Such individuals may or may not be 'natural leaders' in the sense that they command the loyalty and support of followers who regard them as inherently superior, but they may be regarded as 'natural leaders' in the sense that they represent the types of

[1] See Basil Williams, *Oxford History of England: The Whig Supremacy, 1714-60* (2nd edition, revised by C. H. Stuart), Oxford, 1962, pp. 28-30.

leader most likely to emerge in a particular political system. The prominence of members of the legal profession in many legislatures has been attributed to a variety of factors arising out of the political environment: the tendency for legislative representatives to be drawn from groups with relatively high social status; the extent to which legal skills, such as the public presentation of arguments, mediation and the ability to assimilate the principle points of a situation quickly, are useful in a legislative setting; the relative ease with which lawyers adjust their legal careers to the demands of political activity (both in maintaining a legal career whilst politically active and returning to it should such activity lessen or cease); and the extent, especially in countries like the United States, to which lawyers are used as advisers by people generally, and by politicians in particular, on a range of matters which go far beyond mere legal advice. In the case of the United States, a further factor may be added: the fact that the majority of legal and judicial offices are filled by election provides lawyers with an additional incentive to be politically active.[1]

A more limited method by which existing leaders may contribute towards the recruitment of particular types of leaders is by means of co-option. Strictly speaking, co-option involves the election into a body of an individual by existing members, and though this is fairly common in such political institutions as local councils in England and Wales (both through the election of aldermen and as means of augmenting committees), it is less common in this strict sense at higher levels of office-holding. None the less, a process which is basically similar forms the basis of recruitment to the United States Cabinet, and occasionally, to the British Cabinet. Unlike the latter, the President's Cabinet is not chosen from members of the legislature – the separation of powers expounded in the Constitution forbids this – but from wherever he can secure suitable personnel. Thus a president may recruit prominent businessmen and industrialists, members of the academic and legal professions, as well as appointing recognized politicians to his Cabinet. More rarely, a British prime minister may appoint an 'outsider' to his Cabinet or to some post outside

[1] For a discussion of the political role of lawyers in the United States, see Heinz Eulau and John Sprague, *Lawyers in Politics: A Study of Professional Convergence*, Indianapolis, 1964, and Donald R. Matthews, *The Social Backgrounds of Political Decision-Makers*, New York, 1954, pp. 30–2.

the latter. In 1964, for example, Harold Wilson appointed Frank Cousins, general secretary of the powerful Transport and General Workers' Union, as Minister of Technology (with a seat in the Cabinet) and several other non-parliamentarians as ministers outside the Cabinet. In each case, however, steps had to be taken to bring these appointees into Parliament, either by securing them a seat in the House of Commons (as in the case of Cousins) or by making them life peers, so enabling them to sit in the House of Lords. Any attempt on the part of the prime minister to make more than the occasional appointment from outside Parliament, however, would be regarded, if not unconstitutional, at least in contravention of the norms of the British political system.

The methods by which members of the judiciary are appointed is usually subject to less variation than is the case with political and administrative office-holders. Judicial office-holders have normally received legal training, although they are not necessarily practising members of the legal profession at the time of their appointment. In countries like France, members of the legal profession are trained as advocates or for judicial office and the two sections of the profession are separated from the outset. Appointment to judicial office lies in the hands of a special council representing the executive, legislature and judiciary. In Britain, however, no special provision is made for training future members of the judiciary, and these are drawn from the ranks of the legal profession, in practice from barristers. The latter need not be engaged in full-time practice, and it is not unusual for M.P.s who are also barristers to become judges. It is also customary for holders of legal portfolios in any government (such as the Lord Chancellor, the Attorney-General and the Solicitor-General) to hold legal qualifications. These last appointments lapse, of course, with a change of government, but appointments to the judiciary are made by the executive and held during good behaviour, although age-limits have been applied in practice. A different system exists again in the United States, although here some distinction needs to be drawn between members of the federal and state judiciaries. Federal judges, including members of the Supreme Court, are nominated by the president and their appointment is confirmed by the Senate. At state level, however, this method of nomination by the executive and ratification by the legislature is used in only a minority of cases, and in the majority of the states judges are elected by the populace. Even so, judges are drawn from the legal profession, but the use of election illustrates both how methods of selecting the judiciary may vary and, in particular, the extent to which election is used in the United States as a means of recruiting public officials.

For the most part, however, elections are used in political systems as a means of choosing politicians rather than holders of administrative or judicial office, and it is to their use in this respect that we now turn.

An election may be defined as a means of choosing between two or more alternatives by the casting of votes, but this having been said it is important to recognize the infinite variety of electoral systems. They may vary, as far as the election of office-holders is concerned, according to who is elected, by whom and how. Thus elections may be used to choose members of the executive, the legislature or the judiciary. The right to participate in elections may be restricted to varying degrees, and the particular method by which the votes are cast and counted is subject to considerable variation. Some elections may be described as indirect in that the electors cast their votes for a group of individuals who subsequently constitute an electoral college, which proceeds to conduct a second election to decide who shall hold the office at stake. This, technically, is the method by which the President of the United States is chosen – not by direct popular vote, but by an electoral college comprising representatives of the states of the union. In practice, however, the electoral votes of each state are normally cast in favour of the candidate securing the largest popular vote in the state. None the less, this still means that it is possible for a presidential candidate to secure a majority of the electoral college votes but a minority of the nation-wide popular vote.

Most elections, however, involve the *direct* choice of office-holders by the electors, although the choice of the voters is likely to be restricted by the legal qualifications laid down for the holders of political office and by the methods by which political parties select their candidates. In some cases the legal qualifications for office-holders are minimal, demanding merely that they must be adults, citizens of the country concerned, sane and so on, but in other cases they may be more restrictive. The President of the United States must be born a citizen of that country, at least thirty-five years of age and resident in the United States for fourteen years. Similarly, United States senators must also be citizens (though not native-born), at least thirty years of age and resident in the states they represent. We have, of course, already noted other legal restrictions which may limit the circumstances in which an office-holder may be re-elected. On the whole such restrictions are not particularly severe, and other aspects of electoral systems – the extent to which the right to vote (or franchise) is restricted and the way in which votes are cast and counted – are more important.

Universal adult suffrage is the most common basis of electoral franchises, but this is usually restricted by such factors as citizenship, sanity and criminal records. In some political systems these restrictions are taken further and include other criteria, such as literacy, residence and property qualifications. In the past some of these restrictions have been very severe and the electorate has therefore constituted only a minority of the population. Indeed, only as recently as 1920 was the vote granted to women in Canada and the United States, and in Britain full women's suffrage was not granted until 1928, while Switzerland continues to restrict its federal franchise to men. In some cases restrictions on the franchise have been based on philosophic arguments regarding the extent to which members of the electorate should be 'responsible' persons or capable of making rational decisions in exercising the vote, thus stressing the possession of the latter as a privilege involving duties as well as a right. The struggle over the extension of the franchise in Britain constantly revolved around arguments of this sort. In other cases restrictions have been used more crudely to deny the vote to particular sections of the population. This was one of the means used to limit the political participation of Negroes in the southern states of America: literacy tests and the linking of payment of taxes with right to vote were among the most common methods.

Restrictions on the franchise are likely to have an important effect on voting behaviour and therefore on who is elected to political office. This is especially true where restrictions apply to particular sections of the population who are likely to remain unrepresented until they are at least partially enfranchised. This was an important factor, for instance, in limiting working class representation in many countries and Negro representation in the

United States. Furthermore, the sectional extension of the franchise may be linked with the subsequent polarization of electoral behaviour where parties arise specifically to represent these sections of the population. In many European countries the rise of parties seeking to represent and mobilize the working classes have resulted in the latter securing far greater legislative representation than has been the case in the United States, where no viable working class party exists.

Restrictions on the franchise are, for the most part, historically important in helping to explain party alignments and electoral polarization, and their impact is rather different from that of the way in which votes are cast and counted. Electoral systems based on the simple plurality (or 'first past the post') exaggerate the proportion of seats that the winning party secures in the legislature in relation to the votes cast in its support at the expense of its opponents, particularly third or minor parties. Thus in the British general election of 1966, the winning Labour party secured 48·1 per cent of the votes cast and 57·8 per cent of the seats in the House of Commons. Conversely, the Liberal party secured 8·5 per cent of the votes and only 1·9 per cent of the seats. In fact no party has won an absolute majority of the votes cast in a general election since 1935, yet in every election since then either the Conservative or the Labour party has had an absolute majority in the House of Commons. This is because the country is divided into single-member constituencies in which the candidate with the most votes wins – he does not need an absolute majority; he may win by one vote ,or by 20,000, the result is the same. Since the balance between the two major parties is fairly equal and the electoral swing is usually evenly spread and in the same direction over the whole country, the result in a significant number of constituencies is decided by relatively few votes, so that the party winning the general election secures a higher proportion of seats than it does of the national vote. Furthermore, parties like the Liberal party accumulate considerable minority votes in a substantial number of constituencies but do not win a commensurate number of seats. This means that in Britain a general election is, in effect, a choice between the Conservative and Labour parties, and that it is difficult for the Liberal party or any other party or parties to secure enough seats to make the formation of a coalition government necessary. Occasionally the election result is sufficiently close to necessitate a minority government, but coalitions are normally reserved for times of emergency.

In many other countries, coalitions are the norm and their likelihood is often facilitated by electoral systems based on proportional representation. The variety of types of proportional representation is considerable, and each type is associated with particular results: some types favour large parties, some small; others favour well-organized parties, and so on; but each seeks to apportion seats in the legislature in accordance with the support that parties secure at an election. This means that it is more difficult for a party to secure an absolute majority in the legislature than it is in Britain: assuming a minimal degree of distortion in the electoral system, proportional representation demands an absolute majority of the votes cast to secure an absolute majority of the seats.

Countries like Britain and the United States adopted electoral systems that were regarded as simple and obvious, and all subsequent attempts to secure their modification have been successfully resisted, if only because they are advantageous to the major parties. Other countries have chosen systems more deliberately in order to achieve particular results, either a proportional distribution of seats generally, or, more specifically, with the intention of creating some advantage or disadvantage for particular parties. West Germany, for example, uses a mixture of the simple plurality and proportional representation, but no party is allowed any seats in the Bundestag unless it secures a minimum proportion of the votes cast. This system has allowed the larger parties to secure relatively proportional representation in the Bundestag, but has contributed to the exclusion of the extremist N.P.D. France has, throughout its history, experimented with many electoral systems, often seeking to remedy the perennial problems of the fragmented French political system. Australia, on the other hand, adopted the alternative (or preferential) vote in order to avoid the problem of a candidate being elected with a minority of the votes cast in any constituency by taking voters' second preferences into account where no candidate secured an absolute majority. This system, however, has been largely responsible for the failure of the Australian Labour party (A.L.P.) to win an election since 1955, because its rival, the Democratic Labour party, advises its supporters to give their second preferences to the Liberal–Country party coalition. Not surprisingly, the A.L.P. would like to see a reversion to the simple plurality which would facilitate its return to power.

The relationship between electoral systems, voting behaviour and party systems is complex: that there is a relationship cannot be doubted, but it cannot be said, for instance, that the simple plurality causes two-party systems, nor that proportional representation causes multi-party systems. Party systems are the product of the social characteristics of the society concerned, not the electoral system. The latter is likely, however, to facilitate the maintenance of particular party systems: a two-party system is more often associated with the simple plurality; proportional representation is more often associated with a multi-party system. The reverse in each instance is not normally the case: a number of countries use the simple plurality but do not have a two-party system; other countries which use proportional representation and have multi-party systems would probably have such party systems regardless of the type of electoral system used.[1]

A somewhat less important factor is the method of casting votes. Before the introduction of the secret ballot, possibilities and incidence of bribery and corruption were considerable; open voting was clearly an important factor in elections, especially in the era of the limited electorate. Other factors concerning the casting of votes remain important, however. The placing of party labels on the ballot papers clearly assist those electors, probably a majority, who wish to vote for a party rather than a candidate; the introduction of the voting machine in the United States facilitates the practice of 'voting the party ticket' instead of making a large number of individual choices for each office at stake; electoral systems involving preferential voting may create problems for the voter because of their relative complexity and problems for the parties in guiding their supporters in making second or lower preferences; the order in which the candidates' names are placed on the ballot paper may be important where the result is likely to be close, since there is evidence that those higher on the list have an advantage if the voter is uncertain of

[1] For a discussion of the relationship between party systems and electoral systems, see Duverger, *Political Parties*, Book II, Chapter 1, and Douglas Rae, *The Political Consequences of Electoral Laws*, New Haven, Conn., 1967.

which candidate to support; a candidate possessing a name the
the same as or similar to public figures or a name which is clearly
identified with a particular section of the electorate may benefit
electorally; in some countries voting is compulsory, while the
extent to which voting by post or by proxy is allowed may also
be important. These are all examples of how voting methods may
be significant.

In the majority of elections the contest is between *parties* as
much as it is between individual candidates, since the majority
of electors identify themselves with a party. Even those electors
who may be described as 'floating voters' probably see electoral
contests at least partly in party rather than individual terms. A
presidential election in the United States, highly personalized as
it is, rests on a basis of party conflict – independent candidates do
not win. In some countries the party conflict is institutionalized
by the placing of party names on ballot papers, or, more im-
portantly, by the practice of presenting the voters with lists of
party candidates and requiring the voters to choose between
parties rather than individual candidates. This latter practice can
only be introduced in conjunction with a system of proportional
representation and may itself be subject to many variations. Israel,
for instance, treats the whole country as a single constituency: the
electors vote for the party of their choice and seats in the Knesset
are allotted proportionately; a similar process occurs in the
Netherlands. A number of European countries, however, use
party list systems based on multi-member constituencies in which
the seats are allotted proportionately within each constituency
rather than nationally. In the case of Israel, candidates are selected
by the national party organizations, but in most other countries
regional or local party organizations control candidate selection.

The choice made by the parties is therefore important, but its
importance is substantially increased where a party's support is
heavily concentrated, as is likely to happen, in particular constituencies, so that to secure the party's nomination in such a constituency is invariably a guarantee of election. Even in those
constituencies in which the outcome is in some doubt because
the parties are evenly balanced, the effective choice is between the
leading party candidates, minor party and non-party or independent candidates being at a considerable disadvantage. This is
especially true where the electoral system in force is the simple

plurality. Electoral systems based on proportional representation normally provide lesser parties and independent candidates with a greater chance of being elected, of course, but this does not obviate the concept of the 'safe' seat, since in a multi-member constituency based on proportional representation the leading parties can normally expect to secure one or more seats out of those at stake, so that to secure the nomination of these parties remains a substantial guarantee of success. Proportional representation only increases the chances of independent candidates and the majority of those elected are still party nominees, again stressing the importance of party connections.

Securing the nomination and support of a party (preferably a major party) is therefore an important step towards electoral success for individual candidates and an important part of the process of political recruitment. Despite the fact that nationally organized parties normally dominate elections, it is misleading to assume that the selection of candidates is dominated by central party organizations: in most cases responsibility for candidate selection is concentrated at regional or local rather than national level, although in some cases the national organization can formally or informally veto the selection of particular individuals. Even in such cases where a national veto is possible, it is essentially a negative weapon, enabling the party leadership to prevent the nomination of someone it dislikes but denying it the means of securing the nomination of someone it likes. This does not preclude some degree of centralization, but this is usually at regional level (as in West Germany) or at state level (as in the Australian Labour party).

Regional or local control does not necessarily mean the selection of candidates abhorrent to the national party, nor does it exclude co-operation between national and other levels of party organization. It normally means that selection is carried out within a procedural framework common to the party as a whole, and often supervised by the national organization, but it also means that the effective choice of candidate is made at regional or local level. This appears to be the case with the majority of countries for which information is available. There are, of course, significant differences between and within various countries, but these do not invalidate the generalization that candidate selection is subject to substantially local control. Again, in most cases, that control is in the hands of the regional or local *party* organization, but there is a major exception to this rule – the use of primary elections in the United States and, to a lesser extent, local convention in Canada.

Leon Epstein links this major difference to the virtual absence of *organized party membership* in the United States and Canada.[1] To what extent it is a causal relationship is more difficult to say. V. O. Key argues that:

> The adoption of the direct primary opened the road for disruptive forces that gradually fractionalized the party organization. By permitting more effective direct appeals by individual politicians to the party membership, the primary system freed forces driving toward the disintegration of party organizations and facilitated the construction of factions and cliques attached to the ambitions of individual leaders.[2]

Conversely, Epstein suggests:

> Less a cause than a symptom, the primary may have been adopted as an expression of an organizational weakness and individualism that was coming to be widely accepted in American candidate selection. Party organizations must already have been losing what strength they had, if so apparently disruptive a method as the direct primary could have been adopted.[3]

Moreover, as Epstein points out, the most common method of candidate selection in the United States prior to the adoption of the primary was the party convention, a method which is more akin to the primary than to the oligarchical intra-party methods used in most other Western democracies. It is reasonable to argue that where a strong party organization based on mass membership exists, there will be considerable resistance to open the process of candidate selection to the wider electorate, but where the political process is traditionally more open, as in the United States, innovations like the primary are more difficult to resist.

The use of the primary election may be regarded as significant in three respects, compared with alternative methods of candidate selection. First, as practised in the United States, the conduct of primary elections is governed by law (the same is also true of candidate selection by convention) and candidate selection is

[1] See Epstein, *Political Parties in Western Democracies*, Chapter 8.
[2] V. O. Key, Jr, *Politics, Parties and Pressure Groups*, New York (5th edition), 1964, p. 342.
[3] Epstein, *Political Parties in Western Democracies*, p. 210.

therefore subject to public regulation to a degree unknown elsewhere. Secondly, the primary election allows a greater proportion of the electorate to participate in the process of candidate selection than is possible elsewhere. Finally, it provides a means by which a relative 'outsider' can secure a major party nomination.

The fact that primaries are legally required in all but five states, means that would-be candidates must be prepared to fight a public election campaign to secure nomination. The form of the primary varies, however: in some cases the primary is *open*, and any voter may participate, although in most cases he may only vote in one party's primary; in other cases the primary is *closed*, and participation is limited to those who are, by various means, registered as party supporters. Furthermore, although the primary undoubtedly facilitates political participation, it is important to note that turnout varies considerably. As Key points out,

> Comparatively few voters determine who are to be the candidates in the general election campaign. In about three-fourths of the primaries held in a sample of states . . . less than 35 per cent of the potential electorate voted on the nomination of gubernatorial candidates.[1]

Moreover, turnout tends to be highest in the primary of the electorally dominant party and lowest in that of the weaker party, while, where the parties are evenly divided, turnout is often minimized because efforts within each party are made to negotiate agreement on nominations. The provision of fierce intra-party competition in one-party states allows,

> . . . party candidatures [to be] assumed by individuals and groups able to win primary elections. In winning, they are likely to seek at least the informal help of those identified as party leaders or workers, but in much the same way as they seek the help of others outside party ranks. There may be no 'party' to approve or disapprove of candidatures.[2]

Party candidates for most political offices in the United States are chosen by primary elections, although, as we have already seen, not all primaries are of equal significance. The major exception to the practice of selecting candidates by primary elections, at least in the direct sense, is the choosing of presidential candidates. In both major parties this is done by party conven-

[1] Key, *Politics, Parties and Pressure Groups*, pp. 580–1; see also pp. 290–1 and 378–80.

[2] Epstein, *Political Parties in Western Democracies*, p. 205.

tions consisting of delegates from each of the states. It is important to bear in mind, however, that the delegates to a convention may be pledged or at least influenced by the result of a presidential primary which has been held in their state. Approximately a third of the states conduct presidential primaries, some of which allow voters to choose between several candidates for the party nomination; but others are concerned merely with selecting state delegates and offer no opportunity of expressing any direct candidate preference. The influence that these primaries can exert is thus complicated, not only because not all states use them and delegates are often not bound by their results, but because a good or bad showing in one or more of the important primaries can have a crucial effect on a candidate's chance of securing the party nomination at the convention. One of the most striking examples of this was

> . . . the 1952 'Minnesota miracle', when over 100,000 persons took the trouble to write in the name of Eisenhower in the primary [and] Republican leaders all over the land could see that a vote-getter had arrived on the scene.[1]

The primary election is a method of selection peculiar to the United States, and although some Western European countries provide for the participation of party members in the selection of candidates, it is neither as extensive nor as open as the American method. In West Germany, for example, selection may be by a ballot of all party members, but in practice oligarchical control is more common. Similarly, in Norway selection is undertaken by delegate bodies following consultation with local party members. The nearest equivalent to the American primary, however, is found in Sweden and Belgium. In Sweden some parties consult the party membership by means of a postal ballot, and others hold a ballot of all members if this is requested by a quarter of the district delegates. In Belgium parties run primaries which are restricted to party members, who may choose candidates from lists submitted by the party leaders.[2] In no case, however, is selection conducted by means of a public campaign, nor is participation extended beyond party members to those who are merely party supporters.

Canada bears some similarity to the United States in candidate

---

[1] Key, *Politics, Parties and Pressure Groups*, p. 411.
[2] See Epstein, *Political Parties in Western Democracies*, pp. 226–8.

selection in that the two older parties, the Progressive Conservatives and the Liberals, select their candidates through party conventions, and these conventions are sometimes open to all who consider themselves party supporters.[1] Practice varies, however, in both parties, while the New Democratic party (N.D.P.) restricts participation in selection to party members. Nevertheless, there is a further Canadian parallel, and this is the practice of Canadian parties of selecting their leaders through national conventions rather than following the British model of confining this to members of the parliamentary party. As in the American case, the convention consists of delegates from party organizations in each province and is preceded by public campaigning by the aspirants. With the exception of the N.D.P., in which the leadership is subject to election every two years, conventions are held only when necessary, which is normally when the leadership becomes vacant or, more rarely, when the incumbent leader is prevailed upon to allow his position to be challenged, as happened to the Conservative leader, John Diefenbaker, in 1967.

Britain provides an example of the main alternative method of selecting candidates. The two major parties use a two-tier method by which

> . . . a relatively small body examines the applicants [in the Conservative party] or nominees [in the Labour party] for the vacancy and makes certain recommendations to a larger [representative] body, which in turn normally elects one of the recommended candidates . . . selection remains in the hands of comparatively few people, not only within the constituency but within the local party itself.[2]

The control exercised by the national party organizations is basically negative, as we have already noted, and the selection of parliamentary candidates in Britain is subject to considerable local autonomy – a greater degree of autonomy than is often found in other Western democracies, where regional party organizations sometimes have effective control over candidate selection. In countries like Britain, where selection is an internal party affair and not subject to a common legal framework of the sort provided by the American primary system, there are often significant procedural differences between the parties:

[1] See Howard Scarrow, 'Nomination and Local Party Organization in Canada: A Case-Study', *Western Political Quarterly*, **17**, 1964, pp. 55–62.
[2] Rush, *The Selection of Parliamentary Candidates*, p. 276.

Selection in the Labour party is subject to the rules laid down in the party and C.L.P. [Constituency Labour Party] constitutions and no C.L.P. may depart from the prescribed procedure. Under this procedure no individual may *apply* for the vacancy; he must be nominated by a party or affiliated organization. There is no formal procedure for interviewing nominees prior to their appearance before the selection conference and, apart from the general adoption meeting held shortly before the election campaign (which for obvious reasons must be a formality), the decision of the selection conference is final as far as the C.L.P. is concerned. The N.E.C. [National Executive Committee] may overrule the G.M.C. [General Management Committee] and refuse to endorse its choice, but this is the exception rather than the rule. At no time, therefore, is the selected candidate submitted to the approval of the general membership of the C.L.P., other than when the withholding of such approval would be virtually unthinkable.

There is no *formal* selection procedure in the Conservative party, however, although a fairly detailed advisory pamphlet is made available by [the Conservative] Central Office and most local associations follow a basically similar procedure. At the same time, variations in procedure are not only permissible but fairly common. Individuals may apply for vacancies and there is no system of nomination. The interviewing of applicants prior to short-listing is normal, after which successful applicants appear before a body similar in form and composition to the Labour G.M.C. The decision of the executive council [of the local association] is subject to the approval of a general meeting of the association. A *second* general meeting is held at the beginning of the election campaign, when the candidate is formally adopted. The selection is *not* subject to the formal endorsement of the national party, since approval is sought prior to selection.[1]

Procedural differences of this sort are often important in affecting the whole process of selection. For instance, the whole federative nature of the Labour party, with its formal organizational divisions representing trade unions, the Co-operative party, individual members and so on, is reflected in its selection procedure and is the basis of many of the cross-pressures which arise in Labour selections. Similarly, the system of nomination of possible candidates by local party organizations used in the Labour party tends to limit the choice of local parties much more than the system of applications used by the Conservatives.

Despite these differences both within and between political

[1] ibid., pp. 276–7. For a description and discussion of selection in other British parties, see Michael Rush, 'Candidate Selection and its Impact on Leadership Recruitment', in J. D. Lees and R. Kimber (eds.), *Political Parties in Britain: An Organizational and Functional Guide*, London, 1971.

systems in the methods used to select candidates, there is a widespread tendency for the major decisions in candidate selection to be concentrated at local or regional rather than national levels. The principal difference, therefore, between the American primary method and those methods more common to other Western democracies is that in the latter the selection of candidates is conducted *within* the party organization: participation at its very widest is limited to those who are party members – to be a declared party supporter is not enough.

A more significant difference in many respects stems not from the degree of party control over selection, but from constitutional doctrines of the separation and fusion of powers. The separation of powers in the United States (and in those Latin American countries which have adopted American-style constitutions) means that there is a procedural separation in the selection of candidates for the executive on the one hand and the legislature on the other. Thus even though candidates for both executive and legislative positions may be selected by the same or similar procedures, the actual selections are separate and allow the primary electorates (or party organizations in the absence of a primary) a direct voice in the choice of candidates for these positions. In those political systems in which there is a fusion of powers, however, and members of the executives are normally drawn from, and are members of, the legislature, candidates are selected initially as potential members of the legislature rather than the executive. This means that the career patterns of leading office-holders in the two types of system tend to be different.

In Britain the majority of ministers, especially those holding the most important portfolios, are drawn from the House of Commons. They will therefore have had some legislative experience. Most of those ministers who are not M.P.s are members of the House of Lords and will also have had legislative experience. Moreover, the legislative experience of senior ministers usually amounts to at least a decade, while a prime minister is likely to have spent as many as twenty or more years in Parliament before assuming office. Harold Wilson, for example, had been in Parliament for nineteen years when he became Prime Minister in 1964. The majority of his Cabinet colleagues had had at least eleven years' parliamentary experience, while all but a few of those appointed to posts outside the Cabinet had at least five years' experience. Furthermore, depending when the party last held office, a significant proportion of those appointed to ministerial positions (especially those at senior level) may have had previous ministerial experience.

Generally speaking, the longer a party retains office the more likely it is that those who eventually hold senior government posts will have had to work their way up through the ministerial hierarchy. Where a party has had a long period in Opposition, however, the appointment of those without such experience to senior posts (including membership of the Cabinet) is more likely when office is eventually achieved. This was the case with the Labour Government of 1964, of which only two members had previous experience as Cabinet ministers, although a number had held non-Cabinet posts between 1945 and 1951 when the Labour party had last been in power. Those who achieve the office of prime minister usually combine both legislative and ministerial experience. Indeed, the only prime minister in this century to assume office without first having held a Cabinet post was Ramsay MacDonald, the first Labour prime minister, and even he had considerable legislative experience.[1] From time to time individuals with no legislative or ministerial experience are appointed to the Cabinet, but these are the exception rather than the rule.[2]

The career patterns of American presidents and members of their cabinets are likely to be far more varied. Excluding those presidents who succeeded to office as vice-presidents through the death of the incumbent, and who served only the expiry of that term, twenty-two of the thirty-two presidents elected from 1789 to 1968 had had executive and legislative experience prior to election, while seven had had executive experience only, and three legislative experience only. It should be noted, however, that although executive experience includes having held a Cabinet post or having been a state governor, it also includes having held high military command or having been vice-president. If these last two categories are excluded on the grounds that military command is not strictly political experience, and that experience as vice-president varies considerably from one administration to

[1] See Philip W. Buck, *Amateurs and Professionals in British Politics, 1918–59*, Chicago, 1963, Chapter 5 and Appendix 4, Tables 20–3.

[2] See F. M. G. Willson, 'Routes of Entry of New Members to the British Cabinet, 1868–1958', *Political Studies*, 7, 1959, pp. 222–32.

another and is sometimes almost a sinecure, then the number of presidents who have had executive and legislative experience is reduced to fourteen (less than half the total), and those with executive experience only to four. Presidential candidates may be drawn from a wide field, and although often active in politics prior to nomination, their strictly political experience may be limited or negligible. This is even more likely with members of the Cabinet, who may be drawn from a variety of spheres and whose political experience may be non-existent.

This is not to suggest that executive or legislative experience is necessary for these posts, but merely to point out the way in which career patterns may be shaped by the institutional arrangements of the political system. Thus legislative experience is virtually a prerequisite of holding political office in Britain, and executive experience generally precedes appointment to the most senior positions. In the United States, on the other hand, executive and legislative experience, while common, is far from being a prerequisite, especially for those holding Cabinet posts.

Much of what has been said applies to the other Western democracies, although career patterns in these countries have been less widely documented. France, for instance, provides an interesting example of how institutional changes can alter the pattern of recruitment. Under the Fourth Republic there existed a fusion of powers, and ministers were generally members of the National Assembly and career politicians. With the establishment of the Fifth Republic in 1958, however, a modified separation of powers was introduced by which ministers could not be members of the legislature, although they could address it from time to time. This facilitated the recruitment of civil servants, businessmen and other non-politicians as members of the Cabinet, with significant results.

Unfortunately, little is known about the selection of political office-holders in developing countries beyond the fact that the principal vehicles of recruitment are, as in Western democracies, political parties. It seems likely that the processes of recruitment are far less formalized in such systems, since the organizational development of political parties is less extensive and more fragmentary than that found in most industrially advanced countries. Many developing countries are, in territorial terms, of such recent origin that any emphasis on such questions as executive and legislative experience is hardly possible, while the transformation of independence movements into effective political parties presents considerable recruitment problems. Experience is likely to be interpreted in terms of the struggle for independence, but as the achievement of independence becomes accepted, the struggle for power, the responsibilities of government and the problems of social, economic and political development create tension which may fragment the often precarious unity of the former independence movements. Recruitment is likely to be conducted through informal channels based on traditional tribal, ethnic or regional groups. Efforts to avoid social and political fragmentation may be made through the creation of comprehensive nationalist parties seeking to unite as many groups as possible under the aegis of a common ideology – Apter's 'political religion'. This may lead in turn to one-party states of the sort found in Kenya and Tanzania which have, for the most part, sought to absorb and contain opposition elements within a single party. Alternatively, the emphasis may be upon the suppression of these elements, as in Ghana (under Nkrumah) or a number of former French colonial territories. Whatever devices are used, however, the importance of the traditional methods of political recruitment (even through modern institutions such as trade unions, which may be linked with parties) involving informal relationships of kinship and tribal and ethnic origin are likely to predominate.[1]

Although the political systems of those developing countries which have enjoyed independence from colonial domination for many generations (or of those which have never been effectively subjected to colonial rule) have had longer to establish legitimacy, they are, in most cases, subject to as much instability and lack of legitimacy as many more recently-established political systems. None the less, social institutions tend to be less subject to change in such areas as Latin America and parties are often more firmly established there than in other developing areas. Recruitment may therefore be channelled through the more formal party structures, although the social divisions between urban and rural areas, between the traditional and the modern, and the long-standing systems of social stratification almost certainly remain crucial.[2]

[1] See Almond and Coleman (eds.), *Politics in the Developing Areas*, Parts 1–4.
[2] ibid., Part 5.

In contrast to political recruitment in developing societies, where the process tends to be relatively unsystematic, in totalitarian societies it is highly systematized. In addition to exercising general control of the educational system, the totalitarian state seeks to train a party élite for political and governmental office. In Nazi Germany, for example, a three-tier system of élite training was established. At the lowest level the most promising members of the Hitler Youth were sent to Adolf Hitler Schools from the age of twelve and subjected to intensive leadership training. These schools were run by the Hitler Youth. Above these were the National Political Institutes of Education, supervised by the S.S. and providing a combination of strict military training with special instruction in National Socialist ideology. Finally, the leading graduates from these two levels were sent to the *Ordensburgen*, where they received six years' training in the 'racial sciences' as well as political and military instruction.[1]

A similar situation is found in the Soviet Union, although systematic study of the recruitment is inevitably difficult, especially in the field of party recruitment. Fainsod describes three types of party school: (1) Higher Party Schools, 'designed to train leading party officials for republic and oblast level duties and . . . reserved for those having a higher education and considerable experience in responsible [party] work'; (2) Inter-oblast and Republic Higher Party Schools, providing courses for less senior party officials; and (3) Republic and Oblast Schools, dealing with lower level officials.[2]

RECRUITMENT TO ADMINISTRATIVE OFFICE

The systematic training and recruitment of *political* office-holders finds no parallel in Western democracies, but it does bear some comparison with the recruitment of *administrative* office-holders. In Western democracies, the latter are systematically recruited and, usually, trained by the state to fulfil particular roles in the bureaucracy. Recruitment is based primarily on merit, and entrance to the bureaucracy is generally achieved by some form of examination designed to test merit.

[1] See Shirer, *The Rise and Fall of the Third Reich*, pp. 255–6.
[2] Fainsod, *How Russia is Ruled*, pp. 242–4.

Countries like Britain and France, however, differ from the United States in that they adhere to the principle of a politically neutral civil service. Thus leading members of the bureaucracy retain their posts regardless of the party or parties in power, whereas in the United States federal civil service a change of party (or to a lesser extent of president, even though he may be of the same party as his predecessor) means changes of personnel in the higher echelons of the bureaucracy.

It has been estimated that 95 per cent of the personnel of the federal civil service are recruited through the *merit* system, rather than the 'spoils' system, but the importance of the latter (apart from the patronage it places in the hands of the party and president in power) lies in the fact that it is the means by which *key* officials are recruited. It is, of course, grossly misleading to suggest that posts are distributed to party supporters merely in response to the demands of patronage. The latter is more important in rewarding party supporters with minor posts which still remain within the purview of the 'spoils' system, posts such as chauffeurs, stenographers and the like. What the 'spoils' system does mean in political terms is that the highest posts are likely to be filled by 'outsiders' who are not career civil servants.

The philosophy behind this system is not difficult to understand, nor impossible to justify. Although Andrew Jackson was the first prominent politician to give articulate expression to the 'spoils' system, its use was already widespread in many states and by no means unknown at federal level when Jackson gave it the presidential accolade. Patronage, which was the common basis of recruitment in most countries at the time, was rationalized by the argument that changes of personnel were healthy and democratic, that the offices concerned required no special skills, and that the party in power needed bureaucrats who were sympathetic to its aims and would not seek to undermine its actions.

The wholesale use of the 'spoils' system as a means of recruitment has, as the figure mentioned earlier makes clear, been vastly reduced and recruitment on grounds of merit introduced, beginning with the Civil Service (Pendleton) Act 1883. The merit system has gradually been extended by the systematic classification of grades and pay, the introduction of pensions plans (both of which were closely linked with merit schemes) and by direct extension through federal legislation and executive orders.

Following the two world wars, however, the merit system was modified by the preference given to veterans (or ex-servicemen). Thus, between 1920 and 1940, 20 to 25 per cent of those appointed to positions in the federal civil service were veterans, while a decade after the Second World War approximately 60 per cent of those employed by the service had had veterans' preference. The 'spoils' system, however, applies in practice only to a small minority of administrative office-holders (if these veterans are excluded) in the United States, but they are a very significant minority.

Although most civil servants are now recruited through the merit system (veterans still receive preference, but must still reach certain required standards), recruitment is not centralized and each department conducts its own examinations and makes its own appointments. Furthermore, the view that no special skills are required by administrative personnel has militated against the training of civil servants. As the United Comptroller-General remarked in 1910, '. . . it is presumed that officers and employees when appointed and employed have the necessary education to perform the duties for which they were appointed.'[1] This doctrine of initial competence remained inviolate until 1921, when the Graduate School of the Department of Agriculture was established, and this was followed in 1924 by the founding of the Foreign Service School. Thereafter in-service training became more acceptable and widespread, especially with the developments introduced during the New Deal.

Even though Britain and France may be contrasted with the United States in establishing politically-neutral civil services, there are important differences between these two countries. Britain gradually eliminated patronage (though it was not linked with partisan control or turnover of office, as in the United States) during the nineteenth century following the Northcote-Trevelyan Report of 1854 and the establishment of a Civil Service Commission, which was made responsible for the recruitment of all administrative personnel. At the same time, the principle of recruitment by open competition was accepted and subsequently introduced. The civil service was divided into grades according to the nature of the work concerned and personnel for the three

[1] Quoted in Arthur D. Kallen, 'Training in the Federal Service – 170 Years to Accept', *Public Administration Review*, **19**, 1959, p. 37.

main groups (the clerical, executive and administrative classes) were separately recruited through the Civil Service Commission, although internal promotion from one class to another remains an important source of recruits.[1] Open examination of an academic nature are held, but these are supplemented in some cases by intensive interview methods, particularly for the highest group, the administrative class. Occasionally personnel are recruited from outside the civil service, but such appointments are exceptional, although in times of emergency, such as the Second World War, the recruitment of non-career civil servants may assume significant proportions.

Until recently the training of British civil servants was based on the concept of in-service or vocational training, and little in the way of special instruction was provided. The lowest rank in the administrative class, that of assistant principal, is therefore a training grade. This was later supplemented by the establishment of a Centre for Administrative Studies, which provides courses for assistant principals soon after they join the service. The concept of specific training has now been taken further by the founding of a Civil Service College, which will provide a wider basis of training for civil servants.[2] The emphasis remains, however, on in-service training, and therefore upon recruitment based primarily on educational qualifications not necessarily related to or specifically preparation for a civil service career.

France rationalized administrative recruitment rather earlier than Britain, and has, moreover, developed more intensive training techniques for civil servants. French civil servants are recruited by open examination and, as in Britain, the bureaucracy is divided into classes according to their functions. Entry to the higher echelons of the civil service in France differs, however, in that intensive pre-service training forms the basis of recruitment. This pre-service training is provided by the École Nationale d'Administration (E.N.A.) and the École Polytechnique. The E.N.A. was founded in 1945 as part of the extensive civil service reforms carried out in the immediate post-war period. Its role is

---

[1] The present system of classes in the Civil Service is being replaced by a unified grading structure, following the recommendation of the Fulton Report.

[2] See *The Civil Service* (The Fulton Report), Cmd 3683, 1968, Vol. 1, pp. 35–40, and Vol. 4, Section VI. For further discussion and information, see ibid., Vol. 1, Chapter 3, and Vol. 4, Section III.

both to recruit and train higher civil servants, and candidates are selected either by open competition (based on examinations in subjects broadly related to a career in public administration), or by limited competition open to existing civil servants of lower grade. Once they have entered the E.N.A., recruits are salaried civil servants and subsequently undergo a two-year period of administrative training, which includes a year working in a local prefecture and a much shorter period in a private company, as well as various forms of instruction in central administration and policymaking. The E.N.A. thus recruits and trains members of the French civil service who are to fill the chief administrative posts. Recruitment and training of technical specialists for the higher echelons of the civil service is undertaken by the École Polytechnique, although, unlike the E.N.A., the Polytechnique also trains graduates for the armed services and for private industry. The stress in France is thus on training recruits to the bureaucracy specifically for careers in the public service, whereas in Britain and the United States there is less emphasis on training and more on recruiting 'suitable' individuals into the bureaucracy.

Suitability is, in practice, the major factor in administrative recruitment, except where patronage is the sole determinant. Suitability may, however, be variously defined in terms of competence, political loyalty, socio-economic background, ethnic origin and so on. Western democracies tend to emphasize competence, for example, although most demand minimal political loyalty to the state. Socio-economic background is often important in that it is directly or indirectly associated with competence, while ethnic origin is of significance in countries like Canada, where some balance is sought between English- and French-speaking civil servants. In other countries, however, much greater stress is laid upon such factors as political loyalty and ethnic origin. In developing societies formerly subject to colonial rule, strenuous efforts are often made to create a bureaucracy drawn from the indigenous population, although reliance upon members of the former colonial administration is common in the early years of independence. Demands for 'Africanization', for example (demands not necessarily restricted to the bureaucracy), in former British and French colonies often make it difficult to recruit enough competent civil servants. Furthermore, there may be disproportionate recruitment from particular ethnic or tribal groups, as in Nigeria, while the demands of political loyalty, particularly in one-party states, and the extensive use of patronage in some developing countries present additional problems.[1]

Clearly totalitarian societies lay considerable stress on political loyalty, as the Preamble of the German Civil Service Law of 1937 makes clear:

> A professional Civil Service, rooted in the German *Volk*, saturated with a National Socialist commitment, based on personal fealty to the Leader of the German *Reich* and *Volk*, Adolf Hitler, constitutes the pillar of the Nationalist Socialist State.[2]

At the same time, because they are complex modern societies, totalitarian states necessarily emphasize the importance of competence. Thus, in the Soviet Union,

> Every sector of industry and administration has its parallel system of advanced schools and institutes which feed their graduates into the branch of public administration for which they prepare.[3]

The ultimate aim of any totalitarian society, as the Nazi Civil Service Law makes clear, is to create a bureaucracy in which political loyalty is absolute and takes precedence over competence. Indeed, under such circumstances no bureaucrat whose political loyalty is in doubt can be regarded as competent. This, however, presents particular difficulty in periods of change or transition.

When there are fundamental changes in the political system, the accompanying turnover of political and administrative office-holders holders is often considerable. Political office-holders are, of course, subject to a greater turnover, but it is misleading to assume that this is simply the replacement of one group by an opposing one, as Lewis Edinger has shown in his study of the transition from the Nazi régime to the West German Federal Republic. The process is inevitably complicated, and even conscious efforts to replace one 'élite' with another are unlikely to result in a total change of personnel. Thus, despite the efforts of the Allies to control political recruitment in post-war Germany, Edinger found that,

[1] See Richard L. Harris, 'The Role of the Civil Servant in West Africa', *Public Administration Review*, 25, 1965, pp. 308–13; James R. Shuster, 'Bureaucratic Transition in Morocco', *Human Organization*, 24, 1965, pp. 53–8; and Almond and Coleman (eds.), *Politics in the Developing Areas*, Parts 1–5.

[2] Quoted in Elke Frank, 'The Role of the Bureaucracy in Transition', *Journal of Politics*, 28, 1966, p. 742; see also Carl Beck, 'Party Control and Bureaucratization in Czechoslovakia', *Journal of Politics*, 23, 1961, pp. 279–94.

[3] Fainsod, *How Russia is Ruled*, p. 415.

Most members of the 1956 élites were recruited from the ranks of those who had belonged neither to the Nazi élite nor to the counter-élite, who had neither been strong opponents nor strong supporters of the totalitarian régime, neither strongly involved in running that régime nor in fighting it . . . about 24 per cent may be considered to have been supporters of the régime, 57 per cent to have been ambivalent, neutral or oscillating during the twelve years of Nazi rule, and no more than 19 per cent to have been more or less consistently opposed.[1]

Much depends, of course, on the nature of the changes in the political system. Where the transition is from a totalitarian to a non-totalitarian régime, then the changes in personnel may be limited to the holders of the more important political offices, but the establishment of a dictatorial or, more particularly, a totalitarian régime demands more extensive changes of personnel. None the less, it is important to note that even in the latter case (as in the example of developing societies formerly subject to colonial rule) totalitarian régimes are likely to be dependent upon the administrative office-holders of the previous régime. For example:

While trusted Bolsheviks held strategic positions at the top of the administrative pyramid, the lower levels of the bureaucracy were still composed of old-régime carry-overs whose knowledge made them indispensable and whose skills frequently enabled them to determine the policies of the institutions with which they were connected.[2]

Similarly, despite the law of 1937, a study of the German Foreign Office found that the Nazi régime had had to retain most of those already established in the service, and of these approximately a third *never* became members of the Nazi party. This particular study concluded that both the Weimar Republic and the Third Reich were too short-lived to establish bureaucracies which accepted the legitimacy of the régime.[3]

WHO IS RECRUITED AND WHY

The literature on who achieves political and administrative office is extensive. Moreover, as far as modern democracies are con-

[1] Lewis J. Edinger, 'Post-Totalitarian Leadership in Élites in the German Federal Republic', *American Political Science Review*, **54**, 1960, pp. 72 and 75.

[2] Fainsod, *How Russia is Ruled*, p. 92.

[3] Elke Frank, 'The Role of the Bureaucracy in Transition', *Journal of Politics*, **28**, 1966, pp. 725–53.

cerned, there is general agreement that <u>political and administra-</u>
<u>tive office-holders are invariably unrepresentative of the general</u>
<u>population.</u>

Table 25. *Educational background of political and administrative*
office-holders in the United States

HIGHEST LEVEL ATTAINED	Presidents, vice-presidents, Cabinet members (1877–1934)	United States Senators (1949–51)	United States Representatives (1941–3)	State governors (1930–40)
	%	%	%	%
None	–	–	–	–
Grade School	11	3	–	3
High school	10	10	12	20
College	79	87	88	77
Totals	100	100	100	100

HIGHEST LEVEL ATTAINED	Missouri State legislators (1901–31)	High-level civil servants (1940)	Population over 25 years of age (1940)
	%	%	%
None	–	–	5
Grade school	30	–	54
High school	13	7	31
College	57	93	10
Totals	100	100	100

SOURCE: Donald R. Matthews, *The Social Background of Political Decision-Makers*, New York, 1954, Table 6.

Table 25 shows clearly that <u>those who have held various types of</u>
<u>political and administrative office in the United States are educa-</u>
<u>tionally unrepresentative of the general population, and a similar</u>
<u>pattern is found if the occupational backgrounds of some of</u>
<u>these groups is examined</u> (Table 26). <u>A similar pattern emerges if</u>
<u>the backgrounds of political and administrative office-holders in</u>
<u>Britain are examined</u> (Table 27).

The pattern found in Tables 25, 26 and 27 is repeated in other
countries, although there are, as the tables illustrate, important
variations. What is probably of greater significance, however, is
the fact that a similar pattern is found in some developing
countries (Table 28).

Table 26. *Occupational backgrounds of political office-holders in the United States*

OCCUPATION	Presidents, vice-presidents, Cabinet members (1877–1934)	United States Senators (1949–51)	United States Representatives (1941–30)	State governors (1930–40)
	%	%	%	%
Professions	74	69	69	60
Proprietors and officials	21	24	22	25
Farmers	2	7	4	11
Low-salaried workers	1	–	1	1
Wage-earners	2	–	2	1
Servants	–	–	–	–
Farm labourers	–	–	–	–
Unknown, not classified	–	–	2	3
Totals	100	100	100	101

OCCUPATION	State legislators (1925–35)	Labour force (1940)
	%	%
Professions	36	7
Proprietors and officials	25	8
Farmers	22	11
Low-salaried workers	4	17
Wage-earners	3	40
Servants	–	11
Farm labourers	–	7
Unknown, not classified	10	–
Totals	100	101

SOURCE: Matthews, *The Social Background of Political Decision-Makers*, Table 7.

Source and note for table 27

SOURCES: Cabinet ministers: W. L. Guttsman, *The British Political Élite*, London, 1963, Table XV.

M.P.s: J. F. S. Ross, *Elections and Electors*, London, 1955, Tables 71, 77, 87 and 91.

Civil servants: A. H. Halsey and I. M. Crewe, 'Social Survey of the Civil Service', *Fulton Report*, Vol. 3(1), Tables 2.3, 2.7, 2.8 and 2.9.

* The sum of these figures exceeds the total proportion of graduates because of attendance at more than one university.

Table 27. *Background of political and administrative office-holders in Britain*

	Cabinet ministers (1916–55)	M.P.s (1945)		Administrative class civil servants (1967)
(A) CLASS BACKGROUND	%	%	Father's occupation	%
Aristocracy	20	8	Professional and managerial	67
Middle Class	58	} 92	Skilled non-manual and manual	23
Working class	22		Semi-skilled	4
			Unskilled	2
			Other	4
Total	100	100		100

(B) EDUCATIONAL BACKGROUND				
School				
Elementary	20	34	} 42	
Secondary/grammar	20	21		
Public school	52	44	55	
Other	8	–	3	
Totals	100	99	100	

(C) UNIVERSITY BACKGROUND				
Oxford and Cambridge	47 } 59	28* } 42 [1]	49* } 76	
Other	12	18*	28*	
None		41	58	24
Totals	100	100	100	

	Cabinet ministers (1916–55)		M.P.s (1945)	
	%		%	
(D) OCCUPATIONAL BACKGROUND				
Professions	37	Professions	53	
Officials of trade unions, etc.	15	Workers, including TU officials	27	
Commerce and industry	13	Employers and managers	17	
Landowning	12	Unoccupied	2	
Rentier	11			
Civil service, public administration	6			
Armed forces	4			
Manual workers	1			
Totals	99		99	

Table 28. *Occupational and educational background of members of legislatures in Ghana and Nigeria*

		Ghana %	Nigeria %
(A) OCCUPATION			
Education		30 ⎫ 46	30 ⎫ 50
Professions		16 ⎭	20 ⎭
Business		17	27
Farmers		4	6
Manual and clerical workers		6	3
Local government (including chiefs and officials)		16	11
All other		11	3
	Totals	100	100
(B) EDUCATION			
Pre-secondary		44	33
Secondary		42	37
University		14	30
	Totals	100	100

SOURCE: James S. Coleman, 'The Politics of Sub-Saharan Africa', Table 8, in Almond and Coleman (eds.), *Politics of the Developing Areas*, p. 342.

Furthermore, the pattern of recruitment among administrative office-holders, as measured by the occupational class of the fathers of higher civil servants, is similar in modern democracies and developing societies (Table 29).

Table 29. *Occupational class of the fathers of higher civil servants in selected countries*

COUNTRY	Middle class %	Working class %
Denmark (1945)	87	13
Britain (1949–52)	97	3
France (1945–51)	96	4
United States (1959)	81	19
Turkey (1960)	90	10
India (1947–56)	96	4

SOURCE: V. Subramaniam, 'Representative Bureaucracy: A Reassessment', *American Political Science Review*, **61**, 1967, Table 1, p. 1016.

It is, of course, important to bear in mind that in many cases the categories used in these tables are not strictly comparable, especially in dealing with such phenomena as class and educational levels. The validity of the data does not depend on absolute comparability, however, but in demonstrating the extent to which political and administrative office-holders are drawn from particular groups in society, a phenomenon which, it has been argued, is found in all societies in the form of an oligarchy, political élite or ruling class.

Political Recruitment and Élite and Class Theories. In seeking to explain why political and administrative office-holders are drawn substantially from particular social groups in a society, a number of theorists have suggested that these groups constitute élites or classes in whose hands political power is concentrated. Their existence is not accidental but, it is argued, is the result of various forces in society which create some form of social stratification. The basis of social stratification can, of course, vary – it may be based on economic divisions in society, or on the concept of a religious hierarchy, or on some form of status differentiation, or on ethnic divisions and so on. In practice it may well be a combination of these, but particular societies illustrate each type: modern industrial democracies are often cited as societies divided into upper, middle and lower classes according to occupational and other economic criteria; the Hindu caste system is clearly an example of religiously-based stratification; feudal societies were instances of status differentiation; while the position of Jews in Nazi Germany, Negroes in the United States or of Indians in many Latin American countries provide examples of some degree of ethnic stratification. It is further argued that the distribution of power within societies is determined by and directly related to the system of social stratification, and that the particular group wielding such power constitutes a political élite or ruling class.

A similar but separate theory suggests that those who wield power are always a small minority or oligarchy, since all organizations consist of an active minority and an inactive majority. The active minority, it is argued, can always out-manoeuvre the inactive majority because it has the advantage of being organized, and such a minority can only be replaced or overthrown by another minority possessing superior organization. This is Michel's 'iron law of oligarchy'.[1] Thus even an organization

[1] See Robert Michels, *Political Parties*, Part Six.

which, by its rules, grants formal power to its whole membership, is in practice subject to control and manipulation by a minority of active members; or, in the words of one of its leading proponents, Gaetano Mosca:

> In all societies – from societies that are very meagrely developed and have barely attained the dawnings of civilization, down to the most advanced and powerful societies – two classes of people appear – a class that rules and a class that is ruled.[1]

Mosca, however, attributes the dominant position of the minority not only to its organizational advantages, but further argues that the minority possesses these advantages because it consists of superior individuals, superior not necessarily because they are more able, but because they have characteristics which are valued by their particular societies. Mosca calls this minority a *ruling class*; his contemporary and rival, Vilfredo Pareto, calls it a *political élite*. Both Mosca and Pareto agreed that there was a division between rulers and ruled, between the political minority and majority, and that the composition of the ruling class or political élite could change over a period of time, either by the recruitment of members from the non-élite, or by the establishment of a counter-élite, a process which Pareto called the 'circulation of élites'. They differ, however, in that Mosca stresses that the relationship between minority and majority may vary significantly from society to society, whereas Pareto argues that the relationship is fundamentally similar in all societies. Mosca also offers a broader explanation of the circulation of élites.[2]

Other writers have developed the arguments of Mosca and Pareto by arguing that modern industrial societies develop particular types of ruling class or political élite. James Burnham, for instance, suggests that such societies ultimately become dominated by a *managerial élite* whose power rests on their control of the means of production, and that this control is maximized when the state nationalizes all industry.[3] C. Wright Mills, on the other hand, argues (at least so far as the United States is concerned) that

[1] Gaetano Mosca, *The Ruling Class*, edited by A. Livingston and translated by H. D. Kahn, New York, 1939, p. 50.

[2] For a discussion of the theories of Mosca and Pareto, see James H. Meisel (ed.), *Pareto and Mosca*, Englewood Cliffs, N.J., 1965, and T. B. Bottomore, *Élites and Society*, London, 1964.

[3] See James Burnham, *The Managerial Revolution*, New York, 1941.

there is a *power élite*, comprising the heads of the largest business corporations, the political leaders and the leading military personnel, whose dominance rests on the 'coincidence of economic, military, and political power'.[1]

The development élite theories was in many respects a reaction against, and an endeavour to refute, the class theories of Karl Marx. Marx argues that in all societies there is a ruling class and one or more subject classes. These classes are economically based and the power of the ruling class depends upon its control of the means of production, which gives it substantial or absolute control of the means of coercion in society and of the development of ideas. Thus Marx stresses the importance of economic control and organizational advantage, but differs from the élite theorists in arguing that there is an inevitable conflict between classes which will lead not to some circulation of élites, nor to the predominance of a particular élite, but to the dominance of the most numerous class: the working class.

Apart from Marx's assertion that the working class will ultimately secure political power and that, because of working class homogeneity and class consciousness, and because men's basic needs will be satisfied, a classless society will result, there are other differences between the élite and class theories. Both regard the distinction between rulers and ruled as fundamental, but élite theorists attribute this solely to the minority being organized, the majority unorganized, whereas Marx attributes it to the specific organizational advantage of controlling the means of production. According to élite theorists, change is brought about by the circulation of élites, which may occur by a variety of means, whereas Marx attributes change to the conflict between ruling and subject classes. Similarly, both theories assume that the ruling minority is bound together by cohesive social forces, but élite theorists attribute this to a variety of factors, such as similar social background, general identity of interest and so on, whereas Marx is in no doubt that cohesion is based on a common economic interest.[2]

T. B. Bottomore suggests that it is possible to identify various élites as 'groups which have high status (for whatever reason) in a society: a *political class*, consisting of 'all those groups which

---

[1] C. Wright Mills, *The Power Élite*, New York, 1956, p. 278.

[2] See T. B. Bottomore, *Classes in Modern Society*, London, 1965, as well as his *Élites and Society*.

exercise political power or influence, and are directly engaged in struggles for political leadership'; and a *political élite*, comprising 'those individuals who actually exercise power at any given time'.[1] This having been done,

> we can attempt to distinguish between societies in which there is a ruling class, and at the same time élites which represent particular aspects of its interests; societies in which there is no ruling class, but a political élite which founds its power upon the control of the administration, or upon military force, rather than property ownership and inheritance; and societies in which there exists a multiplicity of élites among which no cohesive and enduring group of powerful individuals or families seems to be discoverable at all.[2]

The principal criticism of élite and class theories is that they are both dependent on group cohesion and group consciousness. It is not difficult to establish, as we have already seen, that the holders of political and administrative office are frequently drawn from particular social groups in society; nor is it difficult to demonstrate that members of these groups have common interests by virtue of belonging to their respective groups; but it is an entirely different matter to show that these groups are conscious of those interests and act cohesively in response to them. This is not to say that political élites or ruling classes do not exist in the sense that those who wield political power may be drawn from particular segments of society, but merely to question why they exist.

TOWARDS A THEORY OF POLITICAL RECRUITMENT

The fact that particular groups in society are disproportionately represented among political and administrative office-holders is often attributed to the forces of *demand*. This is clearly so in a limited way with the formal qualifications that are sometimes laid down for candidates at elections, and to a much greater extent in those laid down for administrative office-holders. There may also be less formal demands related to personal background, ability or representativeness, for example. It should be recognized, however, that political recruitment is also a question of *supply*, as the model illustrated in Figure 4 suggests.

[1] Bottomore, *Élites and Society* (Pelican edition, 1966), p. 14.
[2] ibid., p. 44.

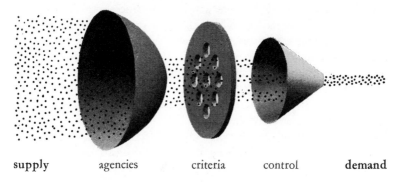

supply   agencies   criteria   control   **demand**

Figure 4. A simple model of political recruitment

Apart from the demand for, say, more women M.P.s in Parliament or fewer lawyers in Congress, it is also important to consider whether supply exceeds or falls short of demand. It does not follow, for instance, that because the demand for women M.P.s is low that this alone accounts for the under-representation of women in Parliament. As far as Britain is concerned, there is evidence that, although supply exceeds demand, the election of *all* those women *seeking* parliamentary candidatures would still leave women considerably under-represented.[1] Conversely, the fact that the legal profession provides a useful basis for a political career may well be a partial explanation of the over-representation of this occupational group in many legislatures – a product of supply as well as demand. Or again, the educational qualifications laid down for higher civil servants are often fairly high and, should it happen that the educational system is such that those who secure these qualifications are disproportionately drawn from particular social groups, then this will be reflected in recruitment to the bureaucracy.

The forces of supply and demand are also influenced by the various agencies of political recruitment, by the criteria that may be applied, and by the degree to which the process is controlled. Some of these agencies work more or less formally (such as administrative recruiting commissions), others entirely informally (such as 'political' families or certain interest groups). Political parties are clearly the most important means in most political

[1] See Rush, *The Selection of Parliamentary Candidates*, pp. 63 and 223.

systems of recruiting holders of political office, although as we have seen the manner in which they do so varies considerably. The importance of parties as agencies of recruitment is illustrated by the extent to which particular parties provide vehicles for the recruitment of working class office-holders: this function is performed, for instance, by the Labour party in Britain, the Communist and Socialist parties in France, the Social Democratic party in West Germany, and the A.L.P. in Australia, whereas the absence of a comparable party in the United States may well account for the much lower proportion of political office-holders of lower socio-economic status in that country.

It is also possible that the general absence of agencies of administrative recruitment comparable to the working class party is partially responsible for the virtual absence of those of lower socio-economic origins from the ranks of administrative office-holders. The principal informal recruiting agencies for the latter are often particular educational establishments which provide individuals with the necessary formal qualifications and the informal incentive to consider a career in the public service. For example, in Britain institutions like Oxford and Cambridge, and in France the Institut des Études Politiques, supply a disproportionate number of higher civil servants, not only because they produce able applicants, but because such a career is traditionally associated with these institutions. Thus, even where an attempt is made to widen the pool of recruitment, as there was in France after 1945, the results may be minimal – in 1966 fifty out of the sixty-five entrants to the E.N.A. came from the Institut.[1]

The agencies of recruitment will normally lay down a variety of criteria embodying the characteristics and skills that they regard as appropriate to the office concerned. These criteria will, of course, reflect demand, but they will also affect supply by encouraging or discouraging those with particular characteristics or skills. It is likely, for instance, that women are discouraged from seeking political office in many countries, and this in itself limits the supply of would-be women politicians. Different parties encourage different types of individual. Donald Matthews suggests, for instance, that American Senators can be divided into four types:

[1] Anthony Sampson, *The New Europeans*, London, 1968, p. 338.

1 *Patricians*, who come from 'political' families of fairly high social status, and found in both parties (7 per cent of the Senators in Matthews's study).

2 *Amateurs*, who are usually of somewhat lower social status, but often wealthy, and supplying rather more Republicans than Democrats (34 per cent).

3 *Professionals*, who have worked their way up through a variety of political offices, and supplying rather more Democrats than Republicans (55 per cent).

4 *Agitators*, who are usually of low social origin and have secured office by their own efforts (4 per cent).[1]

Similarly, the criteria applied by the same party in different electoral districts may vary significantly. In Conservative-held constituencies in Britain, for instance, the type of candidate chosen tends to vary in relation to the safeness or marginality of the seat and the extent to which it is rural or urban. Local Conservative associations in safe seats are more likely than those in marginal seats to select candidates who have attended a public school (especially one of the more prestigious schools), and who are university graduates (especially of Oxford or Cambridge) – tendencies which are reinforced in rural constituencies. In the Labour party candidates sponsored by the trade unions tend to be concentrated in the northern half of the country, those sponsored by the Co-operative party in the southern half, reflecting in both cases the distribution of the membership of these movements. In both parties there are important distinctions between the types of candidate chosen by the party holding the seat and that which does not.[2]

Comparable data may be found in a study of congressional recruitment in Chicago, which found significant differences between the candidates selected by the major parties in the inner city districts (generally safe Democratic areas), the suburban districts (generally safe Republican) and the outer city districts (generally marginal). For example, the safe Democrat districts were usually subject to strict control by the Democratic party machine and individuals prominent within the party organization

[1] Donald R. Matthews, *U.S. Senators and their World*, Chapel Hill, North Carolina, 1960, pp. 61–5.

[2] Rush, *The Selection of Parliamentary Candidates*, Chapters 3 and 6–8.

were most likely to be selected; but in the safe Republican districts, there was less party control and the primary electorate played a more important part, while in marginal districts there was more variation in the types of candidates selected.[1]

The extent to which political recruitment is subject to various types of control is also important in affecting supply and demand. As we have noted, there may be formal qualifications laid down for would-be holders of office. Some of these may be laid down by the agencies themselves, others may be laid down by the state. In either case, this is likely to affect the process profoundly. The educational qualifications normally required for bureaucratic positions reflect not only a demand for a particular type of applicant, but are a limit upon the supply of such applicants. Of more general significance, however, is whether the recruitment process is relatively open or closed. A system of administrative recruitment based on patronage is relatively closed; one based on open examinations is relatively open: both are the results of types of control. Moreover, such control may affect different groups in different ways: a system of patronage will be very open to those who are in a position to influence its distribution, but virtually closed to those who have neither money nor the necessary contacts; whereas an examination system widens the field of possible applicants in some respects and narrows it in others. In the same way some political parties have extensive control over the selection of candidates, others do not. In Britain the *national* party organizations have relatively little control over candidate selection, but there is very considerable *local party* autonomy, so that selection remains effectively under the control of the party. Conversely, in the United States the presence of the primary militates against party control. Nevertheless, in both cases the recruitment process remains relatively open.

This is not the case in totalitarian societies, however, since political recruitment is an area of vital importance and is therefore subject to stringent control. Of course, as we have already seen, extensive changes in personnel normally take time, especially in the administrative sphere, but one of the most important methods of effecting fundamental changes in the political system is through control of the process of political recruitment. Thus the régime in

[1] Leo M. Snowiss, 'Congressional Recruitment and Representation', *American Political Science Review*, **60**, 1966, pp. 627–39.

a totalitarian society endeavours to control the recruitment of all political and administrative office-holders, rather than leave this to autonomous or semi-autonomous agencies. In Germany between 1933 and 1945 and in the Soviet Union the National Socialist and Communist parties respectively are the principal agencies of political recruitment, and as such may fundamentally alter the results of that process. Under the Weimar Republic, for example, recruitment to political office (as measured by the backgrounds of Cabinet personnel) became more open than it had been under the monarchy, but the advent of Hitler resulted in marked changes: the proportion of Cabinet members of aristocrat background increased, those of middle and working class origin declined. Similarly, the proportion of those with military and business backgrounds also increased significantly.[1]

The extent of this control is well illustrated by the U.S.S.R., where significant changes in the composition of the Politburo have occurred since the establishment of the Communist régime in 1917. Most of the leaders of the Russian Revolution and of the Politburo from 1917 to the death of Lenin in 1924 were middle class intellectuals, but between 1924 and 1938, when Stalin was establishing and consolidating his position, the composition of the Politburo changed markedly in terms of the social origins of its members. Whereas the members during the earlier period were typically of middle class, urban origin and had had some higher education, under Stalin the typical member was of lower class, rural origin and had had no higher education.[2] We have, moreover, already seen how the régime has exercised control over the recruitment of party members in the Soviet Union.[3]

The problems of studying political recruitment are well illustrated by the examination of the role of supply in the process. Since this is a more difficult area to examine than demand – the problems of investigating the backgrounds of those who *seek* office are immense compared with the problems of measuring demand – there is a lack of systematic studies of this vital aspect of political

[1] See Maxwell Knight, *The German Executive, 1890–1933*, Hoover Institute Studies, Series B, No. 4, Stanford, California, 1952.
[2] See G. K. Schueller, *The Politburo*, Hoover Institute Studies, Series B, No. 2, Stanford, California, 1951.
[3] See Chapter 3, pp. 108–9 above.

recruitment. Central to the question of supply is finding out what impels individuals to seek or offer themselves for political and administrative office, especially the former. A few studies exist: Philip Buck, for instance, found that of a group of eighty-two British M.P.s, 61 per cent had been invited or persuaded to stand for Parliament (usually by friends or through some other political activity), and 39 per cent had actively sought candidatures.[1] Kenneth Prewitt and his colleagues found interesting differences between the levels of political office and the stage at which individuals became interested in politics in a study of state legislators and city councillors in the United States. The two most important reasons of those who became interested in politics during pre-adult life were 'admiration for particular politicians' and a 'sense of obligation', whereas those whose interest in politics had come in adult life placed 'sense of obligation' first and a 'sense of indignation' second. Thus it was not surprising to find that the 'adults' were more likely to be influenced by local conditions and issues, and the 'pre-adults' by presidential, gubernatorial or senatorial campaigns or particular administrations. Furthermore, 'adults' were more likely to be recruited through non-political activities. Prewitt and his colleagues also found that state legislators were more likely to cite 'admiration for particular politicians' and 'ambition for political power', while city councillors were more likely to cite a 'sense of indignation' or a 'sense of obligation'.[2]

These studies are, however, limited in scope and much remains to be done in this area of political recruitment. Furthermore, the links between supply and demand and the characteristics of those who both seek and secure office remain largely unknown. In another article, Kenneth Prewitt argues that the crucial variable may be *'exposure to politics'* – the extent to which individuals come into contact with political phenomena – and cites a number of studies which show that *political* leaders are subject to a greater exposure to politics than the general population.[3] How far such an

---

[1] Buck, *Amateurs and Professionals in British Politics*, pp. 67–9, and Appendix IV, Table 35.

[2] Kenneth Prewitt, Heinz Eulau and Betty H. Zisk, 'Political Socialization and Political Roles', *Public Opinion Quarterly*, **30**, 1966, pp. 569–82.

[3] Kenneth Prewitt, 'Political Socialization and Leadership Selection', *Annals*, **361**, September 1965, pp. 96–111.

explanation is applicable to *administrative* recruitment and to political recruitment as a whole is not known, but in suggesting political exposure as the crucial variable, Prewitt is in effect arguing that the processes of political recruitment and political socialization are inextricably linked: those links, however, await further investigation.

5 · Political Communication

Political communication – the transmission of politically relevant information from one part of the political system to another, and between the social and the political systems – is the dynamic element of a political system,[1] and the processes of socialization, participation and recruitment are dependent upon it. The communication of knowledge, values and attitudes is fundamental to all three, since it is these which determine the political activity of individuals.

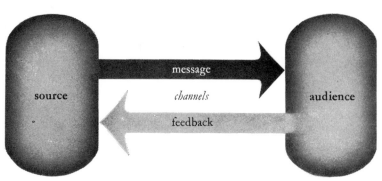

Figure 5. A simple communication model

The elements of a communication system are shown in Figure 5. These comprise the source of the message (or information), the message itself, the channel through which it passes to the audience

[1] See Karl W. Deutsch, *The Nerves of Government: Models of Political Communication and Control*, New York, 1963, *passim*.

(or recipient of the information), and a process known as 'feedback', by which the positions of source and audience may be reversed in the form of a reaction to the message from the original audience to the original source. Thus in a system of political communication, a typical source would be a candidate for election to a political office; his message would be a series of policy proposals; his channel a television broadcast; his audience those members of the electorate who happen to watch the broadcast; and the feedback (or audience reaction) approval or disapproval of his proposals.

The various elements of a system of political communication are not necessarily a structural part of the political system, nor is their role in the process necessarily continuous and it may vary from one situation to another. In one situation an individual is the source of a message, in another he is the audience, and in another he may be the channel through which the message is conveyed. Thus in one case a political office-holder is the source of a message to the electorate, but in the event of some reaction from the latter, their roles are reversed, while in a third situation the office-holder may pass on to the electorate a message from another source. Moreover, some sources are specific, others diffuse: a political leader is an example of the first, an electorate of the second. In any society there is a complex network of communication and a similarly complex network is found in any political system. This network is characterized by a great variety of sources, audiences and channels. It is not simply a question of vertical but also of horizontal communication – communication laterally between individuals and groups who occupy a common level in the political system. For each individual and each group of individuals in the political system, however, there is a discernible communication network.

For a political office-holder, for example, his sources of information will include his immediate colleagues in office, the administrative office-holders associated with his post, various political associates (both supporters and, probably, opponents), a variety of less political contacts (such as interest group leaders), the mass media, and, possibly, periodic contact with other members of society through such devices as electoral campaigns, public speeches and visiting different parts of the country. His audiences and channels of communication will be similarly composed and similarly diverse.

For other, less active individuals sources, audiences and channels will tend to be more limited and the whole process of political communication more intermittent. In spite of differences between political systems it is likely that the channels of information for most individuals are generally similar, as Table 30 suggests.

Table 30. *Main channels of political communications in France, Spain and Iran*

CHANNEL OF COMMUNICATION	France	Spain	Iran
	%	%	%
Newspapers, magazines, etc.	22	38	36
Radio and/or TV	59	37	57
Personal contacts, other sources, etc.	7	22	5
No answer	12	3	2
Totals	100	100	100

SOURCES: France: main channels of information on the presidential campaign, 1965; IFOP, August 1965.
Spain: main channels of information on the plan for economic social development, 1965: IOP, October–November 1965.
Iran: main channels of information about important world events, 1962: NIP, Teheran, Summer 1962– literates only.

Clearly there are some variations from one country to another, as the data in this table shows. For instance, radio and television appear to be considerably less important in Spain and personal contacts and other sources more important than in either France or Iran. None the less, there is a basic pattern in all three countries in which the principal channels of information on political questions are the mass media.

The role of the mass media in political communication illustrates the way in which the whole process is integrated with the societal communication network in that only the more specialized of the mass media are normally wholly or overwhelmingly political in content. Newspapers, radio and television are usually intended to inform their users about a very wide range of matters of which political affairs are a minority, while the entertainment content of radio and television in particular is often predominant. Only particular parts of their output are normally specifically political. Furthermore, there are important differences among the mass media. For example, radio and television audiences tend to be relatively undifferentiated compared with those of the printed mass media. This means that, although particular programmes may be broadcast with a particular audience in mind, radio and television networks are not normally able to cater more or less exclusively for a particular audience in the way that the printed media can and do. Quite apart from specialized publications, such as those serving a particular occupation or interest or seeking to promote specific views, many newspapers have, despite their diffuse contents, clearly identifiable readerships (Table 31).

Table 31. *Newspaper readership, class and party support in Britain*

NEWSPAPER	READERSHIP Predominant class	Predominant voting intention
The Times	Middle	Conservative and Labour
Guardian	Middle	Labour
Daily Telegraph	Middle	Conservative
Daily Mail	Middle and Working	Conservative and Labour
Daily Express	Working and Middle	Conservative and Labour
Daily Sketch	Working	Conservative
Sun	Working	Labour
Daily Mirror	Working	Labour

SOURCE: based on NOP, July 1967.

Given the identity of readership shown in this table, both in terms of class position and party support, each newspaper is able to choose and present its material in the manner best suited to its readership. In other words, each newspaper will normally reach only a particular section of the population and will seek to meet the particular needs of that section. This is clearly the case in Britain, where there are a number of national newspapers whose readerships differ in socio-economic and political identification, and similar differences may be found elsewhere. In some countries, however, the sheer size of the country, involving the existence of time zones, and economic trends in the newspaper industry have reduced, sometimes eliminated, competition between papers, so that one newspaper often enjoys a monopoly in a particular area. Nevertheless, such newspapers still serve a particular readership – in this case identified less in socio-economic or political terms and more by locality. While the same is true of local radio and television networks, it should be noted that these networks, unlike newspapers, often face competition from other networks, and, furthermore, that many programmes that they broadcast (especially television networks) are not of local origin and are not aimed at specifically local audiences.

We have already noted that the significance of the mass media in general and of any one medium in particular varies from one country to another. It is not therefore surprising to find that the extent to which people follow public affairs also varies, often considerably (Table 32).

Table 32. *Proportion of population following accounts of political and governmental affairs in the United States, Britain, West Germany, Italy and Mexico*

FREQUENCY	United States	Britain	Germany	Italy	Mexico
	%	%	%	%	%
Regularly	27	23	34	11	15
From time to time	53	45	38	26	40
Never	19	32	25	62	44
Others and don't know	1	1	3	1	1
Totals	100	101	100	100	100

SOURCE: Almond and Verba, *The Civic Culture*, p. 54.

The number of people who regularly follow public affairs varies in the United States, Britain and Germany, but the major dichotomy shown in this table is between these three countries on the one hand, and Italy and Mexico on the other. Thus, when Almond's and Verba's respondents were asked whether they followed reports of public affairs in newspapers, magazines and radio or television, the proportions replying that they did so at least weekly in respect of newspapers and radio or television, and 'ever' in the case of magazines, were in the range 21 to 58 per cent for the United States, Britain and Germany, but 16 to 31 per cent for Italy and Mexico.[1]

Each political system develops its own network of political communication and the significance of particular sources, channels and audiences will differ accordingly. Except in primitive societies or in those still dominated by traditional cultures, which are characterized by low literacy levels and which lack the technological skills and means to develop modern mass media, the printed word and broadcasting are the major means by which political information is transmitted in any political system. At the same time, other channels of communication are very important

[1] Almond and Verba, *The Civic Culture*, p. 56.

and often more obviously political. Interest groups and political parties, though varying from one system to another, are vital to the communication process by providing channels through which contact between those holding political and administrative office and the general populace can be maintained. Membership of political and quasi-political organizations may involve the individual in only intermittent political communication, but the more active participants are involved in more frequent communication in which information is passed vertically from them to those holding higher positions in the hierarchy of participation and horizontally between members active at a common level, both as members of the same organization and between organizations. Compared with the mass media, which may be regarded as a general means of political communication, interest groups and political parties are more specifically and frequently involved in this process.

Apart from the mass media and formal organizations, there is a third important channel of communication – informal contact between individuals and groups of individuals. Clearly such contact is not in practice isolated from either of the other two major channels, but it is analytically important to deal with it separately, partly because it is not entirely covered by the mass media and formal organizations, and partly because it forms the basis of an important theory of communication.

Informal contact or face-to-face relationships are the most common and frequent means of communication in any society, although its role in *political* communication is probably related more to the formation of *public opinion* than merely to the transmission of political information; and it is in the first of these two roles that the theory of the *two-step flow of communication* has been developed. The two-step flow theory was first postulated by Paul Lazarsfeld and his colleagues in their study of voting behaviour, *The People's Choice*,[1] and it argues that the influence of the mass media is mediated to individuals through 'opinion leaders'. These opinion leaders are 'very much alike and typically belong to the same primary groups of family, friends and co-workers'.[2] Elihu Katz examined a number of studies in both politics and sociology

[1] Lazarsfeld, Berelson and Gaudet, *The People's Choice*, p. 151.
[2] Elihu Katz, 'The Two-Step Flow of Communication: An Up-to-Date Report on an Hypothesis', *Public Opinion Quarterly*, 21, 1957, p. 77.

which sought to test the theory and concluded that inter-personal relations of this type were important in three respects: first, as actual channels of information; secondly, as sources of social pressure upon individuals to adhere to various norms of attitude and behaviour; and thirdly, as sources of support for such norms and therefore for group cohesion. It is important to appreciate, however, that as channels of *information* opinion leaders are primarily subordinate to the mass media and other channels we have mentioned and that their significance is greatest in the realm of public opinion, which involves the evaluation of this information, and with which we shall be dealing later in this chapter.

The particular pattern of communication that a political system develops is, inevitably, dependent upon various factors in society. The most important of these are physical and technological, economic, socio-cultural and political factors. Communication is ultimately dependent upon physical and technological factors, and these stress the importance of examining communication from a temporal point of view. The historical development of communication networks is closely linked to physical and technological factors. In the past the pattern of communication has been largely dictated by the relative ease or difficulty of physical communication and by various technical limitations, which have severely restricted the extent to and speed with which information can be disseminated. Communication networks therefore tended to be relatively isolated and inter-communication between networks was limited. The ability, for example, of the various colonial powers from the sixteenth to the nineteenth centuries to communicate effectively with their colonies was limited by their reliance upon slow-moving sea transport, and there is little doubt that such events as the American War of Independence and wars between the colonial powers were complicated by problems of communication. Even in relatively limited areas in which the physical barriers to communication were not unduly severe, such as a number of European countries, communication was slow and difficult. Newspapers were either non-existent or had only limited circulations, and the dissemination of news was fragmentary and haphazard. Technological advances, however, subsequently overcame many of these problems. In so doing, however, they created not new communication networks but added a further dimension to existing networks.

Physical barriers, such as mountains, deserts, forests, seas, lakes and rivers, are often important in determining an initial pattern of communication. In physical terms, there may exist a natural communication pattern – along rivers, valleys and coastlines, for example – which is subsequently developed into a communications system of land and water transport linking various communities. The relative isolation or integration of these communities within a particular society is obviously profoundly affected by the sort of communication pattern that develops. This was, as we have already suggested, especially true before the development of modern means of communication facilitated by technological advances. Moreover, notwithstanding these advances, physical factors remain of considerable importance in many societies. For instance, the larger a country is the greater the problems of communication, regardless of the existence of natural barriers to such communication. Countries like the United States or Canada, with a considerable east–west span, are divided into time zones which militate against national newspapers and radio and television networks, whereas smaller countries like Britain, or larger ones like Japan even, which fall into a single time zone, are not faced with this problem. Even where a modern communications system exists its affects may be partially offset by physical barriers. The populated areas of Australia, for instance, are mainly around the coastal periphery and its hinterland, with the result that communication is made more difficult. In less advanced countries, physical barriers may constitute even greater barriers to communication, and since many of these countries are in parts of the world which are characterized by formidable physical obstacles, this is a problem common to most developing countries.

In most countries, however, technological changes have reduced many of the problems presented by physical factors and have profoundly altered communication patterns. Modern technology has not only greatly increased the ease and speed with which people and materials can be transported from one place to another, but has also brought about an equal if not greater revolution in the communication of information. The availability of the printed and spoken word has been extended almost beyond measure, while the speed of communication that is now possible across vast distances is itself an important factor. Furthermore, inventions such as the transistor and the miniaturization of communication equipment which it has made possible have also made important contributions.

The extent to which physical barriers are overcome and to which technological advances are significant, however, is closely related to economic development, as Richard Fagen has shown (Table 33).

Table 33. *Relationship between level of economic development and level of mass media development*

MASS MEDIA	GNP *per capita*
Daily newspaper circulation per 1,000 population	·80
Radio receivers per 1,000 population	·85
TV sets per 1,000 population	·75
Cinema attendance *per capita*	·65

SOURCE: Richard R. Fagan, *Politics and Communication*, Boston, Mass., 1966, Table IV.1, p. 58, constructed from data in Russett *et al.*, *World Handbook of Political and Social Indicators*, pp. 272 and 274–5. The figures shown in this table, and in Table 34, are product-moment correlation co-efficients; for an explanation of how they are calculated, see H. Blalock, *Social Statistics*, New York, 1960, pp. 285ff. The closer the figure to 1·00 the more significant the correlation.

As the table suggests, the higher the level of economic development the more extensive the development of the mass media. It is also likely that there will be greater reliance upon the mass media as channels of *information* than upon informal face-to-face contacts, but of greater importance is the relative uniformity of communication that is likely to be found in economically developed societies. Not only are more people involved in the communication system, but they are reached by the same channels and so the information likely to reach them will be more uniform. In developing societies, however, the communication system will usually be more fragmented because it relies less on the mass media and more upon limited and informal channels of communication that reach only particular sections of the population.

These patterns of communication will also be affected by a variety of socio-cultural factors. An obvious factor is the level of literacy (Table 34).

Table 34. *Relationship between level of literacy and levels of the mass media and economic development*

MASS MEDIA AND ECONOMIC DEVELOPMENT	Literacy (Population age 15 and over literate)
Daily newspaper circulation per 1,000 population	·88
Radio receivers per 1,000 population	·80
TV sets per 1,000 population	·69
Cinema attendance *per capita*	·71
GNP *per capita*	·80

SOURCE: Fagen, *Politics and Communication*, Table IV.2, p. 62, constructed from data in Russett *et al.*, *World Handbook of Political and Social Indicators*, p. 283.

Apart from limiting the impact of the printed media, illiteracy also limits the impact of the spoken word since it is inevitably linked to educational attainment. In such circumstances, face-to-face contacts assume immense importance and are the principal means of communication. A study of communication patterns in Egypt vividly illustrates this. The survey on which the study is based was conducted in a number of villages near Cairo. Only a fifth of the respondents were literate. Approximately the same proportion read newspapers, but more than half listened to the radio, and 45 per cent said that they discussed local and national news. Discussion of politics in particular, however, was less important than discussion of village affairs and farming among the men and the least important subject among the women respondents. The most important finding of the survey was that a two-step communication pattern existed between literate and illiterate respondents – the literates passing on news to the illiterates during the day, this being followed by discussion in the evenings.[1]

We have already seen in Table 31 how newspaper readership may vary according to social class and party identification. An American study of the experiences of respondents in an area ravaged by a tornado found that eye-witness accounts varied

[1] Gordon K. Hirabayashi and M. Fathalla El Khalib, 'Communication and Political Awareness in the Villages of Egypt', *Public Opinion Quarterly*, 22, 1958, pp. 355–63.

according to class. Lower-class respondents described the incidents they had seen solely from their own perspective and did not report any accounts of other witnesses. Their narratives were fragmented, their imagery generally concrete and simple, and they usually felt little need to explain the context of their accounts. In contrast, the accounts of middle-class respondents were usually seen from a multiple perspective; their narratives were coherent and organized, their imagery more varied and conceptual, and they frequently explained the context of their remarks.[1]

The whole question of physical, technological, economic and socio-cultural factors is aptly summed up in a study of the communication problems of an island off the coast of Korea. The island, Cheju-do, lies sixty miles off the Korean peninsula and is a province of South Korea. The very fact that it is an island and does lie so far from the mainland presents obvious communication problems as far as contact with the latter is concerned. This physical separation has resulted in the people of Cheju-do regarding themselves as distinct from the people on the mainland, while the island itself is further fragmented by its mountainous terrain. The island's transport system is rudimentary and inadequate, especially as a means of disseminating information, while the mountains reduce the efficiency of radio communication. The effectiveness of the radio network is further reduced because so few people possess receivers, since they are expensive items which are regarded as of little or no use by most of the population. The radio network is, however, supplemented by local newspapers, and both are economically supported by the South Korean government. This provision of mass media is a costly exercise and is further complicated by the high rate of illiteracy on Cheju-do, by the widespread use of the English and Korean languages for oral communication and Chinese characters for written communication. Efforts by the government to surmount some of these problems by the use of simple documentary films and face-to-face contacts have not been successful, largely because of the long history of resistance by Cheju-do to interference from mainland Korea.[2]

[1] Leonard Schatzman and Anselm Strauss, 'Social Class and Modes of Communication', *American Journal of Sociology*, **19**, 1955, pp. 329–38.

[2] Richard A. Garver, 'Communication Problems of Underdevelopment: Cheju-do, Korea, 1962', *Public Opinion Quarterly*, **26**, 1962, pp. 613–25.

It is clear from the case of Cheju-do that political factors – the desire of the Korean government to establish a system of communication which will enable it to disseminate certain political information, and the traditional resistance of the islanders to mainland interference – are often of very great importance in determining the pattern of political communication. In Cheju-do the traditional resistance of the islanders is largely reinforced by the physical, technological, economic and socio-cultural problems of communication in the area. In other cases, however, these problems may be less formidable, and this is more likely in more advanced societies which tend to facilitate rather than hinder technological advance in particular.

In Nazi Germany, for example, the channels of communication were subject to close supervision, and this was largely effective because the régime was able to exert a large measure of control over the content of information in the mass media and to ensure that it secured a wide circulation – the technical apparatus at the government's disposal made it possible. German newspapers received daily instructions from the Propaganda Ministry telling them what to publish, how it was to be presented, what editorials were required, and so on. All editors had to be politically reliable and racially 'pure', and their actions were subject to constant scrutiny. Any newspapers which failed to follow their instructions were either suppressed or suffered appropriate staff changes. The German radio network was subject to even stricter control, which was facilitated in the early days of the Nazi régime by the fact that it was already state-owned. It is a measure of the effectiveness of the Nazi control of political communication that William Shirer, in spite of his access to foreign newspapers and broadcasts, was led to comment:

> A steady diet over the years of falsification and distortion made a certain impression on one's mind and often misled it. No one who has not lived for years in a totalitarian land can possibly conceive how difficult it is to escape the dread consequences of a régime's calculated and incessant propaganda.[1]

The impact of the mass media was reinforced by the face-to-face contacts between individuals, especially those involving party members, who could be relied upon to disseminate only the

[1] Shirer, *The Rise and Fall of the Third Reich*, pp. 247–8.

'truth'. Such a system, as Shirer points out, often results in this 'truth' being so widely believed that to question it is utterly useless.[1]

Substantially the same situation exists in the Soviet Union, for substantially the same reasons:

> The Soviet régime has developed one of the largest and most complex systems of public communication in the world. The Communist party has forged a parallel system of control which is more elaborate and thorough than any other still in existence in the postwar era. Both the system of communication and the control apparatus are oriented toward a single goal. They must serve as instruments through which the party and government mobilize the mind and will of the population; they must see to it that what ought to be done *is* done, what should be thought and felt *is* thought and felt.[2]

The mass media in the U.S.S.R. are subject to strict party and governmental control, and this involves close supervision of all types of newspapers, periodicals and books and their availability, strict control of all broadcasting, and careful scrutiny of all products of the Soviet film industry. This control of the mass media rests firmly on the extensive system of 'agitators' who disseminate party propaganda and political information:

> the . . . agitator makes his contribution to effective party leadership primarily at the level of bringing party policy to the people and seeking to enlist their support. But he plays an important part in bringing the leaders information that they must have as a basis for determining policy, and he has a central role in securing execution of policy.[3]

The role of the 'agitator' in the Soviet Union emphasizes the extent to which political communication consists of a complex network of channels carrying messages between a great variety of sources and audiences, and that such a system involves a process of feedback, by which reactions to messages are received by the original source. The way in which such a system is established has been shown by a study of the development of communication patterns during the Communist occupation of South Korea. The Communist régime concentrated its efforts on three channels of communication: the mass media, the education system and face-to-face contacts. Complete control was exercised over

[1] ibid., p. 248.
[2] Inkeles, *Public Opinion in Soviet Russia*, p. 317. (Original italics.)
[3] ibid., p. 121.

the mass media, and newspapers using the Korean phonetic alphabet (and not Chinese characters) were specially prepared for South Korean consumption. Newspapers were the principal means of mass communication, but their impact was reinforced by radio, posters and parades and demonstrations. The education system was harnessed to propagate political information and great efforts were made to increase literacy levels in order to facilitate the use of printed media. Face-to-face contacts were organized through party organizations, mainly by means of group discussions and instruction. This system was based on three concepts: first, of a *monopoly* (as far as possible) by the authorities of all means of communication: secondly, of *concentration*, on the belief that a message was more effective if it was simple and constantly repeated; and thirdly, of *reinforcement*, the use of all channels for the same message at the same time. The authors of the study suggest that the communication system that developed was more effective as a means of communication from the political authority to the people rather than vice versa. It is likely, however, that this was a function partly of the fact that Korea is and was a developing society and partly of the short period of the Communist occupation. The study none the less illustrates the methods used by a régime intent on securing control of the system of political communication in a society.[1]

The total control of political communication is, of course, one of the major characteristics of a totalitarian society, and political factors are therefore paramount in the development of the pattern of communication in such societies. In modern democracies the degree to which communication is subject to political control, is limited, and total control is neither one of their aims nor one of their characteristics. Political factors remain important, however. We have, for instance, already stressed the importance of face-to-face contacts in all communication systems, and modern democracies are no exception. Thus, much will depend on attitudes towards the dissemination and exchange of political information, as Almond and Verba showed in their five-nation study. They found that not only did the proportion of people who discussed politics vary from 76 per cent in the United States

---

[1] Wilbur Schramm and John W. Riley Jr, 'Communication in the Sovietized State, as Demonstrated in Korea', *American Sociological Review*, 16, 1951, pp. 757–66.

to 32 per cent in Italy (with Britain and West Germany approximating to the American position and Mexico to the Italian), but that there were considerable variations in the degree to which people in these countries felt free to discuss politics. Approximately a quarter of the American and a third of the British respondents did not feel free to discuss politics or felt free to do so with only a few people. Compared with this, more than half the German and Italian respondents and over two-fifths of the Mexican adopted these views.[1] Attitudes such as these are obviously of great relevance to the formation of public opinion, which is one of the major functions of a communication system.

THE FORMATION OF PUBLIC OPINION

We have already seen how totalitarian societies seek to control the communication system in order to control public opinion. Indeed, it is clear that the system itself, or particular parts of it, are deliberately developed to facilitate such control. Richard Fagen notes, for example, that the Committees for the Defence of the Revolution in Cuba were

> first formed by Castro in 1960 to act as a grass-roots defence against counter-revolution. Organized on a geographical basis, they soon became multi-purpose citizen groups used by the leadership for recruiting, administering, and proselytizing in the service of the revolution.[2]

Public opinion is, as the above quotation suggests, formed not in isolation, and is not only an integral part of the process of political communication, but also of the processes of socialization, participation and recruitment. Public opinion is closely involved in each process, because what people know (or think they know) and believe – their knowledge, values and attitudes – is a crucial factor in determining their political behaviour.

It is common to speak of public opinion as though it were massive and united, almost as if it were applicable only to one matter. Even where some division of opinion is acknowledged, it is usually thought to be in clearly-defined groups. In practice, of course, there are an infinite number of 'public opinions' on an infinite range of matters. It is true that on certain matters the

[1] Almond and Verba, *The Civic Culture*, pp. 79 and 83.
[2] Fagen, *Politics and Communication*, p. 34n.

overwhelming majority of people in a society may adhere to a common attitude and hold certain values in common, but that it is not to say that such near unanimity extends to all matters on which the public may have opinions. Thus there may be a general agreement about the 'arrangements of society', but it is less likely that such agreement will apply to matters which affect some individuals (or groups of individuals) and not others, which affect some more than others, and which affects some in one way and others in a different way. It is quite likely, therefore, that public opinion on any particular matter will be divided or, as Robert Lane and David Sears suggest, public opinion will have *direction*.[1] This means that some individuals will be in favour of a particular point of view, others against it. Others, of course, may be uncertain or prefer to qualify their opinion in some way. Various studies have shown, for instance, that the higher a person's level of education, the more likely he is to give a qualified answer to a question. Excluding those who have no view at all on a particular matter, most points of view may be seen on a 'pro-con' basis.

Direction is the fundamental characteristic of an opinion, since it indicates its basic form, but there are two other characteristics which indicate its importance. The first of these is the *intensity* with which the opinion is held. If an individual holds an opinion very strongly, he may be more likely to act upon it than another individual who holds the same opinion less strongly. This is especially important where an opinion is strongly held not just by a single individual but by a group of individuals.[2] Clearly the question of intensity is of importance in political participation in general and recruitment in particular.

The second important characteristic is closely related to intensity, but is also concerned with the relationship between the various opinions that an individual may hold. Since some of these opinions may be more important than others, it is possible to speak of the *salience* of particular opinions.[3] In the case of political behaviour, it is possible than an individual may regard his political opinions as paramount, and this may lead to a high level of participation.

[1] Robert E. Lane and David O. Sears, *Public Opinion*, Englewood Cliffs, N.J., 1964, pp. 6–9.
[2] ibid., pp. 9 and 94–113.
[3] ibid., pp. 15–16 and 78–81.

Saliency is also important, however, in considering another aspect of a person's opinions: the extent to which they may be regarded as consistent. A series of opinions may be inconsistent in either of two ways. First, a person may hold opinions that are to some degree contradictory, and secondly, particular opinions may be inconsistent with the knowledge that a person possesses. For example, 74 per cent of the respondents of a survey in California agreed with the view that the state university and colleges should be independent of the political control of the state governor and legislature, but 63 per cent of the respondents in the same survey also agreed that the 'tax-paying public' should have more say in the way the state university and college system was run (CAL, April 1967). While these views are not entirely contradictory, they are somewhat inconsistent in that the tax-paying public normally exercises the sort of control it appeared to be seeking through its elected office-holders. The relationship between salience and consistency is important, since it often offers an explanation of apparently contradictory attitudes. In April 1966, for instance, a survey in Britain found only 27 per cent of its respondents in favour of the nationalization of the steel industry (SOC, April 1966), yet, a month before, 'public opinion' had returned a Labour government pledged to nationalize steel. In fact, the questions put to the electorate in March 1966, and to the opinion poll respondents in April, received apparently contradictory answers not because of the lapse of time, but because one offered a choice of governments and the other a choice on a single policy. It may well have been that those who voted for the Labour party in 1966, but nevertheless opposed steel nationalization, were prepared to regard the latter as part of the price of Labour victory which they otherwise favoured, or else that they were unaware that it was part of that price.

It is, in fact, misleading to assume that, because people are willing to express opinions on various matters, thay are 'well-informed' or have 'sufficient' information on these subjects. Thus, in 1965, no less than 60 per cent of the respondents in an Italian poll said that they did not know how much Senators and Representatives in Italy were paid. Furthermore, the same proportion said that they had not heard that the pay of Senators and Representatives was a 'public issue'. None the less, nearly 90 per cent were prepared to express an opinion on the issue (DOXA, October

1965). Levels of knowledge may vary very considerably from one country to another, as a series of polls asking the same questions in Norway, Poland and France show (Table 35).

Table 35. *Levels of knowledge in Norway, Poland and France*

	Correct answers			Don't know/No answer		
	Norway	Poland	France	Norway	Poland	France
	%	%	%	%	%	%
Range	37–97	28–88	19–83	2–34	11–48	12–55
Median	73	64	47	14	25	43
Mean	70	61	50	16	29	36

SOURCE: VC, winter 1964–5.

The international survey summarized here asked the respondents in each country a series of *factual* questions on a wide range of political matters. They were asked whether they could name the location of the headquarters of the United Nations; to identify the Test-Ban Treaty; to say which of a series of named countries were members of NATO and the Warsaw Defence Pact; and to identify the political leaders of several countries. It is clear from the table that the highest proportion of correct answers and the lowest proportion of 'don't knows' came from Norway, and the lowest proportion of correct answers and the highest proportion of 'don't knows' from France. The level of knowledge not only varies considerably from one country to another, but, as the table shows, the actual amount of information possessed by an individual on a particular matter may be fairly limited. Thus, in France, as many as 22 per cent of the respondents did not know whether or not France was a member of NATO. But, as we have already pointed out, this does not necessarily prevent people from having and expressing *opinions* on matters of which they may have only limited knowledge. They may, of course, find it easier to hold opinions on some matters than others, as another international survey shows. In this instance respondents in eight countries were asked a series of political questions about whether they thought the power of the United States, the Soviet Union and Communist China would increase or decrease in 1967; and a series of questions asking them to estimate the economic prospects of their countries in 1967.

Table 36. *Level of 'don't knows' on matter of opinion*

	Political questions	Economic questions
	%	%
Range	14–64	3–42
Median	36	17
Mean	38	19

SOURCE: Gallup International, winter 1966–7.

As Table 36 shows, respondents found it easier or were more willing to answer the economic than the political questions: on all three political questions, the proportion of 'don't knows' was higher. Comparing the proportions of 'don't knows' in Tables 35 and 36 is difficult, since the questions and countries vary in the two surveys. None the less, it can be seen that on the whole the proportions of 'don't knows' were lower on factual questions than on political questions, and about the same on economic questions. It is important to bear in mind, however, that although the respondents in this second international survey were being asked their opinions, they were also being asked to make predictions of political and economic developments. This would make these questions almost 'factual' to many respondents and illustrates the closely-woven relationship between fact and opinion. Evidence from other studies shows that, as in the Italian case, informational levels are generally fairly low and 'more people are willing to report on what the government ought to be doing than are able to say what it is doing . . .'[1]

At the same time there is, for any particular opinion, a requisite level of information necessary for its formation. That some minimal point of contact is necessary is clear from an opinion poll in India which asked respondents their attitudes towards various countries: the proportions of 'don't knows' was much higher for countries like Japan, France, West Germany and the United Arab Republic than they were for the Soviet Union, the United States, Communist China and Britain (IIPO, January-February 1966). In this case the respondents found it easier to express opinions on countries with which India had had close contact (friendly or otherwise) than on those countries with which India's relations were more remote.

The whole question of levels of information and willingness to

[1] Lane and Sears, *Public Opinion*, p. 61.

hold opinions is part of the wider problem of *rationality* in the formation of public opinion.

> To be rational [Lane and Sears argue], a man must expose himself to congenial and uncongenial matters alike; he must be able to look at both and perceive them as they are, not merely as what he would like them to be, and he must be able to retain this information in undistorted form.[1]

A rational individual is thus open to information, is able to process it objectively and is able to assess effectively the relationship between his values and the information he receives. Some matters, such as those concerning religious, ethnic or ideological issues or matters involving personalities, are more liable to irrational pressures; while others, such as those based on economic or socio-economic differences, are more subject to rational pressures. Thus certain conditions are more likely to result in irrational responses – situations involving individuals with low social status or subject to poverty, or where there has been an undermining of traditional culture, or where there are problems of family stress, or where the individual is socially isolated, or where educational levels are low, are all examples of such conditions.[2] Much therefore depends upon the societal context and, as we have already argued in our chapter on political socialization, knowledge, values and attitudes are determined by the interaction between social environment and the individual. Public opinion, all opinion, results from the influence of face-to-face contacts and the mass media: from the influence of parents, education, peer groups, work and leisure groups, and opinion leaders on the one hand, and from the influence of newspapers and other printed media, and the broadcasting media on the other. Not all these influences are of equal importance, of course, and much will depend on the *evaluation* of each by the individual.

There is, for example, a good deal of opinion-poll evidence on people's evaluation of the mass media, which, as Table 30 shows, are the main source of information for most people. A Dutch poll found in 1966 that 75 per cent of their respondents regarded newspapers and magazines as giving an accurate or generally accurate picture of events in the Netherlands, but only 56 per cent agreed that this was the case with television (ATTS, August-September 1966). In Norway two-thirds of the respondents in a

[1] ibid., p. 73.   [2] See ibid., Chapter 7.

similar poll said that the newspapers were 'mostly correct' in their reports (PRIO, November-December 1964), but in France only 33 per cent of the respondents agreed that the state-controlled television network (O.R.T.F.) was impartial (IFOP, November 1965). The problem of source evaluation takes on immense proportions during time of national crisis, as the Vietnam war has forcibly demonstrated in the United States. A poll conducted in Minnesota found that 43 per cent of its respondents felt that the mass media were giving an 'honest picture of what is going on in Vietnam', while 47 per cent disagreed, leaving 10 per cent who were uncertain. The reasons why people felt that they were not getting an 'honest picture' were, however, very varied: 35 per cent thought that news was being held back or that war news was inevitably inaccurate; 18 per cent thought that the government was controlling the dissemination of news (possibly for security reasons); 8 per cent said that the true situation was being hidden to avoid public alarm and panic (MINN, September 1966). Thus, even though a substantial minority of these respondents agreed that their news of Vietnam was distorted, they were less united on why this was so. Lack of faith in the mass media or particular sections of it will result either in a low level of information, because the individual ignores this source, or in distorted information, because the individual relies more heavily than usual on his interpretation of the information. In some cases the process may rely very heavily on interpretation or 'reading between the lines' in the manner of the 'Kremlinologist' or 'Pekinologist'.

The question of evaluation, however, applies not only to the audience in its evaluation of the source, but also to the source in its evaluation of the audience. This is particularly the case in political communication, since messages are so frequently calculated to achieve a particular effect. The political leader endeavours to formulate, deliver and address his messages in the manner, at the time and to the audience which will achieve the greatest impact, but in so doing he makes certain assumptions about his message, his audience, his channel of communication, and himself as the source of the message. He assumes that his audience will wish to hear or can be persuaded to listen to his message. Thus, should his message be unpleasant, he assumes that his audience will regard him sufficiently highly as a source to overcome their distaste for it. He assumes that he has chosen the most effective channel of communication and that he will reach his proposed audience, and he assumes that the moment is propitious for the delivery of his message. Often of greatest importance, however, is the relationship between these various assumptions and the changing of public opinion.

The influence of political leaders is not, of course, the only means by which public opinion may change. Indeed, as we suggested in Chapter 2, knowledge, values and attitudes change in response to a great variety of factors. The role of leaders in such change, however, illustrates one of the crucial characteristics of public opinion, that it is both subject to change and a factor in change:

> Public opinion places considerable restraint upon the ability of a leader successfully to advocate important measures which do not accord in some degree with public opinion. Even the most prestigious public figures cannot achieve general opinion change in the face of significant opposition President Roosevelt could not 'pack' the Supreme Court, popular as he was, and Woodrow Wilson was unable to get the United States into the League of Nations. . . . Many an important public figure has fallen from power because he advocated too radical a change, and was himself devaluated by the voters.[1]

The way in which opinion can change in response to events is well illustrated by changing attitudes in India towards Britain and the Soviet Union. Before the war in 1965 between India and Pakistan, 63 per cent of the respondents in a survey of urban centres in India described their attitude towards Britain as 'good' or 'very good', compared with 80 per cent for the Soviet Union. Following the Tashkent talks, in which Russia successfully mediated between the two sides, there was a dramatic change in attitudes towards Britain: only 25 per cent of the respondents now regarded Britain (which had officially adopted a neutral stance during the war) as 'good' or 'very good', 24 per cent regarding Britain as 'bad' or 'very bad'. The change in attitudes towards the Soviet Union was relatively small, but after the Tashkent talks 90 per cent regarded Russia as 'good' or 'very good' and no respondent placed Russia in the two categories of disapproval (IIPO, January-February 1966).

Change in public opinion depends on two factors: firstly, upon the amount of resistance to change that exists, and secondly, on the evaluation of the source or sources of information on which

[1] ibid., pp. 49–50.

the opinion is based. Clearly resistance to change is dependent upon the intensity and salience of opinions: the more strongly opinions are held and the more important they are among the whole range of opinions held by an individual, the less likely is some change of opinion. Similarly, the greater the faith of the individual in the source of information the greater the significance this may have on the likelihood of a change of attitude. It is important to appreciate, however, that faith in a source may be a factor to encourage as much as to discourage change. Resistance to change may be overcome because the source is trusted, and it is on such trust that many political leaders pin their hopes of effecting widespread societal reform. Whether the vehicle and motivating force in such change is a leader, a party or an ideology, its ultimate success depends upon the establishment of a sufficient degree of trust (unless change is, of course, effected by force). This is not to suggest that change may be initiated only from above, although the opportunity for taking such initiative is obviously greater for those holding some sort of formal office. In practice, initiative for change may be taken by those who hold no formal office and who have hitherto been politically inactive. Indeed, the formation of public opinion frequently leads to such initiative, since strongly held opinions may be the decisive factor leading to some form of political participation. It may, for instance, be a factor in the use of violence to effect change, or, as we noted in Chapter 4 in Kenneth Prewitt's study, in the recruitment of state legislators and city councillors in the United States, to take a more specific example.[1] Furthermore, the fact that an opinion is widely held, perhaps by a majority of people, is clearly of importance (regardless of the political system), but this is generally likely to be a reflex factor, a factor of importance not so much in the taking of an initiative but as a reaction to it. It does matter how many people hold an opinion, but it probably matters more *who* these people are. Whatever democratic theory might suggest, the opinions of the prime minister or the president are normally more important than those of the solitary voter; and even at election time the solitary voter is of significance only in combination with his fellow voters – most especially in a marginal situation.

Even so, important as the opinions of certain individuals in a

[1] See p. 158 above.

particular society may be, their level of information may only be marginally greater than that of less important persons, while the degree to which their opinions are rational is not necessarily a function of their importance. Information in any context, but especially in a political context, is seldom 'pure', and in the realm of public opinion it can hardly be expected that it should be. Information, in this sense, means not only the 'facts about a situation', but also 'facts about other people's opinions'. Moreover, the nature and the amount of information received varies considerably from individual to individual, and in each case it must be sifted through the individual's perceptual screen. The result is that each individual has a personalized view of each item of information and develops his opinions accordingly. It is not therefore, surprising to find, as Bernard Cohen did in a study of the development of attitudes towards the peace treaty between the United States and Japan, that 'members of the Executive and Congress received somewhat different images of "public opinion" on the treaty, because different groups and individuals communicated different things to them at different times.'[1] These people received different images, not only because their information, the sources of that information and the times when they received it varied, but also because it is likely that there were existing variations in their perceptual screens – in their knowledge, values and attitudes. We suggested in Chapter 2 that these basic orientations regarding their knowledge, values and attitudes were acquired through the process of political socialization. We also argued, however, that these orientations were subject to possible change under the impact of an individual's experience and that political socialization was a continuous process applicable not only to childhood and adolescence, but also to adult life. If this is so, then changes in particular attitudes or opinions may be accounted for by the same process – by the constant resifting of knowledge, values and attitudes under the impact of experience.

The role of political communication in this process is that of catalyst in that it provides the dynamic element – the means by which politically relevant information reaches the individual and shapes his political orientations. These orientations, which are by no means immutable, may lead in turn to varying degrees of

[1] Bernard C. Cohen, 'Political Communication and the Japanese Peace Settlement', *Public Opinion Quarterly*, **20**, 1956, p. 27.

political participation and ultimately to the holding of political office, and therefore to the consideration of political recruitment: in each of these processes political communication plays its part, but most of all in the process of political, social and economic change. We would therefore agree with Lane and Sears when they assert that 'a political system is shaped and guided by two things: what its members believe, and the way they learn and change their beliefs.'[1]

[1] Lane and Sears, *Public Opinion*, p. 114.

6 · Conclusion

We defined political sociology in Chapter 1 as the examination of the links between politics and society, between social structures and political structures, and between social behaviour and political behaviour; and in discussing its development and the approaches and methods appropriate to its study, we touched upon the problems of objectivity and the study of values and ideas in political behaviour. These are, of course, problems common to the whole of social science – the extent to which its practitioners can be objective in their studies and whether values are of legitimate concern to them. The behavioural approach in particular stresses the need to separate facts from values, though it does not necessarily hold that the latter should be ignored.

The concepts of political socialization and political communication, as we have defined them, are concerned with values, in that they are closely involved with the political behaviour of the individual. No one acts in complete isolation of values, although their existence may not be recognized and may be denied in particular cases. Similarly, a set of values may form a coherent pattern based on a rational process of thought, or appear to be a jumbled mass of contradictory or unconnected reactions to various phenomena. It may, moreover, be difficult, perhaps impossible, to establish any firm or significant relationship between values on, say, political matters on the one hand, and those on economic matters on the other. In a study of the relationship between personal values and political attitudes, for example, Brewster Smith found a correlation between holding *liberty* as a value and concern about the policies of the Soviet Union, but there was no significant relationship between holding *economic security* as a value and attitudes towards the Soviet Union. In 1947, at least, when this survey was conducted, it appeared that attitudes towards Russia in the United States were part of a democratic-totalitarian syndrome rather than an economic syndrome. Smith also found that those respondents holding liberty as a value generally had broad interests and were likely to be active in community affairs, whereas those holding economic security as a value generally had narrower interests and were less likely to be active in community affairs.[1] The political sociologist is therefore deeply concerned with the values held by individuals, with the way in which they are acquired and the way in which they change, since values hold the key to political behaviour; and the problems of studying values in no way lessens that concern.

Political participation and political recruitment can be analysed in terms of the social and other characteristics of the persons involved, but they can only be explained in terms of the values held by those persons. Quite apart from the relative ease with which data on the characteristics of people can be obtained, compared with data on their values, studies of social behaviour suggest that there is often a link between particular characteristics and particular values. Such a link is not necessarily causal, but merely suggests that individuals with certain characteristics are more likely than those with different characteristics to hold certain values. It may well be, of course, that the characteristic concerned, whatever its causal significance, suggests a useful hypothesis to explain the link. In this sense the concern of the political sociologist is primarily with the particular values of the individual or those of groups of individuals.

Values are also important, however, in the form of ideologies, since the development of related values into a consistent or relatively consistent pattern has been, and remains, a powerful force in social and, more especially, political behaviour:

> At the present day, we are better able to recognize the important role of ideologies in social change, because we have the experience of the achievements of Marxism . . . as an ideology which powerfully assists rapid industrialization, and on the other hand, of the retarding influence of traditional creeds in such underdeveloped countries as India.[2]

[1] M. Brewster Smith, 'Personal Values as Determinants of a Political Attitude', *Journal of Psychology*, **28**, 1949, pp. 477–86.

[2] Bottomore, *Élites and Society*, p. 28.

The two examples suggested by Bottomore of the role that ideology can play can, of course, be supplemented by many more, and the very names of many political parties and movements are a convincing testimony of the role of ideas in political behaviour. The very example of political parties, however, serves as a reminder that ideologies and ideas do not function in a vacuum. The relationship between an ideology and the political party which claims to adhere to it is seldom simple: not only may the ideology be silent on many matters, but also, like the party which is its vehicle, it is often subject to change. Such changes are often subtle and difficult to detect, and may even be denied by pro-ponent and opponent alike. Where they are detected they may be subject to exaggeration out of all proportion to the change as the full force of ideological conflict exerts itself. The periodic clashes between left and right in the British Labour party, the brief triumph of the Goldwater forces in the American Republican party in 1964, the conflict between pro-Chinese and pro-Russian elements within various Communist parties and within the world Communist movement, and the formation of the Democratic Labour party in Australia after a split in the A.L.P., are all examples of such conflicts. Where there is little apparent conflict to emphasize ideological commitments it may be more difficult to discern the influence of ideas, and even the names of parties may be confusing: thus it has been suggested that the French Radical Socialist party is neither radical nor Socialist, and the Canadian Progressive Conservative party is neither progressive nor con-servative, while many observers have experienced difficulty in finding any ideological distinction between the Republican and Democratic parties in the United States. The very fact, however, that parties (and other social and political institutions) claim to adhere to particular values or a particular ideology, and that their members (or some of them) believe in them, is of considerable importance in itself. It also illustrates, as Crick points out, that

institutions are the framework of political behaviour and must be studied as the 'institutionalization' of particular styles of politics and social aspirations; political ideas are then the theories and doctrines about how institutions are, can and should be worked.[1]

[1] Crick, 'The Tendency of Political Studies', p. 683.

The political sociologist is thus concerned with the relationship between political institutions and values, with how institutions are shaped by values and how values are shaped by institutions in a reciprocal process of change. Some of the relationships between particular political institutions and values are not difficult to see. For example, a relationship between the British Parliament and the value of liberty as expressed in certain legislation is apparent; while a relationship between the values held by party leaders in Communist-controlled countries and the political institutions that have been established is clear enough. In most cases, however, the relationship is less clear and is extremely complex, especially where institutions have become, on the one hand, semi-independent, developing a life of their own, and on the other, inextricably linked to certain values and to other institutions, so that a complicated process of interaction results. It is at this stage that the problem of values becomes crucial to the political sociologist and to the social scientist generally.

Not only may ideas and ideologies influence political behaviour, but, as Bottomore argues, '. . . every sociological concept and theory has an ideological force by reason of its influence upon the thoughts and actions of men in their everyday life'.[1] The political sociologist is no exception to this rule, and it may be seriously questioned whether objective inquiry in social science is possible. It may, therefore, be necessary to agree with another writer on the subject, 'that it is in the nature of social science that it may be influenced in its methods and results by the character of the observer'.[2]

The two founding fathers of political sociology, Marx and Weber, both believed that they practised a value-free social science, although Weber recognized the importance of values. The standard has since been taken up by the advocates of the behavioural approach to the study of social phenomena. The criticism has not been effectively answered, however, and the problem remains. The fact that the problem is acknowledged rather than ignored is in itself important, and we may agree with Runciman when he suggests that

[1] Bottomore, *Élites and Society*, p. 20.
[2] Leon Bramson, *The Political Context of Sociology*, Princeton, N.J., 1961, p. 152.

... political sociology – that is, an explanation or set of explanations of political behaviour – must depend for its vocabulary on some kind of philosophical position. This derives directly from the fact that the social sciences deal with actions and not events. It does not . . . require us to abandon all notions of scientific method in sociological enquiry; [and though it may be that] complete scientism is unattainable . . . it is nevertheless worth trying.[1]

THE ROLE OF POLITICAL SOCIOLOGY

Our definition of political sociology suggests its principal role – to explain the connection between social and political phenomena. In order to fulfil this role, however, it is necessary to develop theories and methods which will link the social sciences together, particularly sociology and political science. The four concepts which we have defined and discussed in the earlier chapters are an attempt to contribute to the task of developing political sociology as a theoretical and methodological link between sociology and political science. In dealing with each concept, we have endeavoured to draw our examples from as wide a field as possible (while maintaining a degree of continuity to illustrate the way in which the concepts are linked), so as to demonstrate not only the wealth of material available and the need for its systematic treatment, but also to show that political sociology has no inherent ideological commitment, despite our earlier discussion of values. Those values which influence its use are those of the observer, and they therefore vary from observer to observer. It also follows that political sociology is as relevant to the study of political behaviour in the United States or Britain as it is to the study of political behaviour in Ghana or Indonesia, Russia or China. Thus to argue, as some observers have done, that political sociology involves 'a political commitment to the values of democratic institutions',[2] and that its main task is 'the study of the social conditions of democracy as a social system',[3] is unreasonable as well as placing unacceptable limits on political sociology. While

[1] Runciman, *Social Science and Political Theory*, pp. 16 and 66.
[2] Reinhard Bendix and S. M. Lipset, 'Political Sociology', *Current Sociology*, 6, 1957, p. 81.
[3] S. M. Lipset, 'Political Sociology', in R. K. Merton, L. Brown and L. S. Cottrell Jr (eds.), *Sociology Today*, New York, 1959, p. 108.

political sociology has thrown considerable light on the conditions under which democracy is likely to flourish and has done much to illuminate the democratic process, we believe there is sufficient evidence in this book to support the view that political sociology is methodologically applicable to the study of *any* political system.

How far it is possible at present to apply political sociology to *any* political system is a different matter, but this is because

> . . . the establishment of political sociology as a real interdisciplinary approach, as a balanced cross-fertilization, between sociologists and political scientists, is more a task for the future than a current achievement.[1]

This book seeks to contribute to that task.

[1] Sartori, 'From the Sociology of Politics to Political Sociology', p. 200.

Bibliography

GENERAL

Almond, Gabriel A. and Coleman, James S. (eds.), *The Politics of the Developing Areas*, Princeton, 1960.

Almond, Gabriel A. and Powell, G. Bingham, *Comparative Politics: A Developmental Approach*, Boston, 1966.

Almond, Gabriel A. and Verba, Sidney, *The Civic Culture*, Princeton, 1963.

Bendix, Rheinhard and Lipset, Seymour M., 'Political Sociology', *Current Sociology*, 6, 1957, pp. 79–98.

Bramson, Leon, *The Political Context of Sociology*, Princeton, 1961.

Crick, Bernard, *The American Science of Politics*, London, 1959.

Crick, Bernard, *In Defence of Politics*, London, 1962.

Crick, Bernard, 'The Tendency of Political Studies', *New Society*, 3 November, 1966, pp. 681–3.

Dahl, Robert A., *Who Governs? Democracy and Power in an American City*, New Haven, 1961.

Easton, David, *The Political System*, New York, 1953.

Easton, David, *A Framework for Political Analysis*, Englewood Cliffs, New Jersey, 1965.

Easton, David, *A Systems Analysis of Political Life*, New York, 1965.

Herbele, Rudolf, *Social Movements: An Introduction to Political Sociology*, New York, 1951.

Inkeles, Alex, *What is Sociology?*, Englewood Cliffs, New Jersey, 1964.

Janowitz, Morris, 'Political Sociology', in the *International Encyclopedia of Social Science*, New York, 1968, Vol. 12, pp. 298–307.

Johnson, Harry M., *Sociology: A Systematic Introduction*, London, 1961.

Kornhauser, W., *The Politics of the Mass Society*, London, 1959.

Lasswell, Harold D., *Politics: Who Gets What, When and How*, New York, 1936.

Lasswell, Harold D., and Kaplan, A., *Power and Society: A Framework for Political Inquiry*, New Haven, 1950.

Lipset, Seymour M., *Political Man*, Garden City, New York, 1960.

Lipset, Seymour M., *The First New Nation*, London, 1963.

Lipset, Seymour M., 'Political Sociology' in Merton, Robert K., Brown, L. and Cottrell, Leonard S. Jr (eds.), *Sociology Today*, New York, 1959, pp. 81–114.

Mackenzie, W. J. M., *Politics and Social Science*, London, 1967.

Michels, Robert, *First Lectures in Political Sociology*, trans. de Grazia, Alfred, Minneapolis, 1949.

Runciman, W. G., *Social Science and Political Theory*, London, 1965.

Sartori, G., 'From the Sociology of Politics to Political Sociology', *Government and Opposition*, 4, 1969, pp. 194–214.

Weber, Max, *From Max Weber: Essays in Sociology*, trans. and ed. H. H. Gerth and C. Wright Mills, London, 1948.

Weber, Max, *Theory of Social and Economic Organization*, trans. A. M. Henderson and ed. Talcott Parsons, New York, 1947.

Young, Oran R., *Systems of Political Science*, Englewood Cliffs, New Jersey, 1968.

POLITICAL SOCIALIZATION

Aberle, David F., 'Culture and Socialization' in Hsu, Francis L. K. (ed.), *Psychological Anthropology: Approaches to Culture and Personality*, Homewood, Illinois, 1961.

Adorno, T. W., Frenkel-Brunswik, Else, Levinson, Daniel J., and Sandford, R. N., *The Authoritarian Personality*, New York, 1950.

Apter, David E., 'Political Religion in the New Nations', in Geertz, Clifford (ed.), *Old Societies and New States*, New York, 1963, pp. 57–104.

Argyle, M. and Delin, P., 'Non-Universal Laws of Socialization', *Human Relations*, 18, 1965, pp. 77–85.

Bar-Yoseph, Rivkak, 'The Pattern of Early Socialization in the Collective Settlements of Israel', *Human Relations*, 12, 1959, pp. 345–60.

Benedict, Ruth, *The Chrysanthemum and the Sword*, Boston, 1946.

Child, Irvin L., 'Socialization' in Lindzey, G. (ed.), *Handbook of Social Psychology*, Cambridge, Mass., 1954, Vol. 2, pp. 655–92.

Coleman, James S. (ed.), *Education and Political Development*, Princeton, 1965.

Converse, Philip and Dupeux, Georges, 'Politicization of the Electorate in France and the United States', *Public Opinion Quarterly*, 26, 1962, pp. 1–23.

Davies, James C., 'The Family's Role in Political Socialization', *Annals of the American Academy of Political and Social Science*, 361, September. 1965, pp. 10–19.

Dawson, Richard E. and Prewitt, Kenneth, *Political Socialization: An Analytic Study*, Boston, 1969.

Dicks, H. V., 'Personality Traits and National Socialist Ideology', *Human Relations*, 3, 1950, pp. 111–54.

Easton, David, 'The Theoretical Relevance of Political Socialization', *Canadian Journal of Political Science*, 1, 1968, pp. 125–46.

Easton, David and Hess, Robert D., 'The Child's Political World', *Mid-West Journal of Political Science*, 6, 1962, pp. 229–46.

Easton, David and Hess, Robert D., 'The Child's Changing Image of the President', *Public Opinion Quarterly*, 24, 1960, pp. 623–44.

Easton, David and Dennis, Jack, 'The Child's Acquisition of Régime, Norms: Political Efficacy', *American Political Science Review*, 61, 1967, pp. 25–38.

Easton, David and Dennis, Jack, *Children in the Political System: Origins of Political Legitimacy*, New York, 1969.

Eisenstadt, S. N., *From Generation to Generation*, London, 1956.

Estvan, Frank and Elizabeth, *The Child's World*, New York, 1959.

Eysenck, H. J., *The Psychology of Politics*, London, 1954.

Froman, L. A., 'Personality and Political Socialization', *Journal of Politics*, 23, 1961, pp. 341–52.

Fromm, Erich, *Escape from Freedom*, New York, 1941.

Geiger, Kent, 'Changing Political Attitudes in Totalitarian Society: A Case-Study of the Role of the Family', *World Politics*, 8, 1955–6, pp. 187–205.

Goldrich, Daniel and Scott, Edward W., 'Developing Political Orientations of Panamanian Students', *Journal of Politics*, 23, 1961, pp. 84–105.

Greenstein, Fred I., *Children in Politics*, New Haven, 1965.

Greenstein, Fred I., 'Personality and Political Socialization: the Theories of the Authoritarian and Democratic Character', *Annals of the American Academy of Political and Social Science*, 361, September 1965, pp. 81–95.

Greenstein, Fred I., 'Political Socialization' in the *International Encyclopedia of Social Science*, New York, 1968, Vol. 14, pp. 551–5.

Greenstein, Fred I. and Wolfinger, Raymond E., 'The Suburbs and Shifting Party Loyalties', *Public Opinion Quarterly*, 22, 1958, pp. 473–82.

Hyman, Herbert, *Political Socialization: A Study in the Psychology of Political Behaviour*, Glencoe, Illinois, 1959.

Iisager, Holger, 'Factors Influencing the Formation and Change of Political and Religious Attitudes', *Journal of Social Psychology*, 29, 1949, pp. 253–65.

Inkeles, Alex, 'National Character and Modern Political Systems' in Hsu, Francis L. K. (ed.), *Psychological Anthropology: Approaches to Culture and Personality*, Homewood, Illinois, 1961.

Inkeles, Alex, *Public Opinion in Soviet Russia: A Study in Mass Persuasion*, Cambridge, Mass., 1958.

Inkeles, Alex, 'Social Change and Social Character: the Role of Parental Mediation', *Journal of Social Issues*, 11, 1955, pp. 12–13.

Jennings, M. Kent, 'Pre-Adult Orientations to Multiple Systems of Government', *Midwest Journal of Political Science*, 11, 1967, pp. 291–317.

Jennings, M. Kent and Niemi, R. G., 'The Transmission of Political Values from Parent to Child', *American Political Science Review*, 62, 1968, pp. 169–84.

Jaros, D., Hirsch, H. and Fleron, F. J., 'The Malevolent Leader: Political Socialization in an American Sub-Culture', *American Political Science Review*, 62, 1968, pp. 564–75.

Koff, David and van der Muhl, George, 'Political Socialization in Kenya and Tanzania: A Comparative Analysis', *Journal of Modern African Studies*, 5, 1967, pp. 13–51.

Kuroda, Yasamusa, 'Agencies of Political Socialization and Political Change: the Political Orientations of Japanese Law Students', *Human Organization*, 24, 1965, pp. 328–31.

Lane, Robert E., *Political Ideology: Why the American Common Man Believes What He Does*, New York, 1962.

Lane, Robert E., 'The Need to be Liked and the Anxious College Liberal',

Annals of the American Academy of Political and Social Science, 361, September 1965, pp. 71–80.

Langton, Kenneth P., 'Political Partisanship and Political Socialization in Jamaica', *British Journal of Sociology*, 17, 1966, pp. 419–29.

Langton, Kenneth P., 'Peer Group and School and the Socialization Process', *American Political Science Review*, 61, 1967, pp. 751–8.

Langton, Kenneth P. and Jennings, M. Kent, 'Political Socialization and the High School Civics Curriculum in the United States', *American Political Science Review*, 62, 1968, pp. 852–67.

Lasswell, Harold D., *Power and Personality*, New York, 1948.

Levin, Martin L., 'Social Climates and Political Socialization', *Public Opinion Quarterly*, 25, 1961, pp. 596–606.

Le Vine, Robert, 'The Internalization of Political Values in Stateless Societies', *Human Organization*, 19, 1960, pp. 51–8.

Le Vine, Robert, 'Political Socialization and Culture Change' in Geertz, Clifford (ed.), *Old Societies and New States*, New York, 1963, pp. 280–303.

Lipsitz, Lewis, 'Work Life and Political Attitudes: A Study of Manual Workers', *American Political Science Review*, 58, 1964, pp. 951–62.

Litt, Edgar, 'Education and Political Enlightenment in America', *Annals of the American Academy of Political and Social Science*, 361, Sept., 1965, pp. 32–9.

McClintock, Charles G. and Turner, Henry A., 'The Impact of College upon Political Knowledge, Participation and Values', *Human Relations*, 15, 1962, pp. 163–75.

McClosky, Herbert and Dahlgren, Harold E., 'Primary Group Influence on Party Loyalty', *American Political Science Review*, 53, 1959, pp. 757–76.

Maccoby, Eleanor E., Matthews, Richard E. and Morton, Anton S., 'Youth and Political Change', *Public Opinion Quarterly*, 18, 1954, pp. 533–6.

Mann, Erika, *School for Barbarians: Education under the Nazis*, London, 1939.

Murphy, Raymond J. and Morris, Richard J., 'Occupational Situation, Subjective Class Identification and Political Affiliation', *American Sociological Review*, 26, 1961, pp. 383–92.

Nogee, Philip and Levin, Murray B., 'Some Determinants of Political Attitudes among College Voters', *Public Opinion Quarterly*, 22, 1958, pp. 449–63.

Oakeshott, Michael, 'Political Education', in Laslett, P. (ed.), *Philosophy, Politics and Society*, Oxford, 1956, pp. 1–21.

Orren, Karen and Peterson, Paul, 'Presidential Assassination: A Case-Study of the Dynamics of Political Socialization', *Journal of Politics*, 29, 1967, pp. 388–404.

Pethybridge, Roger, 'The Assessment of Ideological Influence on East Europeans', *Public Opinion Quarterly*, 21, 1967, pp. 38–50.

Prewitt, Kenneth, Eulau, Heinz, and Zisk, Betty H., 'Political Socialization and Political Roles', *Public Opinion Quarterly*, 30, 1966, pp. 569–82.

Reading, R., 'Political Socialization in Colombia and the United States', *Midwest Journal of Political Science*, 12, 1968, pp. 352–81.

Riesman, David, *The Lonely Crowd*, New Haven, 1950.

Sigel, Roberta S., 'Some Explorations into Political Socialization: Children's Reactions to the Death of a President', in Wolfenstein, Martha and Kliman, Gilbert (ed.), *Children and the Death of a President*, New York, 1965, pp. 30–61.

Singham, A. W., 'The Political Socialization of Marginal Groups', *International Journal of Comparative Sociology*, 8, 1967, pp. 182–98.

Skrzypek, Stanislaw, 'The Political, Cultural and Social Views of Yugoslav Youth', *Public Opinion Quarterly*, 29, 1965, pp. 87–106.

Szyliowicz, Joseph S., 'Political Participation and Modernization in Turkey', *Western Political Quarterly*, 19, 1966, pp. 166–84.

Tannenbaum, P. H. and McLeod, T. M., 'On the Measurement of Socialization', *Public Opinion Quarterly*, 31, 1967, pp. 27–37.

POLITICAL PARTICIPATION

Abrams, Mark, 'Social Trends and Electoral Behaviour', *British Journal of Sociology*, 13, 1962, pp. 228–42.

Agger, Robert E., Goldstein, Marshal N. and Pearl, Stanley A., 'Political Cynicism: Measurement and Meaning', *Journal of Politics*, 23, 1961, pp. 477–506.

Alford, Robert R., *Party and Society*, Chicago, 1963.

Almond, Gabriel A. and Verba, Sidney, *The Civic Culture*, Princeton, 1963.

Barnes, Samuel H., 'Participation, Education and Political Competence: Evidence from a Sample of Italian Socialists', *American Political Science Review*, 60, 1966, pp. 348–53.

Bauer, Raymond A., 'Some Trends in Sources of Alienation from the Soviet System', *Public Opinion Quarterly*, 19, 1955, pp. 279–91.

Bowman, Lewis and Boynton, G. R., 'Recruitment Patterns among Local Party Officials: A Model and Some Preliminary Findings', *American Political Science Review*, 60, 1966, pp. 667–76.

Brass, P. R., 'Political Participation, Institutionalization and Stability in India', *Government and Opposition*, 4, 1968, pp. 23–53.

Butler, David E. and Stokes, Donald E., *Political Change in Britain*, London, 1969.

Campbell, Angus, Gurin, Gerald and Miller, Warren E., *The Voter Decides*, Evanston, Illinois, 1954.

Campbell, Angus, Converse, Philip E., Miller, Warren E., and Stokes, Donald E., *The American Voter*, New York, 1960.

Erbe, William, 'Social Involvement and Political Activity', *American Sociological Review*, 29, 1964, pp. 198–215.

Gleitman, Henry and Greenbaum, Joseph, T., 'Hungarian Socio-Political Attitudes and Revolutionary Action', *Public Opinion Quarterly*, 24, 1960, pp. 62–76.

Katz, Fred E. and Piret, Fern V., 'Circuitous Participation in Politics', *American Journal of Sociology*, 69, 1964, pp. 367–73.

Key, Jr, V. O., *Politics, Parties and Pressure Groups* (5th edition), New York, 1964.

Key, Jr, V. O., *Public Opinion and American Democracy*, New York, 1961.

Lane, Robert E., *Political Life: Why People Get Involved in Politics*, Glencoe, Illinois, 1959.

Levinson, Daniel J., 'The Relevance of Personality for Political Participation', *Public Opinion Quarterly*, 22, 1958, pp. 3–10.

Lindenfeld, Frank, 'Economic Interest and Political Involvement', *Public Opinion Quarterly*, 28, 1964, pp. 104–11.

Lipset, Seymour M., *Political Man*, Garden City, New York, 1960.

Lipset, Seymour M., Lazarsfeld, Paul F., Barton, Allen H. and Linz, Juan, 'The Psychology of Voting: An Analysis of Political Behaviour', in Lindzey, G. (ed.), *A Handbook of Social Psychology*, Vol. 2, New York, 1954, pp. 1124–75.

Lipset, Seymour M. and Rokkan, Stein (eds.), *Party Systems and Voter Alignments*, New York, 1967.

Litt, Edgar, 'Political Cynicism and Political Futility', *Journal of Politics*, 25, 1963, pp. 312–23.

McClosky, Herbert, 'Political Participation', in the *International Encyclopedia of Social Science*, New York, 1968, Vol. 12, pp. 252–65.

Maccoby, Herbert, 'The Differential Political Activity of Participants in a Voluntary Association', *American Sociological Review*, 23, 1958, pp. 524–32.

McKenzie, Robert T. and Silver, Allan, *Angels in Marble*, London, 1968.

Milbrath, Lester W., *Political Participation: How and Why Do People Get Involved in Politics?*, Chicago, 1965.

Mussen, Paul H. and Wyszynski, Anne B., 'Personality and Political Participation', *Human Relations*, 5, 1952, pp. 65–82.

Nordlinger, Eric, *Working Class Tories*, London, 1967.

Olson, Marvin E., 'Alienation and Political Opinion', *Public Opinion Quarterly*, 29, 1965, pp. 200–12.

Rokkan, Stein (ed.), 'Approaches to the Study of Political Participation', *Acta Sociologica*, 6, No. 1–2, 1962.

Rokkan, Stein, 'The Comparative Study of Political Participation', in Ranney, Austin, *Essays on the Behavioural Study of Politics*, Urbana, Illinois, 1962.

Rose, Arnold M., 'Alienation and Participation: A Comparison of Group Leaders and the "Mass"', *American Sociological Review*, 27, 1962, pp. 834–8.

Rosenberg, Morris, 'Some Determinants of Political Apathy', *Public Opinion Quarterly*, 18, 1954, pp. 349–66.

Srole, Leo, 'Social Integration and Certain Corrollaries: An Exploratory Study', *American Sociological Review*, 21, 1956, pp. 709–16.

Stokes, Donald E., Campbell, Angus and Miller, Warren E., 'The Components of Electoral Decision', *American Political Science Review*, 52, 1958, pp. 367–87.

Townsend, James R., *Political Participation in Communist China*, Los Angeles, 1967.

Truman, David B., *The Governmental Process*, New York, 1951.

Wright, C. R. and Hyman, Herbert H., 'Voluntary Association Memberships of American Adults: Evidence from National Sample Surveys', *American Sociological Reviews*, 23, 1958, pp. 284–94.

POLITICAL RECRUITMENT

Barber, J. D., *The Lawmakers: Recruitment and Adaptation to Legislative Life*, New Haven, 1965.

Beck, Carl, 'Party Control and Bureaucratization in Czechoslovakia', *Journal of Politics*, 23, 1961, pp. 279–94.

Bottomore, T. B., *Elites and Society*, London, 1964.

Bottomore, T. B., *Classes in Modern Society*, London, 1965.

Buck, Philip W., *Amateurs and Professionals in British Politics*, 1918–59, Chicago, 1963.

Burnham, James, *The Managerial Revolution*, New York, 1941.

The Civil Service (The Fulton Report), Cmd. 3683, HMSO, London, 1968.

Downs, Anthony, 'A Theory of Bureaucracy', *American Economic Review*, Papers and Proceedings of the American Economic Association, 55, 1965, pp. 439–46.

Diament, Alfred, 'A Case-Study of Administrative Autonomy: Controls and Tensions in French Administration', *Political Studies*, 6, 1958, pp. 147–66.

Edinger, Lewis J., 'Post-Totalitarian Leadership in Élites in the German Federal Republic', *American Political Science Review*, 54, 1960, pp. 58–82.

Epstein, Leon, *Parties in Western Democracies*, New York, 1967.

Eulau, Heinz and Sprague, John, *Lawyers in Politics: A Study in Professional Convergence*, Indianapolis, 1964.

Frank, Elke, 'The Role of Bureaucracy in Transition', *Journal of Politics*, 28, 1966, pp. 725–53.

Guttsman, W. L., *The British Political Élite*, London, 1963.

Harris, Richard L., 'The Role of the Civil Service in West Africa', *Public Administration Review*, 25, 1965, pp. 308–13.

Kallen, Arthur D., 'Training in the Federal Civil Service – 170 Years to Accept', *Public Administration Review*, 19, 1959, pp. 36–46.

Kim, Young C., 'Political Recruitment: the Case of Japanese Prefectural Assemblymen', *American Political Science Review*, 61, 1967, pp. 1036–52.

Knight, Maxwell, *The German Executive*, 1890–1933, Hoover Institute Studies, Series B, No. 14, Stanford, California, 1952.

Lasswell, Harold D., Lerner, Daniel and Rothwell, C. Easton, *The Comparative Study of Élites*, Stanford, California, 1952.

Marvick, Dwaine, *Political Decision-Makers*, Glencoe, Illinois, 1961.

Marvick, Dwaine, 'Political Recruitment and Careers', in the *International Encyclopedia of Social Science*, New York, 1968, Vol. 12, pp. 273–82.

Matthews, Donald R., *The Social Background of Political Decision-Makers*, New York, 1954.

Matthews, Donald R., *U.S. Senators and their World*, Chapel Hill, North Carolina, 1960.

Meisel, James H. (ed.), *Pareto and Mosca*, Englewood Cliffs, New Jersey, 1965.

Michels, Robert, *Political Parties*, originally published 1911, first English edition 1915; latest edition, translated by Eden and Cedar Paul, with an introduction by Seymour M. Lipset, New York, 1962.

Mills, C. Wright, *The Power Élite*, New York, 1956.

Mosca, Gaetano, *The Ruling Class*, ed. A. Livingstone and trans. H. D. Kahn, New York, 1939.

Pareto, Vilfredo, *The Mind and Society*, ed. A. Livingstone and trans. Andrew Bongiorno and A. Livingston, New York, 1935.

Prewitt, Kenneth, 'Political Socialization and Leadership Selection', *Annals of the American Academy of Political and Social Science*, 361, September 1965, pp. 96–111.

Rae, Douglas, *The Political Consequence of Electoral Laws*, New Haven, 1967.

Ranney, Austin, *Pathways to Parliament*, London, 1965.

Ross, J. F. S., *Elections and Electors*, London, 1955.

Ross, J. F. S., *Parliamentary Representation* (2nd edition), London, 1948.

Rush, Michael D., *The Selection of Parliamentary Candidates*, London, 1969.

Rush, Michael D., 'Candidate Selection and Its Impact on Leadership Recruitment', in J. D. Lees and R. Kimber (eds.), *Political Parties in Britain: An Organizational and Functional Guide*, London, 1971.

Scarrow, Howard, 'Nomination and Local Party Organization in Canada: A Case-Study', *Western Political Quarterly*, 17, 1964, pp. 55–62.

Schueller, G. K., *The Politburo*, Hoover Institute Studies, Series B, No. 2, Stanford, California, 1951.

Seligman, Lester G., 'Political Recruitment and Party Structure', *American Political Science Review*, 55, 1961, pp. 77–86.

Seligman, Lester G., 'Élite Recruitment and Political Development', *Journal of Politics*, 26, 1964, pp. 612–26.

Shuster, James R., 'Bureaucratic Transition in Morocco', *Human Organization*, 24, 1965, pp. 53–8.

Snowiss, Leo M., 'Congressional Recruitment and Representation', *American Political Science Review*, 60, 1966, pp. 627–39.

Subramaniam, V., 'Representative Bureaucracy: A Reassessment', *American Political Science Review*, 61, 1967, pp. 1010–19.

Weber, Max, 'Politics as a Vocation', in *From Max Weber: Essays in Sociology*, trans. and ed. H. H. Gerth and C. Wright Mills, London, 1948, pp. 77–128.

POLITICAL COMMUNICATION

Almond, Gabriel A. and Verba, Sidney, *The Civic Culture*, Princeton, 1963.

'Attitude Change', *Public Opinion Quarterly* (special edition), 24, 1960, pp. 163–365.

Barker, Anthony and Rush, Michael D., *The Member of Parliament and His Information*, London, 1970.

Bauer, Raymond, Inkeles, Alex and Kluckhorn, Clyde, *How the Soviet System Works*, Cambridge, Mass., 1965.

Berelson, Bernard R., Lazarsfeld, Paul F. and McPhee, William N., *Voting: A Study of Opinion Formation in a Presidential Election*, Chicago, 1954.

Childs, H. L., *Public Opinion*, Princeton, 1965.

Davison, W. Phillips, 'On the Effects of Communication', *Public Opinion Quarterly*, 23, 1959, pp. 343–60.

Cohen, Bernard C., 'Political Communication and the Japanese Peace Settlement', *Public Opinion Quarterly*, 20, 1956, pp. 27–38.

de Sola Pool, Ithiel, 'Political Communication' in the *International Encyclopedia of Social Science*, New York, 1968, Vol. 3, pp. 90–5.

Deutsch, Karl W., *Nationalism and Social Communication: An Enquiry into the Foundations of Nationality*, New York, 1953.

Deutsch, Karl W., *The Nerves of Government: Models of Political Communication and Control*, New York, 1963.

Dexter, Louis Anthony, 'What Do Congressman Hear in the Mail?', *Public Opinion Quarterly*, 20, 1956, pp. 16–27.

Fagen, Richard R., *Politics and Communication*, Boston, 1966.

Garver, Richard A., 'Communication Problems of Underdevelopment: Cheju-do, Korea, 1962', *Public Opinion Quarterly*, 26, 1962, pp. 613–25.

Hirabayashi, Gordon K. and El Khalib, M. Fathalla, 'Communication and Political Awareness in the Villages of Egypt', *Public Opinion Quarterly*, 22, 1958, pp. 355–63.

Jacobs, Milton, Farzanegan, Farhad, and Askenazy, Alexander R., 'A Study of Key Communicators in Urban Thailand', *Social Forces*, 45, 1966–7, pp. 192–9.

Katz, Elihu, 'The Two-Step Flow of Communication: An Up-to-date Report on an Hypothesis', *Public Opinion Quarterly*, 21, 1957, pp. 61–78.

Katz, Elihu and Lazarsfeld, Paul F., *Personal Influence: The Part Played by People in the Flow of Mass Communication*, Glencoe, Illinois, 1955.

Klapper, Joseph, T., *The Effects of Mass Communication*, Glencoe, Illinois, 1960.

Lane, Robert E. and Sears, David O., *Public Opinion*, Englewood Cliffs, New Jersey, 1964.

Lazarsfeld, Paul F., Berelson, Bernard R. and Gaudet, Hazel, *The People's Choice: How the Voter Makes Up His Mind in a Presidential Election Campaign*, New York, 1948.

Packard, Vance, *The Hidden Persuaders*, New York, 1957.

Pye, Lucian W. (ed.), *Communication and Political Development*, Princeton, 1963.

Schatzman, Leonard and Strauss, Anselm, 'Social Class and Modes of Communication', *American Journal of Sociology*, 60, 1955, pp. 329–38.

Schramm, Wilbur, *Mass Communication* (2nd edition), Urbana, Illinois, 1960.

Schramm, Wilbur, *Mass Media and National Development: the Role of Information in Developing Countries*, Stanford, California, 1964.

Schramm, Wilbur and Riley Jr, John W., 'Communication in the Sovietized State, as Demonstrated in Korea', *American Sociological Review*, 16, 1951, pp. 757–66.

Smith, Bruce Lannes, Lasswell, Harold D., and Casey, Ralph D., *Propaganda, Communication and Public Opinion: a Comprehensive Reference Guide*, Princeton, 1946.

Smith, M. Brewster, 'Personal Values as Determinants of a Political Attitude', *Journal of Psychology*, 28, 1949, pp. 477–86.

Sussman, Leila A., 'F.D.R. and the White House Mail', *Public Opinion Quarterly*, 20, 1956, pp. 6–16.

Index